ADVANCE PRAISE FOR

the GENDER BINARY is a BIG LIE

"At this moment in time, when campaigns of misinformation seek to discredit and dehumanize trans and nonbinary folks, especially children and youth, Wind's accessible and informative deep dive into the history (and the now) of gender around the world will open eyes and minds. Filled with historical facts, biographical vignettes, terms and definitions, and so much more, *The Gender Binary Is a Big Lie* will guide the next generation of young people (and many open-minded adults) to create a world that not only accepts, but celebrates those who exist beyond the binary."

—Rob Bittner, LGBTQ+ literature advocate and educator

"This book will save lives. By normalizing the existence of gender diversity through time and space, by sharing a beautiful array of stories, by interrogating the tyranny of the gender binary in such a gentle yet forceful way, Lee Wind offers inspiration and encouragement at a time when it is most needed."

—Dreya Blume, psychotherapist and author of *Voices from Hawai'i's Māhū and Transgender Communities*

"This book is a must-read for anyone interested in gender & the history of gender diversity around the world. As a Brit intersex, non-binary & transmasc creativity & mental health coach in Hollywood, I feel seen and happy to know more of our contributions to humanity—lots to be proud about!"

—Seven Graham, producer, writer, actor

"Lee Wind uses an easy-to-understand, engaging voice to teach young readers the important truth that there have always been more than two genders. While also developing the reader's skills for thoughtful historical analysis on any subject, Wind shares well-researched, fascinating stories and concepts for any well-rounded education. *The Gender Binary Is a Big Lie* belongs in every classroom, library, and bookshelf."

—Sarah Prager, author of *Queer, There, and Everywhere*, *Rainbow Revolutionaries*, and *A Child's Introduction to Pride*

THE QUEER HISTORY PROJECT

the GENDER BINARY is a BIG LIE

INFINITE IDENTITIES AROUND THE WORLD

LEE WIND

ZEST BOOKS
MINNEAPOLIS

FOR EVERYONE READING THIS, OF EVERY GENDER:
YOU BELONG.

Zest Books™
An imprint of Lerner Publishing Group, Inc.
241 First Avenue North
Minneapolis, MN 55401 USA

For reading levels and more information, look up this title at www.lernerbooks.com.
Visit us at zestbooks.net.

Illustrations on pages 237 and 238 by L. Whitt.

Designed by L. Whitt.
Main body text set in Janson Text LT Std. Typeface provided by Linotype AG.

Library of Congress Cataloging-in-Publication Data

Names: Wind, Lee, author.
Title: The gender binary is a big lie : infinite identities around the world / Lee Wind.
Description: Minneapolis : Zest Books , [2023] | Series: Queer history project |
    Includes bibliographical references. | Audience: Ages 11–15 | Audience: Grades
    7–9 | Summary: "Author Lee Wind takes readers across the globe to examine
    gender identity and representation throughout history. Learn how cultures both
    past and present debunk the idea of a gender binary" —Provided by publisher.
Identifiers: LCCN 2022023600 (print) | LCCN 2022023601 (ebook) |
    ISBN 9781728414539 (library binding) | ISBN 9781728414546 (paperback) |
    ISBN 9781728486093 (ebook)
Subjects: LCSH: Gender identity—Juvenile literature. | Gender nonconformity—
    Juvenile literature.
Classification: LCC HQ18.552 .W56 2023 (print) | LCC HQ18.552 (ebook) |
    DDC 305.3—dc23/eng/20220526

LC record available at https://lccn.loc.gov/2022023600
LC ebook record available at https://lccn.loc.gov/2022023601

Manufactured in the United States of America
1-48623-49057-4/1/2024

There are as many genders as there are people in the world.

—Alok Vaid-Menon

BEFORE WE START

A note on the title: It's not that the categories of gender we call men and women don't exist. The lie is that we are told gender is binary—that those two ways to be human are all that ever has or ever will exist—and that's just not true.

The false idea that gender is a binary with no other options affects every one of us, regardless of whether we fit (or are perceived to fit) in one of the two boxes dominant culture tells us are our choices.

How did the idea of gender get so limited?

What do more expansive definitions of gender look like?

Who are the societies that understand and define gender with many more options?

Where and when have individual people lived outside the boundaries of gender?

I write this as a cis gay man, a child of immigrants, a husband, a father, a Jew, a spiritual atheist, a vegetarian, and an ally to all the other groups represented by the queer community's LGBTQIA2+ acronym, as well as to women, people of color, Indigenous people, disabled people, and everyone who's under-resourced, under-respected, and undervalued.

> Short for *cisgender*, *cis* means my internal sense of gender and my physical body match.

Like every author, I'm a very specific person. I don't know that I'm the perfect person to write this book, but I do know it's the book that demanded to be written. Because while many people feel comfortable with the binary, that is not all there is.

And it turns out, breaking that mental model is a liberation for us all.

CONTENTS

HOW MANY COLORS ARE IN A RAINBOW?

Even though we can be pretty sure that rainbows in the sky haven't changed physically since our most distant ancestors first saw them, the answer is, "It depends."

On what?

On where and when you are.

Ask a bunch of kids in twenty-first-century America, and you'll hear that rainbows in the sky have seven colors: red, orange, yellow, green, blue, indigo, and violet.

The years 2001–2100

Go back in time more than 2,350 years to Aristotle, the famous philosopher and scientist in ancient Greece, and he taught that a rainbow **"is three-coloured . . . red, green . . . [and] purple"** but admitted that sometimes there were four: **"between the red and the green an orange colour is often seen."**

Early Islamic scholars said they saw three colors. Ancient Chinese scientists and philosophers saw five colors. So did Isaac Newton, who saw "red, yellow, green, blue and violet."

Not Aristotle's three—they saw "red, green and yellow."

Isaac Newton is maybe most famous for the legend of getting bonked on the head by an apple, which helped him develop the law of universal gravitation—what we call gravity.

THE GENDER BINARY IS A BIG LIE

Until around 1665 CE, when Isaac got the idea to connect the colors in the rainbow "to notes on a Western musical scale,"—adding orange and indigo. That got us to a consensus among European scientists—inherited by those in the "West"—that there are seven colors.

Modern science tells us that most humans can see about one million distinct colors in the visible spectrum of light—including those bending out of water droplets to create a rainbow. But a rainbow in the sky doesn't have its colors separated by coloring-book lines. As science writer Ethan Siegel explained, "The gradation of color in a rainbow is continuous—there are no stripes. Humans, however, like to organize things, including colors, to make sense of them." This means it is our expectations—what we have been trained to see—that guides our brains to organize those hundreds of thousands of hues into distinct bands of color when we see a rainbow.

Most humans have three types of cones, the cells in the eye that detect color. People whose eyes have two types are often called color blind, and those whose eyes have four types can see extra colors— one hundred million separate colors!

The same can be said of gender.

Gender is an idea held by a group of people. Some—but not all— societies teach that gender is a binary that matches a person's physical body; people who have male bodies are men, and people who have female bodies are women. This results in public buildings generally having two kinds of bathrooms, girl things and boy things, and babies dressed in pink or blue depending on what's

The idea is that there are only two possible options.

Many restrooms reinforce the false idea that a gender binary includes everyone, showing only two options: a women's room and a men's room.

under their diapers. But many societies had—and still have—very different ideas about gender.

BUGI

The Bugi people of southern Sulawesi, Indonesia, recognize and honor three physical sexes (male, female, and intersex) and five genders—"men [oroani], women [makkunrai], calabai, calalai, and bissu." As reported on the PBS Map of Gender-Diverse Cultures, "Calabai are biological males who embody a feminine gender identity. Calalai are biological females who embody a male gender identity. Bissu are considered a 'transcendent gender,' either encompassing all genders or none at all. The bissu . . . serve ritual roles in Bugi culture and are sometimes equated with priests."

In a 2002 article for the International Institute for Asian Studies, director of the Herb Feith Indonesia Engagement Center Sharyn Graham Davies writes about the "Wedding Mother" role many calabai play in Bugi culture. Davies also describes a calalai member of the Bugi people, Rani. As Davies said, "Rani works alongside men as a blacksmith, shaping *kris*, small blades, and other knives; wears men's clothing; and ties *hir* sarong in the fashion of men. Rani also lives with *hir* wife and their adopted child. While Rani works with men, dresses as a man,

Hir, in italics, is the pronoun used for Rani by Davies.

smokes cigarettes, and walks alone at night, activities women are not encouraged to participate in, Rani [has a female body and is] therefore not considered a man. Rani does not wish to become a man. Rani is *calalai*."

Davies explains that bissu present themselves in ways that combine feminine and masculine, "A bissu may carry a man's *badi'* (knife) but wears flowers in *hir* (his/her) hair like a woman." Bissu are also seen to combine human and spirit elements, as people "who can be and often are possessed by spirits in order to confer blessings."

Bissu spirit mediums in Sulawesi, Indonesia

As Pooang Matoa, a bissu high priest, explained to a *National Geographic* documentary crew, **"There are five genders, and we don't need to separate people based on their gender because everything must live in harmony. . . . If one of the genders is separated then the world would become unbalanced."**

For Bugi people, in the past and still today, there are more than two ways to be a human.

What if we look back in history? Really far back, like nearly five thousand years ago?

NEOLITHIC AGE EVIDENCE

About 7,000 miles (11,265 km) from Indonesia, archaeologists working in a suburb of Prague in the Czech Republic made a discovery in 2011. They were excavating grave sites that dated back to 2800 BCE. People of the Corded Ware culture at that time had very specific, and different, burial rites for men compared to women. Men were buried on their right side, with their heads pointing west. They would have weapons and flint knives buried with them. Women would be buried on their left side, with their heads pointing east. They would wear necklaces and earrings, and be buried with jugs and a pot shaped like an egg near their feet.

At a press conference, archaeologists explained that they had unearthed a skeleton of someone whose body was male who had been buried mostly in the way women were traditionally buried—on their left side but with their head facing west. And while they weren't buried with weapons, jugs were in the grave site with them, including a pot shaped like an egg near their feet. Archaeologist Katerina Semradova was quoted as saying, "We believe this is one of the earliest cases of what could be described as a 'transsexual'

Today we'd say transgender.

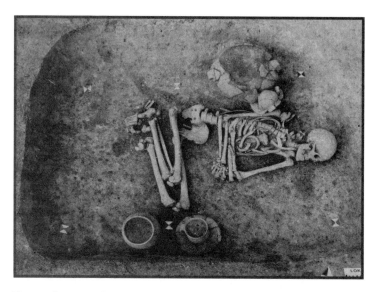

The gender nonconforming Corded Ware grave uncovered in Prague, Czech Republic

or 'third gender grave' in the Czech Republic." News reports spoke of the discovery of a "Gay Caveman." That's wrong on both counts. We have no idea if this person was gay—we don't know who or if they romantically loved anyone, or how they identified. And *cavemen* were about fifteen thousand years earlier. But it does seem clear that in that society nearly five thousand years ago, this life outside the gender binary was lived and honored!

READING BETWEEN THE LINES

One of the main challenges we face when looking at the history of gender diversity across the globe is that the recording was often done by people outside of those communities.

A false belief of European colonialism that started around the 1500s was that the other people and societies the colonists encountered were on a progressive journey to modernize and eventually "catch up" to the colonists' culture. The colonists believed they were advanced, "civilized," and more worthy than everyone else they met on their expeditions. This let them rationalize terrible practices such as slavery, stealing land, and even genocide—because the people they were doing these things to were seen as backward and *less than* themselves.

Historian Will Roscoe noted 157 Indigenous societies in North America whose members include people with male bodies who dress as women and perform many of the tasks generally done by women (sometimes referred to as a third gender role and identity) and people with female bodies who dress as men and perform many of the tasks generally done by men (sometimes referred to as a fourth gender role and identity.)

But to see the truth of other genders in history, sometimes we have to interpret hostile primary sources— and read between the lines. Here's a powerful example from the 1700s, when people from the Spanish missions encountered different genders in Indigenous societies living inside the boundaries of what would eventually be called California in the United States. While recording these differences, the author of this primary source also reveals how the colonists worked to destroy these age-old cultural practices:

Some third gender and fourth gender Indigenous people, as well as other queer-identified Indigenous people in North America, use the term *two-spirit* for themselves. That's where we get the 2 (sometimes rendered as 2S) in the LGBTQIA2+ acronym. You can learn more about gender being more than binary in many North American Native nations in the chapter about We'wha of *No Way, They Were Gay?*

THE GENDER BINARY IS A BIG LIE

Francisco Palou's Life and Apostolic Labors of the Venerable Father Junípero Serra, Founder of the Franciscan Missions of California

At Mission Santa Clara, 1777

The Father Missionaries of the Mission noticed that among the gentile women (who always worked separately and without mixing with the men) there was one who, by the dress, which was decorously worn, and by the heathen headdress and ornaments displayed, as well as in the manner of working, of sitting, etc., had all the appearances of a woman, but judging by the face and the absence of breasts, though old enough for that, they concluded he must be a man, so they asked some of the converts. They said that it was a man, but that he passed himself off always for a woman and always went with them and not with the men, and that it was not good that he should be found there.

Gentile was the word used to identify people from outside the faith. In the 1970s and '80s Philadelphia suburbs where I grew up, members of my Jewish community used the term to refer to non-Jews.

Heathen is another religious-coded word. More negatively charged, this reveals the colonial belief that those with different (and thus "wrong") spiritual beliefs needed to be "saved" and converted to the same religion as the colonists.

There are two ways to read this. The first: Not good that this third gender person be found there with the women is a judgment, siding with the missionary colonists against the traditional acceptance of this third gender role in their Native society. The second: Not good that this third gender person be found there with the men speaks to their acceptance of this different gender role in their community.

As the Fathers judged there was some trickery about it they decided to investigate. . . . This the corporal did and on taking off his aprons they found that he was more ashamed than if he really had been a woman. . . .

After he had been warned that it was not right for him to go about dressed as a woman and much less thrust himself in with them, as it was presumed that he was sinning with them, they let him go. He immediately left the Mission and never came back to it, but from the converts it was learned that he was still in the villages of the gentiles and going about as before, dressed as a woman. But it was impossible to find out what the reason for it was.

I'd get out of there too—wouldn't you if you were told you couldn't be yourself? And still, how interesting that this third gender Native person didn't stop being their authentic self; they just went somewhere safer.

Mission San Antonio de Padua in Monterey County, California

THE GENDER BINARY IS A BIG LIE

TRANS-EXCLUSIONARY RADICAL FEMINISTS MAKE THE SAME MISTAKE

It's revealing that the only interpretation the missionaries had as to why this person with a body they saw as male would be hanging out with the women would be to physically take advantage of those women. It didn't occur to them that the person in question knew their authentic identity—their true gender—in a way that transcended their body's physical characteristics.

The same mistake is made today, with some trans-exclusionary radical feminists and some lawmakers falsely accusing trans women of wanting access to women's bathrooms to take advantage of women. Trans people want access to bathrooms to use the bathroom! The people who are really in danger when they have to use a public bathroom are trans people, who, as the National Center for Transgender Equality reports, face "extraordinary levels" of violence.

In the same hostile primary source, the colonists think they've figured out the reason. They report from Mission San Antonio in Monterey County, where they explain how a missionary father, with soldiers, entered a house and interrupted the private time of an Indigenous couple who the missionaries perceived as two men. The colonists, the report says, punished them both, though not as severely as they deserved, and tried to show them what an ugly sin they were committing. The gentile replied that the other man was his *Coia*, or his wife. After the punishment they received, they were not seen again in the Mission, nor in any place near by, nor have any such execrable people been found since in any of the Missions.

Only they say that in the stretch of land along the Channel of Santa Barbara there are to be found many *Coias*, and that it is rarely you can find a village where there are not two or three. But we trust in God that as the country is gradually being filled with the Missions, these detestable people will be eradicated and that this most abominable of vices will be exterminated, and in its stead will be planted the Catholic faith, and with it all the virtues, for the greater glory of God and for the better welfare of these poor degraded people.

The bias of the author comes through loud and clear.

Showing how normative, and accepted, their relationship was in their society.

Knowing how the missionaries saw and treated third gender people and their spouses, it's not surprising they would keep their distance from the missions.

Every village had two or three of these third gender people living among them. They were accepted and part of their communities!

It's tragic and horrible that the colonists saw these people who seemed so different and called them detestable and abominable. And in the name of the missionaries' god and religion they set out to eradicate and exterminate not just this gender role but also the people who lived it. It's one painful piece of the colonization of the United States by Europeans that displaced Indigenous people and nations with violence, land seizures, and cultural suppression. These many injustices continue to resonate and impact Indigenous people and nations.

As hard as it is to read this hostile primary source, it's also amazing proof that nearly every village of Indigenous people these colonists encountered in an area that spanned over 100 miles (161 km) included multiple people living these third gender roles! It shows us how European colonists imposed the binary idea of only two genders onto the Indigenous people and nations of Turtle Island.

Turtle Island is the name some Indigenous people use for North America.

Geo Neptune (*left*) is a Passamaquoddy two-spirit artist and activist who reminds us that two-spirit people and identities are a vibrant part of Native nations and societies today.

GENDER ACROSS TIME

So in traveling throughout time and around our world, we see that gender is diverse and much more than a simple binary. As a social construct, something that society has taught us (like the colors we see in a rainbow), gender is also a moving target. It means that gender for you—in your family, in your culture—may be different from what it was for your elders when they were your age and for their elders before them.

Even little things, such as the colors pink and blue, have been coded with gender meaning, but not always in the way you might expect. Over a hundred years ago in the US, pink was the recommended color for boys! Advice in the June 1918 *The Infants' Department* (later *Earnshaw's*) magazine read, **"The generally accepted rule is pink for the boys, and blue for the girls. The reason is that pink, being a more decided and stronger color, is more suitable for the boy, while blue, which is more delicate and dainty, is prettier for the girl."**

WHY IS THIS SO IMPORTANT?

Because many of us have been lied to all this time. It's like being taught that there are only two colors (or even seven) in a rainbow, so when you look at one in the sky, that's all you think you see.

When the Viking-age grave (labeled Bj 581) of a warrior was discovered in the late 1880s, and the skeleton was surrounded by "a sword, an axe, a spear, armour-piercing arrows, a battle knife, two shields, and two horses, one mare and one stallion" along with "a full set of gaming pieces [that] indicates knowledge of tactics and strategy," it was seen as "the complete equipment of a professional warrior . . . a high ranking

Between about 800–1066 CE

THE GENDER BINARY IS A BIG LIE

Originally published in 1889, this sketch by Hjalmar Stolpe is of the misgendered Viking warrior's grave, labeled Bj 581, in Birka, Sweden.

officer." The archaeologists of the time just assumed the warrior had been a man. In 2014 scientists reported that their study of the bones actually suggested the warrior had a female body. Another study published in 2019 in the *American Journal of Physical Anthropology*, "A Female Viking Warrior Confirmed by Genomics," used DNA from the warrior's teeth and bones to confirm that their physical body had been female.

Even though there had been stories of battle-tested and victorious female Viking warriors since the Middle Ages, in the 1880s the idea of real female warriors in history was seen as nothing more than myth. The male archaeologists just applied their own gender lens to the past. And it took 125 years for us to see the warrior buried in Bj 581 more clearly—and we still don't know how that Viking warrior understood their gender.

When someone's gender is unclear or unknown, I'll use the gender neutral "they" pronoun to show respect.

Going directly to the primary sources can help us see beyond the binary and uncover our historical legacy—and today's reality—of the many ways we humans define, honor, and live gender. Why? Because knowing gender is *not* just binary can change lives, and our world, for the better. Starting now.

THIS ISN'T THE WHOLE STORY

Often books that talk about history, societies, and culture for young people are prescriptive, as if things work only one way and everything you'll ever need to know about that topic is inside. That's not what this book is. Don't think of it as an encyclopedia of gender but as a taste, a preview. I hope you'll get excited about what we discover together and then dig in on your own. Find new histories and stories about gender

that inspire you. There are so many primary sources to explore, so many people living their authentic gender expansively, and so many societies that celebrate a multiplicity of gender roles and identities that include and go beyond the binary!

Our gender diverse history—and world—is out there. Waiting for you. And for us all.

ON LABELS AND GENDER

Terms of gender identity are constantly evolving and can hold different meanings for different people. It's important to let each person define themself with their own term or terms of identity or, if they choose, none at all. Here are some terms and definitions to get you started:

AFAB—the acronym (sometimes pronounced as "ay-fab") for someone whose body is "assigned female at birth"

affirmed gender—a person's true gender (which can be different from the gender they were assigned at birth)

agender—someone who doesn't identify with or experience any gender

AMAB—the acronym (sometimes pronounced as "ay-mahb") for someone whose body is "assigned male at birth"

androgyne/androgynous—someone who feels their gender is either a combination of genders, in-between genders, both binary genders, or neither binary gender

bigender—someone who feels their gender fully includes two or more genders

cisgender—someone who feels their internal sense of gender matches their body's physical characteristics, also called cis

cross-dresser—someone who wears clothes or accessories associated with a gender other than their own but generally does not identify with that gender

demigender—someone who feels their gender partially includes a specific gender

drag—a performance art form that subverts and challenges the gender binary

drag king—someone who publicly performs a gender expression that highlights and sometimes deconstructs gender expectations of masculinity

drag queen—someone who publicly performs a gender expression that highlights and sometimes deconstructs gender expectations of femininity

gender fluid—someone who feels their gender changes or shifts over time

gender nonconforming—someone who expresses their gender in a way that is outside of society's expectations, also called GNC

genderqueer—someone who feels their gender is outside the boundaries society places on all of us

intersex—someone born with external and/or internal characteristics that are "more diverse than stereotypical definitions for male or female bodies." Some intersex people also identify their gender as intersex, in parallel to how male/female sex is also part of man/woman gender construction and experience. And some intersex people identify within the gender binary and others do not.

Genderqueer is sometimes seen as a political statement as well as an identity. Laura A. Jacobs, a psychotherapist who identifies as genderqueer, explains that to her, the term represents **"a deliberate playing with gender in a very political sense, and being provocative around gender norms to highlight the gender stereotypes of our culture."**

LGBTQ—the acronym for the lesbian, gay, bi, trans, questioning, and queer community; sometimes with IA2+ (as LGBTQIA2+) including intersex, asexual, and two-spirit people. The + is added to include everyone who feels they are part of the queer community but don't see themselves reflected in the specific identities in the acronym.

nonbinary—someone who feels their gender identity is outside the binary of male/boy/man and female/girl/woman, sometimes called ENBY or NB, though NB can also refer to non-Black

pangender—someone who feels their gender encompasses all genders

polygender—someone who feels their gender encompasses multiple genders

queer—a person who feels their love, gender, or both are different from what is expected by society; also an umbrella term for the LGBTQ+ community. The word *queer* used to be a slur, and while it has been reclaimed and is seen by many as empowering, some older folks remember it being said to them with hate. Thus, PFLAG recommends not labeling other people queer unless they've claimed the label themselves. But everyone who does so with respect is welcome to use the term *queer* when speaking of the LGBTQ+ community, as the "queer community."

third/fourth gender—sometimes used in cultures to acknowledge there are multiple categories of people and individuals whose identity is neither male/boy/man nor female/girl/woman

trans boy or trans man—someone who identifies as trans whose gender is boy or man

transgender/trans—someone who feels their internal sense of gender does not match their assigned sex at birth.

Some trans folks affirm their gender by changing their physical bodies, while others do not. And some trans people identify within the gender binary (as a man or woman) while others do not, and some identify as nonbinary.

trans girl or trans woman—someone who identifies as trans whose gender is girl or woman

two-spirit—someone who identifies as an Indigenous queer person of Turtle Island—what Western culture calls North America. Sometimes shown as 2S, or the numeral 2, in the queer community acronyms LGBTQIA2+ and LGBTQ2S+. Geo Neptune defines two-spirit as, "an umbrella term that bridges Indigenous and Western understandings of gender and sexuality" and explains that different nations have different definitions of two-spirit.

SOME LABEL ADVICE

James Baldwin wrote in a 1985 essay, **"Once you have discerned the meaning of a label, it may seem to define you for others, but it does not have the power to define you to yourself."**

We are all many things—there are worlds within us, just as we are part of an infinite world and universe around us. Rather than hemming us in, let terms open us up to better understand ourselves and others.

RETIRED TERMS

Some of these are offensive—you may see them used in older resources, but unless you identify within one of these groups and are reclaiming the word politically and artistically, avoid using them:

berdache—an old term for "two-spirit"

hermaphrodite—an old term for "intersex." There is a movement by younger intersex activists to reclaim the term in the same empowering way activists reclaimed the word *queer*.

transexual—an old term for "transgender," which was sometimes used to indicate a person's gender journey included medical assistance (such as gender affirming hormones or surgery)

transvestite—an old term for "cross-dresser"

LOSE THE -ED

A person is intersex (not intersexed), cisgender (not cisgendered), or transgender (not transgendered).

The point is to respect the person as an active subject without implying something has been done *to* them for them to have that identity.

Dr. Johanna Olson-Kennedy, medical director of the Center for Transyouth Health and Development at Children's Hospital Los Angeles, explains the problematic usage, "It's similar to if you said someone was 'Asianed' to describe them as Asian."

It's a good guideline for all terms of identity. Lose the -ed.

GOOD STUFF TO KNOW

There's a lot to unpack when we explore gender. This part of the book shares some basics so we'll have a common language and foundation from which we can build.

We'll start with some biology (looking at what does and doesn't defines "male" and "female"), then lay out the many social categories of gender, talk language (including pronouns and neopronouns), share different mental models for thinking about gender, dip back into biology (nothing is "natural" about the idea that a gender binary includes everyone), and end with acknowledging that certain genders have been afforded privileges and rights—while others have not.

BIOLOGY PART 1: WHAT'S THE DIFFERENCE BETWEEN MALE AND FEMALE?

In *Evolution's Rainbow: Diversity, Gender, and Sexuality in Nature and People*, Professor Joan Roughgarden, a transgender biologist, says that **"to a biologist, 'male' means making small gametes, and 'female' means making large gametes. Period!"**

Gametes are cells with half of the genes to make a new individual.

In humans, bodies that make small gametes (sperm) are called male, and bodies that make large gametes (eggs) are called female. A single sperm (small gamete with half a set of genes) and a single egg (large gamete with half a set of genes) can come together to make a new cell with a full set of genes. Biologists call that new cell a zygote, and in humans that fertilized egg can grow into a new human.

An egg is about one million times larger in size than a sperm.

What about bodies that don't currently make either gamete? They're too young, or they're past the age to parent biological children. Western culture bends time forward or backward to get those bodies into a "male" or "female" box.

What about bodies that don't make any gametes?

Or bodies that are set up to make and/or deliver both types of gametes?

The term for all the bodies that don't fit neatly into the male category or female category is intersex. Roughgarden explains what this means for mammals: **"Although the gametes-size binary implies that only two sexed functions exist, many body types occur, ranging from all-sperm parts, through various combinations of both sperm- and egg-related parts, to all-egg parts."**

We humans are mammals too.

So, gametes—that's the whole difference between male and female? Yup. **"The key point,"** Roughgarden says, **"is that 'male' and 'female' are biological categories, whereas 'man' and 'woman' are social categories."**

And I would add, intersex.

A body has a biological sex, or type: male, female, or intersex. A person has a gender: boy/man, girl/woman, trans, genderqueer, gender questioning, gender fluid, nonbinary, and other gender diverse identities. Each of those is a social category, something defined by culture, not biology.

BIOLOGY PART 2: AREN'T THERE OTHER PHYSICAL DIFFERENCES THAT DETERMINE A BODY'S BIOLOGICAL SEX?

In *Sex Itself: The Search for Male & Female in the Human Genome*, Sarah S. Richardson offers a more expansive definition of what determines a body's biological sex. Richardson says that many scientists understand that **"human biological 'sex' is not diagnosed by any single factor, but is the result of a choreography of genes, hormones, gonads, genitals, and secondary sex characters."**

WHAT ABOUT CHROMOSOMES?

Human cells have a nucleus. Inside that nucleus are "packages of DNA" called chromosomes. Humans have twenty-three pairs of chromosomes. The twenty-third pair (an XY, XX, XYY, X, or Y) is typically described as the sex chromosome. But Richardson explains that popular belief isn't based on science. It was a response to Western culture's **"revolution in gender roles"** from the 1960s onward and the rise in society and politics of women, lesbian, gay, and bi people, as well as trans and intersex people. **"In the midst of gender chaos, some take them [the XY or XX chromosome] to represent the essence of maleness and femaleness and the ultimate naturalness, and hence rightness, of social customs and practices organized around the different roles, interest and capacities of the two sexes."**

> Here again is the false idea that everyone is included in a gender binary.

Richardson makes the case that we should adopt a different, "sex-neutral" name for this twenty-third pair because the idea of XY and XX matching the view of gender as solely binary has warped the science. **"Gendered assumptions have led geneticists to bypass standard**

methodology, ignore alternative models, privilege certain research questions, and skew their interpretation of evidence."

As scientists dig into the data offered by the complete human genome sequence, Richardson warns we're in danger of repeating those mistakes. If you're only looking for difference, then you're likely to miss the similarities. And if you only research "men" with male bodies and "women" with female bodies, then you're missing all the people who don't identify within that binary.

In fact, we have to break free from two false binaries: the idea that bodies can only be one of two biological types and the idea that people can only be one of two culturally determined genders.

The word for all the genes and genetic material of an organism is *genome*. Completed in 2022, the international effort to map the human genome found there are about three billion pieces of information in a specific order that help make up each of us.

SO WHAT IS GENDER?

Gender is a social category that encompasses many realms of a person's being. Gender includes the following:

YOUR INTERNAL IDENTITY

When you close your eyes and picture yourself, you have an idea of who you feel you are. Maybe that self-image has a gender, and maybe it doesn't.

YOUR BODY

When you open your eyes and look at your body without clothes, your body has characteristics—some that you see and some that you don't—that are often used to define a body's biological sex. Intersex people throughout history and around the world remind us that there are many more than just the two categories of male and female.

THE INTERPLAY BETWEEN YOUR INTERNAL IDENTITY AND YOUR BODY

People whose body matches their internal gender identity can call themselves cis or cisgender. *Cis* is Latin for "on this side."

People whose body does not match their internal gender identity can call themselves trans or transgender. *Trans* is Latin for "on the other side."

YOU AS PART OF NATURE

One beautiful definition of gender is by author, illustrator, and activist Maya Gonzalez in their book *The Gender Wheel: A Story about Bodies and Gender for Every Body*. It reads, **"Gender is part of our connection to nature. In a sense it is how nature connects to our hearts and dances through our bodies."**

YOU IN THE WORLD OF PEOPLE

Drag queen and television personality RuPaul has a great line, **"You're born naked, and the rest is drag."** This means that all the choices we make in how we present ourselves to the world add up to a performance of gender. For RuPaul, wearing a brightly patterned men's suit and appearing with a shaved head is as much a performance as wearing a sequined women's dress and appearing with a giant pink wig.

Everything external about how you perform (or don't perform) gender is your gender presentation.

The organization Gender Spectrum calls this your social gender.

YOU IN LANGUAGE

Words can also signal a person's gender. Often people make assumptions about someone's gender based on their name

RuPaul

Also RuPaul

or things they see in that person's gender presentation, but those guesses can be wrong. Being misgendered can be painful and even dangerous for some people. (Sadly, some people feel they have the right to police the gender binary by forcing other people to conform to it.)

When you are addressed as a gender you don't identify with

The respectful thing to do when you don't know someone's pronouns is to ask—or, if that feels awkward, consider shifting your language so you default to the gender-neutral singular "they."

MORE ON THE LANGUAGE OF GENDER

THE SINGULAR "THEY"

Merriam-Webster crowned the singular "they" as 2019's Word of the Year. Their editors wrote, **"More recently . . . they has also been used to refer to one person whose gender identity is nonbinary, a sense that is increasingly common in** published, edited text, as well as social media and in daily personal interactions between English speakers. There's no doubt that its use is established in the English language, which is why it was added to the Merriam-Webster.com dictionary this past September."

This new definition was added.

NEOPRONOUNS

Neopronouns and noun-self pronouns were featured in the *New York Times* in a 2021 article by Ezra Marcus. "A Guide to Neopronouns" explained the growing movement to create new words or use nouns as pronouns specifically because they are not gendered. The article featured self-portraits by artists who use neopronouns. Katetorias uses pri/prin/prins/princeself. Steven goes by two other names as well, Jupiter and Juno, and uses a number of neopronouns, including cosm/cosmos/cosmself, star/stars/starself, and ey/em/eir/eirs/emself.

A 2020 survey of 40,001 queer youth by the Trevor Project found that "1 in 4 LGBTQ youth use pronouns or pronoun combinations that fall outside of the binary construction of gender." While the most common nonbinary pronoun used was "they" (often in combination with he, she, or both he and she), the researchers found that "4% of LGBTQ youth reported the use of pronouns such as 'ze/zir' 'xe/xim,' and 'fae/faer,' or combinations of these terms with other pronouns."

METAPHORS FOR GENDER

Mental models can help us better understand how something functions. The challenge is when those ideas prevent us from seeing the larger picture or have bias baked in. Let's look at some different ways people think about what gender is and how we live it.

ONE EASY WAY TO BE AN ALLY
TO EVERY GENDER

Consider changing your online profiles to include your pronouns. For example, I add (he/him) after my name. (Sometimes there's no good spot and it can be added after your last name). Including your pronouns signals a few things:

1. You recognize that people shouldn't assume someone else's pronouns just by seeing their name or photo.
2. You acknowledge that someone might use multiple possible pronouns. And you're taking the time to share yours.
3. You are a safe person for someone who uses pronouns that are different from what other people might assume based on their name, appearance, or both.
4. You are making space at the table for intersex, trans, genderqueer, gender questioning, gender fluid, nonbinary, and other gender-diverse people.

Sharing your pronouns in the real word (such as on a name tag or when introducing yourself) signals the same things.

(THINK OUTSIDE THE) TWO BOXES

The gender binary is presented in Western culture as two boxes everyone "should" fit inside: one box for people with male bodies and a boy/man gender identity and the other box for people with female bodies and a girl/woman gender identity. But when we know that not everyone fits in those two boxes, it makes us see how limiting the idea of boxes is.

A SPECTRUM

One idea that challenges the gender binary puts "male" at one end of a line and "female" on the other, with a range of people in between. The problem with this model, explained by gender-fluid activist Lucy (who also goes by Benji), is that it privileges those extremes of "male" and "female" to be somehow more legitimate than everyone else.

Points

STARS

The metaphor Lucy prefers is **"a cloud or stars in the universe, where you have a lot of different vertices each possessing its own spot of importance, as opposed to having male on one side and female on the other and those holding, sort of grounding everything, and everything else sort of circulates around that. And it sort of makes the others less legitimate. . . . Male exists, female exists, rock on if those are for you. But giving respect to the other ones and not just defining them in regards to male and female is really important."**

Lucy's words are a great reminder that the way we talk about gender diversity can privilege the binary or challenge it.

THE GENDER UNICORN

Designed by the team at Trans Student Educational Resources, the Gender Unicorn includes five different areas: gender identity, gender expression/presentation, sex assigned

The Gender Unicorn

Graphic by: **TSER**

Gender Identity
- Female/Woman/Girl
- Male/Man/Boy
- Other Gender(s)

Gender Expression/Presentation
- Feminine
- Masculine
- Other

Sex Assigned at Birth
- Female
- Male
- Other/Intersex

Physically Attracted To
- Women
- Men
- Other Gender(s)

Romantically/Emotionally Attracted To
- Women
- Men
- Other Gender(s)

To learn more go to:
www.transstudent.org/gender

Design by Landyn Pan
Illustration by Anna Moore

at birth, physically attracted to, and romantically/emotionally attracted to. Gender identity has three ranges that travel from neutral to more of each identity: female/woman/girl; male/man/boy; and other gender(s). These can change over time, and they can be felt simultaneously. Similarly, gender expression/presentation also has three ranges that travel from neutral to more of each expression of identity: feminine, masculine, and other. And sex assigned at birth offers three options as well: female, male, and other/intersex. It's a much more robust and dynamic way to think about identity, expression, and our physical bodies.

THE GENDER CIRCLE

A Native American elder speaking at the Montana Two Spirit Society's annual gathering in 2016 said, **"The medicine wheel represents men on one side and women on the other. But there's a space in between that is for the Two Spirits. We join the men and women and complete the circle. That is our place in life. That is the Creator's purpose for us."**

THE GENDER WHEEL

Inspired by the circular Mayan and Aztec calendar, Maya Gonzalez offers a vision of gender as a wheel of four circles, one inside the other. The center star represents each person as part of nature. The first circle around that represents the person within a culture and is called the pronoun circle. Gonzalez's examples include she, he, they, ze, and tree. Next is a person's inside self for how you feel your gender is inside you, with places on the circle for gender fluid, trans femme, agender, boi grrl, and many more. Next is the body circle, including trans, intersex, and cis bodies. And the outermost circle is the relationship circle, for how we relate to others. Gonzalez says that **"the wheel is alive. All of the circles turn to show the infinite dance that includes every body inside and outside, as well as out in the world. . . . When any of the circles of the wheel turn just a tiny bit in either direction, another place in the dance opens up, another place where someone belongs."**

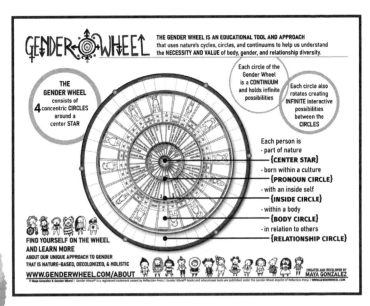

THE GENDER BINARY IS A BIG LIE

GENDER AS A JOURNEY

In their "create-a-path" book *She/He/They/Me: An Interactive Guide to the Gender Binary*, Robyn Ryle sees gender as a journey over **"shifting terrain."** Ryle writes, **"The more you know about gender, the more gender becomes like a path that you get to create for yourself."**

This idea of gender being more than a quality of who we are but an adventure that we live gives us all more agency and parallels a suggestion of queer theory: to view *queer* as a verb (an action word) rather than a noun (a word to describe a person or community). In their comic-style nonfiction *Queer: A Graphic History*, academic Meg-John Barker and cartoonist Jules Scheele share this lesson from queer theory: **"Try to avoid polarizing into either/or binaries: male/female and straight/gay. . . . Remember queer = doing, not being."**

> *Queer theory* is the name for ideas that challenge putting people into categories, challenge the idea of binaries such as gay/straight and male/female, show how many things depend on where and when you are, and look at the power relationships behind how people and systems function.

CREATING OUR GENDER ACROSS OUR LIVES AND IN RELATION TO OTHERS

Professor Joy Ladin writes in her essay, "Torah in Transition" about how **"gender is not only an image in which we are created: it is an image in which we create, and recreate, ourselves, through our relationships to one another."** Speaking of how the gender of a single person changes at the different ages of their lives (think child, teen, getting married, being a parent, being a grandparent) and the context of where they are (at home or at work), Ladin notes that **"gender is something we bring out of ourselves, shaping and reshaping it in response to changing needs for completeness, companionship and a place in the world . . . our genders are fluid, shifting in nuance and emphasis as we move in and out of contact with people we know and need in different ways."**

GENDER AS ENERGY

Malidoma Somé, a member of the Dagara Tribe of Burkina Faso, explained gender in Dagara culture this way in a 1993 magazine interview: **"Among the Dagara people, gender has very little to do with anatomy. It is purely energetic. In that context, a male who is physically male can vibrate female energy, and vice versa. That is where the real gender is. Anatomic differences are simply there to determine who contributes what for the continuity of the tribe. It does not mean, necessarily, that there is a kind of line that divides people on that basis."**

Somé also spoke of the special role gay people have in Dagara culture—though he quickly clarified that it is not their physical or romantic attraction to others that define them. **"Any person who is at this link between this world and the other world . . . with the gods and with the spirits who dwell there . . . experiences a state of vibrational consciousness which is far higher, and far different, from the one that a normal person would experience. This is what makes a gay person gay."**

GENDER AND TIME

Anne Fausto-Sterling, professor of biology and gender studies, suggests we consider gender identity **"as a stable process, not a fixed state."** In her book *Sexing the Body: Gender Politics and the Construction of Sexuality*, Professor

THE GENDER BINARY IS A BIG LIE

Fausto-Sterling uses the analogy of a glass of water on a table that once set down is still—or stable—and then, if the table is bumped or some liquid added or removed, the water jostles about for a bit until it calms and becomes stable again. It's a way to acknowledge that our—and others'—gender identity can be different at different times.

Is there a metaphor for gender you like best? Or do you have one of your own?

And maybe, as queer theory suggests, we can hold multiple metaphors for gender in our minds at the same time.

BIOLOGY PART 3: IDENTITIES BEYOND A GENDER BINARY ARE NATURAL

Nature is wildly diverse when it comes to gender. Across ecosystems and around the world, many animals and organisms have more than two biological categories, more than two social categories, or more than two of both.

Let's start with a few examples of diversity in biological categories:

White-tailed deer have six biological categories: (1) male body type with hard bony antlers, (2) male body type with velvet-horn antlers, (3) male body type with no antlers, (4) female body type with no antlers, (5) female body type with hard bony antlers, and (6) another distinct female body type with antlers. As Roughgarden says in *Evolution's Rainbow*, many humans have a prejudice that to be intersex means nature has made a mistake, but the scientific evidence shows just the opposite. **"The frequency of velvet-horns in white-tailed deer is around 10 percent in some areas and can reach as high as 40 to 80 percent."**

She also writes about a tropical ginger plant from China, one of eleven families of flowering plants where **"some individuals are male in the morning, making pollen, while** others are female in the morning, receiving pollen. Then they switch sexes in the afternoon." There's even a name for this switching of biology: flexistyly.

Roughgarden offers the bluehead wrasse as an example of fish that have three biological categories: males who are male for life, females who are female for life, and **"individuals who begin as females and later change into males."** For the cleaner wrasse fish, researchers have observed that **"when a large sex-changed male is removed from his harem, the largest female changes sex and takes over. Within a few hours, she adopts male behavior, including courtship and spawning with the remaining females. Within ten days, this new male is producing active sperm."**

Nature also offers abundant examples of a vast diversity of social categories—what we call gender.

There are hundreds of species of fish with multiple expressions of "male." Roughgarden tells us about the plainfin midshipman, a singing fish with three genders:

(1) a large male that **"emits a low humming sound for as long as fifteen minutes"** to attract (2) a female fish to enter his territory to lay her batch of eggs, as well as (3) a small, silent male that darts in to fertilize the eggs in a large male's territory. The biology and social strategy of the two male types are vastly different. Another example is sunfish, who have four physical and social categories—three types of males and one female. The large males (1) are aggressive and make nests for eggs in their territories. Small males (2) dart in to fertilize some of the eggs released by the female (3) while the large male is distracted chasing

The scientific name is *Porichthys notatus*, and it has rows of bioluminescent spots that look like buttons on a navy uniform.

away another small male. The medium male (4) can then enter the large male's territory without any aggression, initiating a courtship between the medium male and the large male. Then, when a female approaches a medium male and large male pair, **"the three of them jointly carry out the courtship turning and mating."** The three types of male sunfish even have different life spans.

The side-blotched lizard, studied in California, has three male and two female genders. Roughgarden explains there are orange-throated males (1) that are very aggressive with large territories that **"overlap the home ranges of several females."** Blue-throated males (2) are less aggressive, with territories that are smaller and include only one female. Yellow-throated males (3) don't defend territories. Orange-throated females (4) lay many small eggs and are very territorial. And yellow-throated females (5) **"lay fewer but bigger eggs"** and are **"more tolerant of each other."**

Hummingbirds, Roughgarden says, may be **"the best documented example of transgender expression in birds."** The coloring of feathers on the throat and upper chest of forty-two species of hummingbirds revealed that eighteen species included **"masculine females," "feminine males,"** or both. Among those eighteen species, the **"distribution of masculinity among females was gradual . . . from most feminine to most masculine"** but among males, **"the great majority were masculine, with no intermediates and a small second peak at the most feminine category."**

Nature has more diversity than we've been taught—both in biological categories (the sex, or types, of organisms' bodies) and in social categories (the gender roles those organisms live). So it shouldn't be surprising that human beings also, naturally, have more than two biological categories of bodies and more than two social categories of gender.

QUANTUM PHYSICS (ALSO KNOWN AS QUANTUM MECHANICS) SHOWS US THE NONBINARY NATURE OF, WELL, EVERYTHING

A retired scientist and engineer who worked on space exploration for more than thirty years, Blair shares a short lesson on the nonbinary nature of every fundamental particle: **"According to Quantum Mechanics, the universe is inherently non-binary. Electrons, photons, quarks, etc. can all seem to be particles at some times, waves at other times, and something else at still other times. It all depends on the context and how they are being observed. But regardless, they are always themselves."** Then Blair relates it to their own nonbinary identity. **"We non-binary gender-diverse people, we're the normal ones! It's the nature of the universe. Get over it!"**

WHAT ABOUT HUMANS?

Professor Roughgarden sums it up: **"Our species isn't divided into two classes, normal and different. Our species is naturally a rainbow of normalcies in every bodily detail. . . . Apart from gamete size and associated plumbing, nearly every male trait is naturally possessed by some female, and nearly every female trait is naturally possessed by some male. Claims of a gender binary in humans based on small statistical differences against a backdrop of great overlap amount to social myths."**

THE GENDER BINARY IS A BIG LIE

WHAT MAKES GIRLS AND BOYS (AND WOMEN AND MEN) ACT DIFFERENTLY?

In *The Lenses of Gender*, Sandra Lipsitz Bem discusses many different elements of gender formation, calling out androcentrism and the binary nature of gender in our American culture. Bem says, **"By polarizing human values and human experiences into the masculine and the feminine, gender polarization not only helps to keep the culture in the grip of males themselves; it also keeps the culture in the grip of highly polarized masculine values."** These are values such as prioritizing war over peace, risk-taking over nurturing, and dominating nature over living in harmony with nature.

Andro is Latin for "man," so androcentrism is when things are structured to center on men's needs and interests.

One of the causes of girls and boys behaving differently that Bem cites is revealed in a 1985 study of a toddler playgroup by Beverly Fagot, which found that **"the twelve-month-old boys and girls communicated to their teachers and to one another in very similar ways; but the teachers, because of their gender stereotypes, unwittingly reinforced the girls for communicating more gently and reinforced the boys for communicating more assertively. As a result of this different treatment, those same boys and girls displayed dramatically different styles of communicating when they were again observed some twelve months later."**

Calling out the systems that transform **"difference into disadvantage,"** Bem calls for the dismantling of both androcentrism and gender polarization, imagining a future where **"biological sex would no longer be at the core of individual identity and sexuality."**

Professor of history and philosophy of science Cordelia Fine, in her book *Delusions of Gender*, said, **"Our minds, society, and neurosexism create difference. Together, they wire gender. But the wiring is soft, not hard. It is flexible, malleable, and changeable."**

Neurosexism is an insulting argument that if women accomplish less than men, it's because of their lesser brain capacities.

This means we *learn* gender. Fine says, **"Social structure, media, and peers offer no shortage of information to children about masculinity and femininity."**

And if we learn gender is only two options, then we can unlearn it.

THE LIMITS OF USING PHYSICAL CHARACTERISTICS TO DEFINE GENDER

Babies born in the United States with genitalia that don't match the two options of "male" or "female" have often had surgeries to make their bodies conform. Of course, as babies, they cannot consent to this. Some of those who experienced this have spoken out as adults. Patient activist Cheryl Chase wrote, **"If I label my postsurgical anatomy female, I ascribe to surgeons the power to create a *woman* by *removing* body parts."**

Iain Morland considers this in the essay "Why Five Sexes Are Not Enough," saying that **"bodies that cannot be easily described as either male or female"** can be seen *not* as having an **"'ambiguous' combination of male and female genitalia . . . but rather a perfect, and perfectly comprehensible, set of intersexed genitals."**

Morland suggests that we look at Suzanne Kessler's observation that gender is something we *perform* rather than the configuration of our physical bodies under our clothes. Kessler expressed what almost all of us experience daily: **"In the everyday world, gender attributions are made without access to genital inspection."**

Ultimately, Morland wants us to consider that for those of us with **"non-intersexed anatomies"** claiming the identity "male" and "female" is **"morally indefensible because they constitute a commitment to the descriptivism that disenfranchises intersexed individuals."**

> Assuming that a person's gender identity describes their body under their clothes

> Since Morland wrote this in 2007, language has evolved and the usage intersex (without the —ed) is seen as more respectful as I write this. See Lose the "-ed" on p. 29.

Morland makes two points here. First, check out how Morland uses language to center intersex people, referring to those who aren't intersex as people with "non-intersexed anatomies." Language is so powerful!

And second, for those of us with bodies that, when described, match our "boy/man" or "girl/woman" gender, is our privilege blinding us to the harm done by this system? Because it directly impacts people who are intersex.

As Morland says, **"It is specifically unwanted genital surgery—with its aim of making genitals describable—that causes the cultural dominance of descriptivist accounts of identity to be agonisingly disenfranchising for people with unusual sex anatomies."**

> Painfully excluded

GENDER PRIVILEGES AND RIGHTS

Many cultures have set up multiple systems to advantage some people and disadvantage others depending on their gender. Voting rights, military service, whose last name gets passed down to the next generation, who can play what sport—in all of these realms and many others the false idea that everyone fits inside a gender binary had and still has a lot to say about who can do what.

The deck has been stacked in other ways as well, depending on people's wealth, skin color, heritage, country of origin, religion, and on and on.

One example is voting rights. In the US, women didn't get the right to vote until 1920. Seventy-seven years earlier there was a local election in Salisbury, Connecticut. In 1843 only white men who owned land there could vote. Levi Suydam was white, owned land, and applied to vote as a Whig, but the opposing party objected saying Levi was "more female than male." After a medical exam, Dr. William

The Nineteenth Amendment includes, **"The right of citizens of the United States to vote shall not be denied or abridged by the United States or by any State on account of sex."** But people of color (including women) were still prevented from voting by many state laws until the Voting Rights Act of 1965.

One of the political parties at that time

Barry pronounced Levi a man, and the Whigs won that election by a single vote—Levi's vote. A few days later, the doctor learned that Levi also menstruated. We don't know what happened then. Professor Fausto-Sterling tells us that after this story was made public in 1990, when a fact-checker called an official in Salisbury to verify the story, they were told the family and local residents wanted to "keep the family name quiet."

PAT—THE ANDROGYNOUS, DROOLING, SOCIALLY AWKWARD OUTSIDER JOKE

In the early 1990s, Julia Sweeney played the character Pat O'Neill Riley on the hit sketch comedy TV show *Saturday Night Live*. The joke was that Pat was androgynous, and the people around Pat couldn't figure out Pat's gender and didn't want to offend Pat by asking. The character was popular, and in 1994 a Pat movie came out (it wasn't a commercial or critical success). That's when Sweeney retired the character.

But what she didn't expect is that Pat persisted in popular culture, becoming, as the *New York Times* reported, "an all-purpose insult hurled at people who do not fit conventional definitions of masculinity or femininity."

Joey Soloway, who created the television show *Transparent* and identifies as nonbinary, said that the character Pat **"was shame embodied and turned into an it—a thing, not a person."**

In 2019 Sweeney acknowledged that the character wouldn't work today. **"You'd be able to say, 'What are your pronouns?' And Pat would say, 'I'm so offended, they're obviously—' And then the joke would be over."**

A measure of progress.

WHAT WE THINK WE KNOW

Often the things we are *sure* we know are defined by our experience.

What's cool is that when we learn about someone else's experience that's different from our own, it helps us rethink what we know. It expands our worldview. It makes us wiser. And more willing to question other things we're so sure of.

And that journey of questioning, exploring, and thinking about gender is what this book is all about.

Ahead are seven in-depth chapters and six shorter profiles that look at cultures that have more than two genders, at individuals who lived outside the gender binary, and at how gender in dominant culture has been colonized and policed so much that many people think the binary is all there is or ever was . . . and how that's simply not true.

Ready? Let's jump in.

THE GENDER BINARY IS A BIG LIE

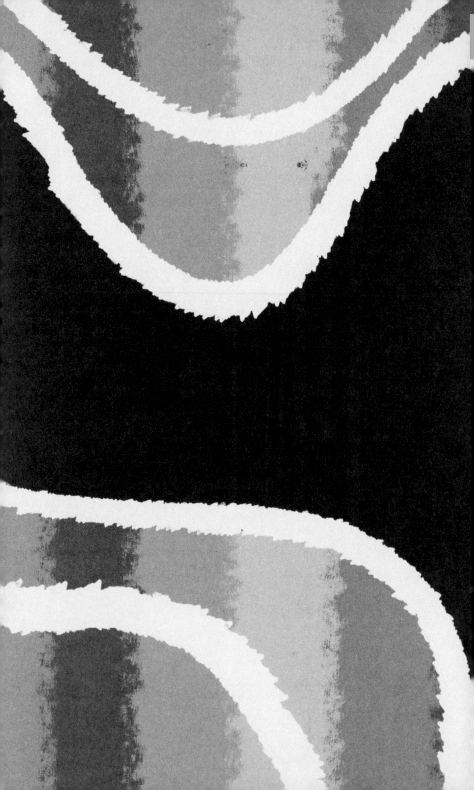

CHAPTER 1

EUNUCHS

GREEK, ROMAN, AND BYZANTINE EMPIRES

ABOUT 386 BCE TO 1453 CE

FROM WHICH IT AROSE THAT, WHEN AT A LATE PERIOD HE RETIRED TO ROME, AND FIXED THERE THE ABODE OF HIS OLD AGE, BEARING WITH HIM THE COMPANY OF A GOOD CONSCIENCE, HE WAS LOVED AND RESPECTED BY MEN OF ALL RANKS.

—Ammianus Marcellinus, on the heroism of the
eunuch Eutherius in 356 CE

GENDERS IN THE ANCIENT ROMAN EMPIRE

Genders were very tied up in the social hierarchies of Roman culture in the about two hundred years that covered the change from late classical antiquity to the early Middle Ages, also known as the time of the decline and then fall of the Roman Empire. Mathew Kuefler, professor of history, explains in his book *The Manly Eunuch: Masculinity, Gender Ambiguity, and Christian Ideology in Late Antiquity* that Roman culture included multiple genders of men. Among them were masculine men (often the ones in power) and unmasculine men, called infames. Infames were a completely different social and legal class of men. As Kuefler wrote, "to distinguish between the manly and the unmanly was to delineate clearly the boundaries of power through gendered identity."

That's Latin, and a lot like our English word *infamous*, or "famous for being terrible."

A lot of the qualities we think of as masculine or markers of toxic masculinity can be traced back to the ideas of what made a manly man back in the times of the Romans and the Greeks before them. Being aggressive or violent, not showing any emotions, being rational, smart, courageous, and having a desire to dominate and be the most powerful were "masculine" traits celebrated by those in power.

Women were portrayed by Roman historians as passive, emotional, irrational, cowardly, not as smart—and following the misogynistic logic of the time—because of all these lesser "feminine" traits, they deserved their lesser social status. As Kuefler put it, in Roman times there was a "moral division of human nature between masculine goodness and feminine wickedness."

Misogyny is the fear and hatred of women.

In Roman society some men were enslaved, and they belonged to a completely different social and legal class of men. Intersex people who had penises were included as men in whichever class they belonged—manly man, unmanly man, or man who was enslaved. Additionally, Roman culture during this time had other genders: women, women who were called infamis, women who were enslaved, and eunuchs.

Pronounced "YOU-nic."

EUNUCHS

Eunuchs did not have fully functioning male genitals, meaning they could not have (or could no longer have) biological children as a father. Or, going back to what we learned earlier about what makes a body male, their body could not produce (or could no longer produce) small gametes. Professor of history Sarah Bond, in a *Forbes* article, explained that the term *eunuch* comes from the Greek word εὐνοῦχος, a combination of the word meaning "bed" and the word meaning "to guard over." Originally, eunuchs watched over women, children, and royalty.

Pronounced "Ev-new-hos"

But another definition of eunuchs, by researcher Mark Brustman, is that eunuchs also included men who didn't have any interest in physical intimacy with women that might lead to their having children. Making them an ancient category of gay men! As Brustman puts it, "What we moderns think of as eunuchs, namely castrated men, were simply a limited subset of the category, referred to at the time as 'man-made eunuchs.' Incredible as it sounds today, society in the past valued gay men so much for their inherent qualities that the market used to try (without success) to manufacture them!"

> *Castration* means "to make someone unable to have children"—here, it's about the removal or disconnection of the testicles in people who have them.

Ulpian, a legal expert and imperial official for the Roman emperor Lucius Septimius Severus from 222 to 228 CE, wrote in Latin that there were three types of eunuchs, **"those who are eunuchs by nature, those who are made eunuchs, and any other kind of eunuchs."** Those three categories could translate to 1) males not physically attracted to women, a.k.a. gay males, as Brustman suggests; 2) castrated males; and 3) people whose bodies appeared male in some ways (including some intersex people) and yet could not produce small gametes.

> The job—and Ulpian's life—ended when he was murdered by officers who were supposed to be under his command in 228 CE.

Kuefler says that Ulpian used Greek words in his Latin text to further break down category 2—those who are made eunuchs—explaining some of the different ways a person might be "made" a eunuch: surgery to remove their testicles, penis, or both; tying their scrotum tight enough to cut the connection between the testicles and the rest of the body; and crushing their testicles.

Because eunuchs couldn't, or wouldn't, have kids (or at least new kids) of their own, they were often seen by the people

The idea of eunuchs being safe around women and acting as guardians, caretakers, tutors, and even being enslaved in the service of noble women has lasted thousands of years. We can see it in this oil painting from the 1700s, *The Sultana Served by Her Eunuchs* by Charles-Amédée-Philippe van Loo.

in power as more trustworthy—less likely to overthrow the current ruler to install their own new dynasty. Sometimes eunuchs were put in positions of power over others (in the government, military, or royal household) because of that trust—but their power was almost always given by the rulers and less than what the rulers had themselves. Eunuchs were generally seen as safe to be around women—they wouldn't get a woman pregnant—and having that control over women's bodies was important for the men in power.

One terrifying example of this cultural belief in practice is from around 200 CE. Plautianus was a prefect, a high-ranking Roman official, who the Roman historian Cassius Dio tells us, in a translation by Herbert Baldwin Foster, **"enjoyed the special favor of [Emperor] Severus."** Plautianus was a man—clearly a manly man—who **"wanted everything, asked everything from everybody, and got everything."** Cassius tells us that **"at home he [Plautianus] castrated one hundred nobly born Roman citizens."** Why? **"His object was that Plautilla his daughter (whom [the**

Emperor Severus's son] Antoninus afterward married) should be waited upon entirely by eunuchs . . . and also have them to give her instruction in music and other branches of art."

There would later be laws against castrating people to make them eunuchs, but it was clear that the rules only applied to castrating people *within* the Roman Empire. The loophole was that males could still be castrated outside the Roman Empire and then brought into or come to the empire.

In Roman culture, eunuchs had a "confused legal status," Kuefler wrote, and "could associate with women and participate in feminine activities even in the most intimate of domestic surroundings, but they also traveled freely among men and in public and held offices and wielded authority reserved to men."

The Roman emperor Severus Alexander (who ruled from 222–235 CE) called eunuchs a **"third kind of human being."**

Eunuchs empowered noble women by making them more independent. Kuefler explains, "In the ancient Roman world, a woman of the upper classes was not permitted to travel in public except in the presence of men . . . [who] were her relatives." Eunuchs created an exception to that rule, because upper-class women could travel with them.

For people who were "made" eunuchs, the manner and timing of their castration—in particular if it was before or after puberty—changed things. If their testicles were removed or disconnected before puberty, then many of the male secondary sex characteristics would not occur. Their bodies and faces might remain hairless, and their voices might not change. Fat could distribute differently on their bodies, gathering at their buttocks, belly, and chest, which led to the ancient writer Sidonius Apollinaris referring to eunuchs whose breasts **"hang down like a mother's paps."** Their arms and legs could grow extra long, and Kuefler reflects on how modern science supports ancient texts that described the different bodies of eunuchs, adding "susceptibility to curvature of the spine and osteoporosis, [and] sallow skin prone to premature wrinkles" to eunuchs' possible physical differences.

Eunuchs who were castrated after puberty might appear externally much like manly or unmanly men—they could have beards and body hair, as well as low voices. When telling that same story of Plautianus having one hundred nobly born Roman citizens castrated to protect and teach his daughter, Cassius wrote, **"He castrated not merely boys or youths, but grown men, some of whom had wives. . . . So we beheld the same persons eunuchs and men, fathers and impotent, gelded and bearded."**

Instead of *castrated*, Cassius's translator, Foster, chose *gelded*—a term used to describe horses that have been castrated. Maybe Foster chose it because it referenced an animal, so it better conveyed the disdain of the original Latin.

THE HERO EUTHERIUS, IN CONTRAST

Like women and unmanly men, eunuchs of all kinds were stereotyped with a lot of negative traits. Ammianus Marcellinus, who wrote a history of Rome "during the reigns of the Emperors Constantius, Julian, Jovianus, Valentinian, and Valens," praised a eunuch Eutherius for a heroic act—while at the same time revealing the negative light in which eunuchs were seen.

SOME HELPFUL BACKGROUND

These events, we're told by Marcellinus, with a translation by C. D. Yonge, happened in 356 CE. The Roman emperor at that time was Constantius. Julian was Caesar, the chosen successor to Constantius. If you think of Constantius as a king, then Julian was the crown prince. Julian was fighting to **"re-establish the province, and to reunite the fragments that had been broken from it."** At one point in the description of his battles and successes, Julian was in the walled city of Sens without most of his troops, who were staying in nearby towns. That's when Sens was attacked. Julian couldn't really fight back because he didn't have the troops with him. After a siege of thirty days, the enemy gave up. But Marcellinus tells us that **"Marcellus, the master of the horse, who was posted in the immediate neighbourhood, omitted to bring him any assistance, though the danger of the city itself, even if the prince had not been there, ought to have excited his endeavours to relieve it from the peril of a siege by so formidable an enemy."**

THE HEROISM OF EUTHERIUS

When Emperor Constantius heard that Marcellus was able to help but hadn't when Julian was trapped, the emperor fired him. Marcellus was upset and decided to go to the emperor to trash-talk Julian. Here's where Eutherius, the eunuch who would be praised so highly, comes in. Let's let Marcellinus tell us what happened: **"Therefore, when he departed, Eutherius, the chief chamberlain, was immediately sent after him, that he might convict him before the emperor if he propagated any falsehoods. But Marcellus, unaware of this, as soon as he arrived at Milan, began talking loudly, and seeking to create alarm, like a vain chatterer half mad as he was. And when he was admitted into the council-chamber, he began to accuse Julian of being insolent, and of preparing for himself stronger wings in order to soar to a greater height."**

Marcellus was trying to make the emperor believe Julian was plotting to overthrow the emperor. Let's pick up the story:

While he was thus uttering his imaginary charges with great freedom, Eutherius being, at his own request, introduced into the presence, and being commanded to say what he wished, speaking with great respect and moderation showed the emperor that the truth was being overlaid with falsehood. For that, while the commander of the heavy-armed troops had, as it was believed, held back on purpose, the Caesar having been long besieged at Sens, had by his vigilance and energy repelled the barbarians. And he pledged his own life that the Caesar would, as long as he lived, be faithful to the author of his greatness.

Eutherius was the hero who saved the day. He told the emperor that Julian was loyal to the emperor, pledged it on "his own life," and called out Marcellus's lies. Five years later, Julian became the next Roman emperor.

THE LIFE OF EUTHERIUS

It's pretty telling that the beginning of Marcellinus telling us about Eutherius is all about how terrible most eunuchs were perceived to be. Marcellinus wrote: **"The opportunity reminds me here to mention a few facts concerning this same Eutherius, which perhaps will hardly be believed; because if Numa Pompilius or Socrates were to say anything good of a eunuch, and were to confirm what they said by an oath, they would be accused of having departed from the truth. But roses grow up among thorns, and among wild beasts some are of gentle disposition."**

Even if someone as famous as Socrates were to say something good about a specific eunuch—and swear it was true—they would be called a liar! But Marcellinus hopes we believe him.

Marcellinus tells us Eutherius's life story:

[Eutherius was] born in Armenia, of a respectable family, and having while a very little child been taken prisoner by the enemies on the border, he was castrated and sold to some Roman merchants, and by them conducted to the palace of Constantine, where, while growing up to manhood, he began to display good principles and good talents . . . displaying extraordinary acuteness in discovering matters of a doubtful and difficult complexion; being remarkable also for a marvellous memory, always eager to do good, and full of wise and honest counsel . . . he was always sober and consistent, cultivating those excellent virtues of good faith and constancy to such a degree that he never betrayed any secret, except for the purpose of securing another's safety; nor was he ever accused of covetous or grasping conduct, as the other courtiers were.

From which it arose that, when at a late period he retired to Rome, and fixed there the abode of his old age, bearing with him the company of a good conscience, he was loved and respected by men of all ranks.

We spell *marvelous* in the US differently, but this was translated back in 1911 in England. You'll notice British spelling of words in a number of the translations quoted in this book.

It's a pretty glowing report. And then, just to make sure we understand that Marcellinus was telling us about an exceptional person (great *even though* he was a eunuch), Marcellinus reinforces many of the Roman cultural stereotypes about eunuchs in his final words about Eutherius:

"though men of that class generally, after having amassed riches by iniquity, love to seek secret places of retirement, just as owls or moths, and avoid the sight of the multitude whom they have injured.

Iniquity means to do something in an unfair, illegal, or terrible way.

"Though I have often ransacked the accounts of antiquity, I do not find any ancient eunuch to whom I can compare him." He then lists the faults of the other eunuchs of note that "they were apt to be either rapacious or else boorish, and on that account contemptible; or else ill-natured and mischievous; or fawning too much on the powerful; or too elated with power, and therefore arrogant. But of any one so universally accomplished and prudent, I confess I have neither ever read nor heard, relying for the truth of this judgment on the general testimony of the age."

THE NASTY POEM ABOUT EUTROPIUS

What do you do when your friend doesn't get the opportunity they wanted and someone else gets it instead?

Well, if you're the poet Claudian, you write a pretty nasty poem about the guy who got the job Claudian's boss wanted. Some forty years after Eutherius saved the day for Julian, the eunuch Eutropius was rewarded for leading a very successful military campaign. Eutropius was celebrated in Constantinople (the capital of the Eastern Roman Empire) and was given the honor of being named consul for 399 CE. The issue Claudian had with Eutropius wasn't really what Eutropius had done—the issue was that he was a eunuch.

The opening lines of Claudian's "Against Eutropius" poem, translated by Maurice Platnauer, set the ugly tone:

Let the world cease to wonder at the births of creatures half human, half bestial, at monstrous babes that affright their own mothers, at the howling of wolves heard by night in the cities, at beasts that speak to their astonied herds, at stones falling like rain, at the blood-red threatening storm clouds, at wells of water changed to gore, at moons that clash in mid heaven and at twin suns. All portents pale before our eunuch consul. O shame to heaven and earth! Our cities behold an old woman decked in a consul's robe who gives a woman's name to the year.

Astonied is an old word for "dazed or frozen in confusion."

It continues in the same vein, and then Claudian says, **"Had a woman assumed the fasces though this were illegal it were nevertheless less disgraceful. Women bear sway among the Medes and swift Sabaeans; half barbary is governed by martial queens. We know of no people who endure a eunuch's rule."**

A symbol of power that looks like a bundle of sticks with an axe head poking out of the top. One is on display in the chamber of the US House of Representatives in Washington, DC.

Political moves behind the scenes got Eutropius out of power, exiled, and executed for treason. Claudian put it this way in the preface to book 2 of his "Against Eutropius":

That name erased, our annals breathe once more, and better health is restored to the palace now that it has at last vomited forth its poison. His friends deny him, his accomplices abandon him; in his fall is involved all the eunuch band, overcome not in battle, subdued not by strife—they may not die a man's death. A mere stroke of the pen has wrought their undoing, a simple letter has fulfilled Mars' savage work.

THE GENDER BINARY IS A BIG LIE

But it's still fascinating that Eutropius, as a eunuch, rose to such prominence.

Eunuchs weren't just part of society during the decline and fall of the Roman Empire. We can also travel back in time in that same culture to discover . . .

SPORUS, THE EUNUCH SPOUSE OF EMPEROR NERO

About three hundred years earlier than Eutropius and Eutherius, there was another famous eunuch. Back in 54 to 68 CE, Nero was the Roman emperor. He was married to a woman named Sabina who was obsessed with her appearance. The historian Cassius even described how **"not fancying her appearance in a mirror one day, she prayed that she might die before she passed her prime."**

Nero may have been emperor, but he was no prince, as the saying goes. Cassius, who didn't have much good to say about Nero, told us what happened:

> **Sabina also perished at this time through an act of Nero's. Either accidentally or intentionally he had given her a violent kick while she was pregnant. . . .**
> **Nero missed her so that . . . because a boy of the liberti class, named Sporus, resembled Sabina, he had him castrated and used him in every way like a woman; and in due time he formally married him though he [Nero] was already married to a freedman Pythagoras. He assigned the boy a regular dowry according to contract, and Romans as well as others held a public celebration of their wedding.**

Someone who had been enslaved who was now free

A public wedding between a eunuch and an emperor!

This was in 65 CE, and Emperor Nero was married to a eunuch and also to a man!

Cassius was an ancient historian with a sense of humor—willing to repeat a good joke: **"While Nero had Sporus the eunuch as a wife, one of his associates in Rome, who had made a specialty of philosophy, on being asked whether the marriage and cohabitation in question met with his approval replied: 'You do well, Caesar, to seek the company of such wives. If only your father had had the same ambition and had dwelt with a similar consort!'—indicating that if this had been the case, Nero would not have been born, and the government would have been relieved of great evils."**

Sporus survived Nero's death in 68 CE and would also be the companion of Emperor Otho—who ruled the Roman Empire for just ninety days. The next emperor was Vitellius, and things didn't end well for Sporus. Cassius doesn't tell us what happened to Pythagoras, Nero's other surviving spouse. But the historical record does include this fascinating story of a teenager made a eunuch in 65 CE who was the spouse of one emperor and the companion of another before dying just four years later in 69 CE.

Emperor Nero killed himself when he lost power.

Even before the Roman Empire, there's evidence of eunuchs rising to prominence and power. Some even became rulers! The portrait on this coin is of Philetairos, a eunuch who became the ruler of the city of Pergamon in 282 BCE. (On a map, Pergamon would be in Turkey, across the Mediterranean Sea from Athens in Greece.) Philetairos is acknowledged as the founder of the Attalid dynasty, an empire that lasted nearly 150 years.

MEN IN POWER ROMANTICALLY LINKED TO EUNUCHS WAS NOTHING NEW

Centuries before the Roman Empire, Alexander the Great conquered nearly all the world known to the Macedonians and Greeks, forging an empire across Europe, the Middle East, and Asia. Alexander's spreading of Hellenism (Greek culture and thought) was so far and wide that we can still see its effects in our culture—such as in democracy, jury trials, geometry, lighthouses, and even the Olympics!

Alexander was married to three different women, but Hephaestion, a childhood friend who grew up with Alexander and became one of his most trusted generals, is believed by some historians (including me) to be the love of his life. Others don't agree.

At the same time, the ancient historian Plutarch tells us, in a translation from the original Greek by Aubrey Stewart and George Long, about a moment Alexander had with a eunuch named Bagoas: **"At the capital of Gedrosia, Alexander again halted his army, and refreshed them with feasting and revelry. It is said that he himself, after having drunk hard, was watching a contest between several choruses, and that his favourite Bagoas won the prize, and then came across the theatre and seated himself beside him, dressed as he was and wearing his crown as victor. The Macedonians, when they saw this, applauded vehemently, and cried out to Alexander to kiss him, until at length he threw his arms round him and kissed him."**

LATE ROMAN EMPIRE LAWS AGAINST MANLY MEN HAVING RELATIONSHIPS WITH EUNUCHS

Back to the Late Roman Empire, in 342 CE a law created under the Emperors Constantius II and Constans "imposed the death penalty" on men who married eunuchs. In 390 CE a law expanded the penalty to apply to any man who was physically intimate with a eunuch. Often, when we look back at laws prohibiting behavior, it lets us know the behavior was happening in that society at that time—otherwise, they wouldn't have made a law to try to stop it!

The researcher Mark Brustman says that those laws were put in place as a political move by the church, who had identified eunuchs with their power and influence as enemies of Christian doctrine. Through the church's influence, the definition of what made someone a "man" shifted from interest in intimacy with women to simply having a male body. This criminalized gay men (eunuchs by nature) and became, as Brustman said in the title of one article, "The Historic Origins of Church Condemnation of Homosexuality."

The Christian church would eventually win the struggle for power, and the story of the "Baptism of the Eunuch," as Philip was said to have done in the New Testament, became a theme of Renaissance art—symbolic of the church welcoming foreigners and eunuchs. Here, Louis Chéron's etching (we don't know when it was created, but Chéron was a French artist who lived from 1660 to 1725 CE) includes a Roman-styled chariot as part of the scene. The eunuch here doesn't appear to be Ethiopian.

EUNUCHS WERE A DISTINCT GENDER FOR CENTURIES

"Though the western half of the Roman Empire crumbled and fell in 476 . . . [CE], the eastern half survived for 1,000 more years," according to the editors at History.com.

Historians call the eastern half of the Roman Empire the Byzantine Empire. In 330 CE, Roman emperor Constantine I declared a "New Rome" and named its capital,

Another version of Philip's Baptism of the Eunuch, by Rembrandt, in 1626 CE. Yeah, that Rembrandt—the famous Dutch painter.

Constantinople, after himself. Five years earlier, the emperor established Christianity as the official religion of the Roman Empire.

Today it's called Istanbul.

Kuefler says in *The Manly Eunuch* that the success of Christianity was due, in part, to a gender crisis—a crisis eunuchs had helped create by doing things like leading men into battle and displaying "manly" virtues. Kuefler suggests that large numbers of Roman men "were attracted to Christianity because they found in it a means to reaffirm their manliness and to reclaim their separateness from and domination of women."

In the essay "Living in the Shadows: Eunuchs and Gender in Byzantium," Kathryn M. Ringrose, a lecturer in history at the University of California, San Diego, discusses eunuchs occupying a distinct gender identity in Byzantine society between the third and twelfth centuries CE. Speaking of the unique cultural roles filled by eunuchs, Ringrose writes,

"Many of these roles were considered to be unmasculine or else involved tasks that were performed by women outside an aristocratic society . . . such as bookkeeping, managing money, and speculating in real estate." Other roles "required that eunuchs supervise boundaries, especially those charged with religious or supernatural elements." And still other eunuchs "frequently appeared in important positions normally held by males in the army and navy."

RECENT EXCAVATIONS, NEW POSSIBILITIES

When archaeologists were working on a burial site in Quesna, Egypt, in the late 2010s, they discovered two skeletons (they labeled the remains B21 and B26) from before the Roman Empire—sometime between 332 to 30 BCE. Kristina Killgrove tells us in the 2017 *Forbes* article, "Skeletons of Two Possible Eunuchs Discovered in Ancient Egypt," the archaeologists noted that B21 was buried in a different direction: "with the head to the south, rather than the typical head-north orientation of the period." And B21's growth plates for their leg and arm bones had not fused. B21 was "taller than average, even though they were not

fully grown." There are other possible medical explanations, but the archaeologists suspected

This woodcut illustration of General Narses (a eunuch) is from a book printed in 1493 in both Latin and German, Hartmann Schedel's *Liber Chronicarum* (or *Nuremberg Chronical*). It's probably just a guess of what Narses looked like, as it was made over nine hundred years after he lived. The Latin title of the woodcut translates as "Narses Eunuch."

B21 might have been a eunuch (a made eunuch) whose castration before puberty caused these physical differences. Killgrove said, "As more archaeologists begin to identify potential intersex individuals in ancient graves, it is likely that our understanding of the highly variable and socially constructed nature of sex and gender roles in past populations will dramatically increase." Well said!

And maybe the different burial direction was a reflection of that person's different gender.

Before, during, and after the Late Roman Empire, multiple kinds of eunuchs had a distinct social and legal status—though that status changed over time. From about the time of Alexander the Great (356–323 BCE) to the Late Roman Empire (250–450 CE) through to the end of the Byzantine Empire (with the fall of Constantinople and the death of Emperor Constantine XI in battle, both on May 29, 1453), for over eighteen hundred years both natural and human-made eunuchs were seen as separate genders in these cultures.

Does knowing about eunuchs in Greek, Roman, and Byzantine societies change how you see history?

When you separate masculine traits from male bodies and acknowledge these traits can be found in other bodies, does it help you better see the stereotypes we live with?

CASTRATI

ITALY

1500s TO 1900s

As we leave the Roman Empire, let's recognize that genders in a specific culture—and how people live within those genders—can dramatically change over time. In Italy, from the 1500s through the early 1900s, castrating young boys who could sing was a path many families took hoping their children would achieve wealth and fame as castrati—the rock stars of their day.

And some other parts of Europe

Adoring crowds, overcome with emotion as they cheered castrati performances, are reported to have shouted, **"Eviva il coltello!"** In English: "Long live the knife!" They meant the knife that had operated on the young boy before puberty to disconnect his testicles from his body to prevent his voice from dropping in pitch. The idea was castration made castrati able to sing in a high register like a female but with the muscle power and lung capacity of an adult male body—one that wouldn't have secondary sex characteristics that happen to male bodies in puberty like their voice changing, growing an Adam's apple, and facial hair. No one talked much about the intense vocal training the best castrati went through—the focus was all about "the knife."

The Catholic Church's ban on women singing in church choirs was broadened in the mid-1500s to ban women singing anywhere in public. But what about opera? What about church music? For hundreds of years, the answer for opera fans, composers, and the church became castrati—at one point an entire choir of castrati performed in the Vatican's Sistine Chapel. ← Just one example: The 1607 opera *L'Orfeo* by Claudio Monteverdi had four roles for castrati. By 1640 every major choir in Italy included castrati singers. And the famed composer George Frideric Handel, living in London between 1712 and 1759, wrote a number of operas around the star appeal of different castrati, such as Francesco Bernardi, who was known as Senesino, and Giovanni Carestini.

The same chapel where Michelangelo painted his frescos from 1508 to 1512. (Learn more about Michaelangelo and how he was a man who loved another man in *No Way, They Were Gay?* page 12.)

The most famous castrato of all was Carlo Broschi, known as Farinelli. In the 1700s Farinelli was a superstar across Europe, and was celebrated by composers, nobility, and the public. The *Encyclopedia Britannica* reports that for almost ten years starting in 1737, Farinelli sang the same songs every night to the Spanish king Philip V because it soothed the king's "deep-seated melancholia." At performances in London, fans reportedly shouted, **"One God, one Farinelli!"** And in 1770, after Farinelli had retired to a villa outside Bologna, he was visited by a fourteen-year-old Mozart, who had traveled to meet the famous singer.

Depression ↗

In a male body that isn't castrated, in late adolescence the bones fuse and stop growing. Farinelli was so famous that in 2006 anthropologists dug up his remains to see what they could learn. From his bones—that indeed had not fused—they estimated he was very tall for the time, maybe 6 feet 3 inches (1.9 m). A different kind of anthropology was done by the opera

Yup. That Mozart— Wolfgang Amadeus Mozart.

singer Cecilia Bartoli, whose 2019 album *Farinelli* featured works specifically composed for the famous castrato at the height of his career. In the *Guardian*, Bartoli says the songs "tell us quite precisely about Farinelli's unusual vocal range (around three octaves), his masterful singing technique (virtuosic passages and extended slow phrases that competitors could not keep up with), his exceptional breath control (some phrases ranging between forty seconds and a minute), and his powers as an interpreter (the depth of emotion expressed in these arias)."

A portrait from 1734 to 1735 of the famous castrato Carlo Broschi—whose stage name was Farinelli—by Jacopo Amigoni. The singer is shown being crowned by the muse of music, Euterpe, and the winged angel with the trumpet represented Farinelli's fame.

The only castrato we have audio recordings of today is Alessandro Moreschi, who was part of the Sistine Chapel Choir. Moreschi's singing voice was thought to be angelic, and people called him the Angel of Rome. One person who heard Moreschi sing at the height of his fame wrote of the performance, **"His voice rose above the choir in a crescendo [and] overpowered [them] as completely as a searchlight outshines a little candle."**

Some of the castrati who achieved fame were demanding in their stardom—Luigi Marchesi would only agree to perform in an opera if he made his first appearance onstage riding a horse and singing a specific aria. But their voices and public appeal had composers clamoring to work with them—and the public would pack theaters to see them perform.

In a parallel to today's rock stars, some castrati were also seen as romantically and physically desirable. Giacomo Casanova, who was famous for writing about his romantic and physically intimate exploits, wrote in his diary about one castrato performance: **"In a well-made corset, he had the waist of a nymph, and, what was almost incredible, his breast was in no way inferior, either in form or in beauty, to any woman's. . . . To resist the temptation, or not to feel it, one would have had to be cold and earthbound as a German."**

Living and loving in the 1700s, Giacomo Casanova was Italian and not above playing on stereotypes.

While some castrati did become famous and wealthy, most did not. Poor families often took the gamble. One estimate, reported by Alan Riding in the *New York Times*, is that in the 1730s about four thousand boys were castrated *every year*.

Castrating young boys was technically against church law, but parents and surgeons made up excuses—a fall from a horse, a bite from an animal—and castrati sang for the church and opera for hundreds of years. It wasn't until the early 1900s that Pope Pius X banned castrati from singing in the Vatican—including Alessandro Moreschi, who became a choir director instead. That was a turning point for the fate and fortune of all castrati. And in 1940 Johannes Kley's edition of the *Repertorium Rituum* acknowledged that for church choirs, **"women, too, are now generally admitted."** But even with no new castrati made by families hoping for their child's chance to be a rock star, the *Guardian* reported that the Vatican employed the suspected castrato Domenico Mancini as a private singer from 1939 to 1959.

CHAPTER 2

THE SIX GENDERS OF CLASSICAL JUDAISM

1 TO 199 CE

[AN INTERSEX PERSON] IS IN SOME WAYS LIKE MEN, AND IN OTHER WAYS LIKE WOMEN. IN OTHER WAYS [THEY ARE] LIKE MEN AND WOMEN, AND IN OTHERS [THEY ARE] LIKE NEITHER MEN NOR WOMEN.

—Mishnah Bikkurim, 4:1

> I've updated this translation (and others in this chapter) to be more respectful to intersex people.

GENDER DIVERSITY THEN, BUT NOT SO MUCH NOW

In researching this book, I was maybe most surprised that one of the cultures that included genders beyond the binary was the one I had been raised in! Growing up in a Reform Jewish household in a Philadelphia suburb in the 1970s and '80s, the child of immigrants from Israel, everything in Jewish culture and religion that I experienced presented gender as a binary that included everyone. But it turns out it wasn't always that way.

The Mishnah is a study book of Jewish law, a collection of oral laws and arguments designed to train people to think and work their way through different issues of Jewish religious law. It was put together and first published around 200 CE. The Gemara is another text that contains additional writings and discussions about what's in the Mishnah. Together, the Mishnah and the Gemara are called the Talmud. And in the Talmud, there are *hundreds* of references to multiple genders beyond men and women.

> There are two different Talmuds, the Babylonian Talmud and the Jerusalem Talmud. The Mishnah is similar in both, but the Gemara has many differences.

In this 2012 photo of people praying at the Western Wall, you can see the division between men on the left of the fence and women on the right.

But there's no sign of that when you visit one of the most holy places in Judaism, the Western Wall in Jerusalem (sometimes called the Wailing Wall), where the gender binary is on prominent display. Religious people go to the wall, which is believed to be the last standing part of the wall surrounding the ancient Temple, and pray. Some write their prayers on slips of paper that they stick between the stones in the wall. A fence divides access to the wall. Men are allowed on the left side (believed to be the more holy area), which has a "The Prayer Plaza Men," sign, and women are allowed on the right side, which has a "The Prayer Plaza Women" sign. No crossing to the other side is allowed. In a different area a short walk away, gender isn't supervised and you can pray on a platform about 50 feet (15 m) away from the wall. There are no signs, and you cannot get close enough to touch the stones or stick a prayer inside.

THE GENDER BINARY IS A BIG LIE

UNCOVERING A LEGACY BEYOND THE GENDER BINARY

When Elliot Kukla was twenty years old and a student at an orthodox Jewish school, he took a class on the Mishnah. Here's what he said:

> I found a startling text buried in a sheaf of handouts. I learned about someone who takes an ascetic vow. This vow will be valid if, and only if, a son is born to him. However, if the baby turns out to be a daughter, a *tumtum* or an *androgynos*, he is not bound by this vow (Mishnah Nazir 2:7).
>
> As soon as I read this perplexing text I called over my teacher and excitedly asked her: "Who is this *tumtum*?" "Oh," she answered, "The *tumtum* is a mythical beast that is neither male nor female—kind of like a unicorn—that our Sages invented in order to explore the limits of the law." Even though I knew next to nothing about Jewish texts and traditions, I had a feeling that my learned teacher might be wrong. I instantly identified with the *tumtum*. I had spent a lifetime feeling homeless and adrift between the modern categories of "male" and "female." When I met the *tumtum* I finally came home.

An ascetic is someone who denies themself everything but the most simple things, usually for religious or spiritual reasons.

Kukla went on to become a rabbi in 2006, and that same year he came out as trans. One of the people behind the online resource TransTorah, Rabbi Kukla explained in his 2006 essay "A Created Being of Its Own" that between 1 and 199 CE, the rabbis of the Mishnah identified four different physical body types: zachar (male), nekevah (female), androgynos (intersex), and tumtum (undetermined). The rabbis identified two other gender categories: aylonit (someone born with a female body who later develops masculine traits), and saris (someone born with a male body who later develops feminine traits). That added up to six genders. If you count the two different kinds of saris, maybe seven.

An article in My Jewish Learning adds a second type of aylonit, making their number eight.

Here's one example Rabbi Kukla cites in his 2006 resource "Gender Diversity in Halacha (The Way We Walk): Mishna and Tosefta (1st–2nd Centuries CE)," from the Tosefta Megillah, which is about the duty of reading the story of Esther for the Purim holiday:

All are obligated for the reading of the Scroll of Esther [on Purim]: Priests, Levites, converts, freed slaves, disqualified priests, *mamzarim*, a born *saris*, a saris by human action, those with damaged testicles, those lacking testicles—all of them are obligated. And all of them have the power to fulfill the obligation of the community [if they read the Scroll of Esther to the community as a whole]. A *tumtum* and an *androgynos* are obligated [to read the Scroll of Esther]. But they do not have the power to fulfill the obligation for the community as a whole. The *androgynos* has the power to fulfill the obligation for his own kind [another *androgynos*] and does not have

Often translated as "bastard," it means someone born from a forbidden relationship such as incest or adultery.

THE GENDER BINARY IS A BIG LIE

the power for one who is not his own kind. A *tumtum* does not have the power to fulfill the obligation for others, whether they are of his own kind or not of his own kind. Women, slaves, and minors are exempt. Thus they do not have the power to fulfill the obligation of the community.

With different religious obligations for people in each category, we can see that ancient Jewish tradition understood—and lived the reality—that gender is not simply binary. Let's explore the different genders in ancient Jewish tradition further:

ANDROGYNoS—INTERSEX

Androgynos was the term used in the Talmud for people who we would call intersex, people whose physical bodies have a combination of male and female characteristics and/or traits. Intersex folks are mentioned 149 times in the Talmud, as in these excerpts from the Mishnah Bikkurim 4: **"[An intersex person] is in some ways like men, and in other ways like women. In other ways [they are] like men and women, and in others [they are] like neither men nor women."**

Then the text lists the differences, including these:

In what ways [are they] like men? . . . [They] can take a wife but not be taken as a wife. . . . And [they] must perform all the commandments of the Torah, like men.

And in what ways [are they] like women? . . . [They] must not be secluded with men. . . . And [they are] disqualified from being a witness, like women. . . .

In what ways [are they] like both men and women? One who strikes [them] or curses [them] is liable. . . . And [they] may inherit any inheritance, as in the case of men and women.

And in what [ways are they] different from both men and women? . . . [They are not] liable for entering the temple while impure, . . . [and they] must not be sold as a Hebrew slave, unlike men or women.

This section of the Mishnah ends with a quote from Rabbi Meir (sometimes attributed to Rabbi Yosi) that **"the androgynos he is a created being of her own."** Hebrew is a very gendered language, and the use of both "he" and "her" to refer to a single intersex person here is clearly intentional. As Rabbi Kukla and Rabbi Reuben Zellman say in "Created by the Hand of Heaven: Making Space for Intersex Jews": "This Hebrew phrase blends male and female pronouns to poetically express the complexity of the *androgynos'* identity."

A created being of its [their] own, Rabbi Kukla says **"is a classical Jewish legal term for exceptionality . . . it is a proclamation that God creates diversity that is far too complex for human beings to understand. . . . Every one of us must be appreciated as a 'created being of its [our] own.'"**

Diving into a quote and exploring the many meanings it can have is a technique of Jewish study. Rabbi Kukla sees the "created being of our own" quote as a call to action: **"the basis of a liberation theology for men, women, transgender people, and everyone else. . . . God wants and needs difference. Holiness comes from diversity, as opposed to sameness. . . . It asks us to throw away the expectations that our bodies or our souls are containable within two categories. It allows us to see**

A religious theory or body of study

each and every other person as a uniquely created being." It's a profound declaration that the ancient Jewish inclusion of people with genders like intersex can free us all from the idea that a gender binary is all there ever is or was.

And ourselves

TUMTUM—UNDETERMINED OR NONBINARY

Tumtum is another type of gender diversity in ancient Judaism. Rather than being seen as their bodies having a combination of male and female characteristics (like intersex people) tumtum are people whose physical characteristics are undetermined or obscured. This means their bodies don't appear male, female, or intersex. Tumtum are mentioned 181 times in the Talmud.

In the Mishnah Bikkurim 4, Rabbi Yose (which may be an alternate spelling of Yosi) speaks about someone being tumtum, saying **"sometimes he is a man and sometimes he is a woman."** We'd translate it as "sometimes they are a man and sometimes they are a woman."

Religious Jews may wear tzitzit—fringes tied to each corner of a rectangular prayer shawl or other garment. The fringes serve as a reminder, as the editors of My Jewish Learning explain, "to think of God at all times." In the discussion of the rules for wearing tzitzit, different rules apply to people who are tumtum (as well as to people who are androgynos). Mishneh Torah, Fringes 3 says:

> **Women and slaves and children are exempt from fringes from the Torah. But it is from the words of the [rabbis] that every child who knows how to wrap himself is obligated [to wear] fringes, in order to educate him in the commandments. And women and**

slaves that want to wrap themselves with fringes, may wrap themselves without a blessing. And so [too] other positive commandments that women are exempted from; if they want to do them without a blessing, we do not protest against them. A *tumtum* (a person with recessed sexual organs) and an *androginos* (a person with both male and female sexual organs) are obligated in all [of these commandments] because of a doubt. Therefore, they should not recite a blessing, but rather do them without a blessing.

AYLONIT—TRANS OR GENDER NONCONFORMING

In addition to bodies that appear different from male and female at birth, ancient Judaism acknowledged other gender categories as well. The term used in the Talmud for what today we might call trans or gender nonconforming was aylonit (sometimes *ay'lonit*). It's been defined as people who are assigned female at birth who later develop masculine traits or characteristics. Aylonit people are mentioned eighty times in the Talmud.

In Yevamot 80b:6, the answer to who is aylonit has a lot of various definitions: **"It is anyone who is twenty years old and has not yet grown two pubic hairs. And even if she grows pubic hairs afterward, she is still considered a . . . underdeveloped woman with regard to all her matters."** The text continues with different rabbis sharing their "signs," such as **"she lacks the cushion of flesh that is usually situated above a woman's genitals"** and **"anyone whose voice is deep, so that it is not evident from it whether she is a woman or a man."** They may not agree on exactly who fits in the category of people who are aylonit, but it's very cool to see trans and gender nonconforming people acknowledged and discussed.

And in a section about marriage contracts, there's guidance about when an aylonit cannot marry a man—and when an aylonit can, reading: **"an aylonit is not entitled to a ketubah"** which is followed shortly with this exception, **"If from the outset he had married on the understanding that she is an aylonit she is entitled to a ketubah."**

A marriage contract

There was more disagreement about who aylonit were allowed (or not allowed) to marry. In Mishnah Yevamot 6:

"A common priest may not marry a[n] . . . [aylonit], who is incapable of bearing children, unless he already has a wife and children. Rabbi Yehuda says: Even if he has a wife and children, he may not marry [an aylonit]." The important part seems to be the person's ability to have children or not—and if they could not bear children, *that* would be the reason they're not supposed to marry a priest.

Jewish religious leaders were called priests—an inherited position of authority—through the 200s to 300s CE when rabbis and patriarchs rose to dominate Jewish religious life.

SARIS—TRANS OR GENDER NONCONFORMING AND EUNUCHS

There is also evidence in the texts about folks in the category of saris—people assigned male at birth who later develop feminine traits or characteristics, lack a penis or testicles, or a combination of these. There is the distinction of saris by nature (saris hamah) and saris by human intervention (saris adam). Saris by nature is translated as "sun eunuch"—the idea that the person was a saris from the first moment (or even before) the sun shone on them. Saris by human intervention refers to people who have been castrated. *Adam* is the Hebrew word for "man"—and yes, it's the same name as Adam, from the Bible's creation story. Saris people are mentioned 156 times in the Talmud.

Pronounced ah-DAHM

In Yevamot 80b again, saris by nature are defined this way: **"The Sages taught: Who is considered a eunuch by natural causes? It is anyone who is twenty years old and has not yet grown two pubic hairs. And even if he grows pubic hairs afterward, he is still considered a eunuch by natural causes with regard to all his matters. And his signs are as follows: Whoever does not have a beard, and his hair is defective, unlike that of ordinary individuals, and his skin is smooth, i.e., hairless."** Different rabbis and teachers cited many other traits that defined a eunuch by natural causes, such as urine that foamed or not giving off steam when someone bathed in the rainy season or even someone whose voice was neither masculine nor feminine.

Not a lot of consensus but definitely space for those who are saris **"by the hand of Heaven,"** as the rabbis and sages who wrote the Yevamot said.

Later in Mishnah Yevamot 8:4, we hear from Rabbi Elazar, who in speaking of the ceremony to release a widow from the obligation of marrying the brother of her dead husband distinguishes between a "seris-chammah" (saris by nature) saying they can be "healed" and a "seris-adam" (saris by human intervention) who "cannot be healed." How might a saris by nature be healed?

Researcher Mark Brustman has a possible answer in his different take on who a saris by nature, or a eunuch by nature, might have been. As Brustman said at the Eunuchs in Antiquity and Beyond conference held at Cardiff University in 1999, "The interruption of procreative power which is characteristic of eunuchs is equivalent to that which is characteristic of exclusively 'homosexual' men." So a gay man who married a woman and had children with her would be one possible answer to Rabbi Elazar's statement that a saris by nature might be "healed." While being intimate with a woman doesn't change someone being gay, there's a long history of men whose primary emotional and physical attraction was to other men being "in the closet"—hiding their true feelings in a homophobic culture, sometimes by marrying a woman and having children together.

> Procreative means "to have children."

Saris by human intervention had different rules of Jewish religious law that applied to them, including the ruling that they were not allowed to marry. Eliezer Melamed explains in "Pearls of Jewish Law" that this went back to the rule from the Bible: **"No one whose testes are crushed or whose penis is cut off shall be admitted into the congregation of the Lord."** (Devarim 23:2) Melamed also stated, "Even a married man who becomes a saris must divorce his wife." In line with these teachings, the imperative to have children comes up in many of the rules about saris.

SIXTEEN HUNDRED YEARS OF GENDER DIVERSITY

While so far we have focused on gender diversity in classical Judaism between 1 and 199 CE, the references to people who are androgynos, tumtum, aylonit, and saris continue in classical midrash and Jewish law codes all the way through the 1500s CE.

> Classical Jewish midrash is, as the website My Jewish Learning explains, "the process of interpretation by which the rabbis filled in 'gaps' found in the Torah."

From 201 through 1600 CE there were 350 references to people who were androgynos in classical midrash and Jewish law, 335 references to people who were tumtum, 40 references to people who were aylonit, and 379 references to people who were saris. With the 566 references in the first two hundred years CE, it adds up to more than 1,600 references to gender diversity in classical Jewish texts in about the same number of years!

A little more references, 1,670, than years, 1,600.

Traditional Jewish men include one prayer in their morning prayers that specifically thanks God for their gender. As the prayer goes, they thank God "who has not made me a woman." The instruction for the trio of prayers of gratitude that God made the Jewish man not a gentile, not a woman, and not a slave is set down in the Talmud, credited to Rabbi Judah bar Ilai in the second century. Some modern scholars have seen a parallel to an even more ancient tradition of Greek men thanking their Gods for three things: "that I was born a human and not a beast, a man and not a woman, a Greek and not a Barbarian."

Contrasting this misogyny is a trans prayer from 1322 CE—a powerful primary source example of gender diversity in historic Judaism.

Qalonymos ben Qalonymos was born in 1286 CE in Arles, a city that had one of the oldest Jewish communities in France. Like his father, Qalonymos (sometimes spelled Kalonymus), had the honorary title of "Nasi," which translates as "prince." Qalonymos was a translator, writer, and scholar, and at one point went to Rome. Some historians think Qalonymos was the one who, in 1321, pleaded "the cause of the Roman Jews before the pope at Avignon."

In 1322 Qalonymos wrote a manuscript, the *Eben Boḥan*, and it was first published over 150 years later, in 1489. In it, Qalonymos includes a prayer where they wish to have been created as "a fair woman" rather than their body's male form. Some historians think it was written as satire, while others read it and see a trans person writing from their heart. Read this translation by author and activist Abby Stein, and see what you think:

What an awful fate for my mother
that she bore a son. What a loss of all benefit! . . .
    Cursed be the one who announced to my father:
    "It's a boy! . . ." Woe to him who has male sons
Upon them a heavy yoke has been placed
restrictions and constraints. Some in private, some
    in public
some to avoid the mere appearance of violation
and some entering the most secret of places. Strong
    statutes and awesome commandments
six hundred and thirteen
who is the man who can do all that is written
so that he might be spared? Oh, but had the artisan
    who made me created me instead - a fair woman.
    Today I would be wise and insightful. We would
    weave, my friends and I
and in the moonlight spin our yarn
and tell our stories to one another
from dusk till midnight
we'd tell of the events of our day, silly things
matters of no consequence. But also I would grow
    very wise from the spinning

and I would say, "Happy is she who know how to
    work with combed flax and weave it into fine
    white linen." And at times, in the way of women,
    I would lie down on the kitchen floor, between
    the ovens, turn the coals, and taste the different
    dishes. On holidays I would put on my best
    jewelry. I would beat on the drum
and my clapping hands would ring. And when I was
    ready and the time was right
an excellent youth (husband) would be my fortune. He
    would love me, place me on a pedestal
dress me in jewels of gold
earrings, bracelets, necklaces. And on the appointed
    day, in the season of joy when brides are wed,
    for seven days would the boy increase my delight
    and gladness. Were I hungry, he would feed me
    well-kneaded bread. Were I thirsty, he would
    quench me with light and dark wine. He would not
    chastise nor harshly treat me, and my . . . pleasure
    he would not diminish
every Shabbath, and each new moon
his head would rest upon my breast. The three
    husbandly duties he would fulfill
rations, raiment, and regular intimacy. And three
    wifely duties would I also fulfill, [watching for
    menstrual] blood, [Sabbath candle] lights, and
    bread . . .
Father in heaven
who did miracles for our ancestors
with fire and water
You changed the fire of Chaldees so it would not
    burn hot

THE GENDER BINARY IS A BIG LIE

You changed Dina in the womb of her mother to a girl
You changed the staff to a snake before a million eyes
You changed (Moses') hand to (leprous) white
and the sea to dry land. In the desert you turned rock
    to water
hard flint to a fountain. Who would then turn me from
    a man to woman? Were I only to have merited this
being so graced by goodness. . . . What shall I say?
    why cry or be bitter? If my father in heaven has
    decreed upon me
and has maimed me with an immutable deformity
then I do not wish to remove it. the sorrow of the
    impossible
is a human pain that nothing will cure
and for which no comfort can be found. So, I will bear
    and suffer
until I die and wither in the ground.

Wow. What a prayer. And how amazing that we can read it today.

GENDER LIBERATION CAN BENEFIT EVERYONE

The editors of and contributors to TransTorah write that "TransTorah is not just about transgender people. We believe that our society's narrow beliefs about sex and gender are harmful to all people, and that gender liberation benefits everyone. We write with a vision of a world in which we all have more freedom to be our full selves. We all suffer when we are forced to conform to gender expectations that do not reflect the richness of our identities and gifts."

WRESTLING WITH—AND REINTERPRETING—BIBLICAL TEXT

One of the traditions of Jewish scholarship is to break down every word of a teaching, trying to understand it from multiple angles and perspectives, to get to the essence of what is being said.

Let's consider the biblical verse from Deuteronomy 22:5, **"A man's clothes should not be on a woman, and a man should not wear the apparel of a woman: for anyone who does these things, it is an abomination before God."**

Rabbis Kukla and Zellman say in their essay, "To Wear Is Human: Parshat Ki Teitze," in the 1000s CE, the biblical commentator Rashi said that the point of this Torah teaching was to prevent cross-dressing being used as a trick to have an intimate relationship outside a person's marriage. About one hundred years later, Maimonides said it was intended to prevent folks from sneaking off to worship idols. Rabbis Kukla and Zellman sum up the classical scholars' interpretation that cross-dressing is only wrong **"when it is for the express purpose of causing harm to our relationship with our loved ones or with God. The prohibition that we learn from this verse is very specific: we must not misrepresent our true gender in order to cause harm."**

Credited with being "the greatest Jewish philosopher of the medieval period"

Rabbis Kukla and Zellman see Deuteronomy 22:5—a verse that on its face seems so rigidly against gender nonconformity—as **"a positive *mitzvah*, a sacred obligation to present the fullness of our gender as authentically as possible. Unfortunately, not everyone is able to fulfill this mitzvah without endangering their life or livelihood. . . . However, the Torah wants us to be true to ourselves."**

While the technical definition of the word means "commandment," *mitzvahs* are understood to be good things that you (and others) do.

By being true to ourselves (and letting others be true to themselves), we can avoid causing harm. Rabbis Kukla and Zellman say, **"When we cover up our true souls and muffle our divine reflection under clothes that feel 'wrong', we are harming God's creation. This is what our Torah prohibits!"**

Seeing those biblical words as an affirmation of gender diversity rather than a critique is a powerful empowerment for gender-diverse Jews.

Rabbi Kukla says, **"Although Jewish Sages often tried to sort the world into binaries, they also acknowledged that not all parts of God's creation can be contained in orderly boxes."** As an example, he quotes the Babylonian Talmud on the uncertainty of twilight, the time in between day and night, **"As to twilight, it is doubtful whether it is part day and part night, or whether all of it is day or all of it is night. . . . Rabbi Yosi said: Twilight is like the twinkling of an eye as night enters and the day departs, and it is impossible to determine its length."**

In his 2006 sermon, "The Holiness of Twilight," given on the eve of Rosh HaShanah, Rabbi Zellman said,

The Jewish
New Year

Our rabbis believed that twilight held great and unique power. Demons abounded in these minutes between night and day. One was especially vulnerable to the many forces of evil.

With their concern about demons, we might expect that our rabbis would have warned us of the grave dangers of twilight. Perhaps we should not leave our houses at the time of sundown. . . .

Instead, the rabbis taught that twilight, and dawn, are the best times to pray. They concluded that these times that are in-between and indefinable are when our prayers are most likely to be heard. The place in the middle that made them afraid was also for them the place where miracles were most likely, where divine forces rise, where transformation is the most possible. Rather than shutting down the twilight hour, they opened it and elevated it. It is not a degraded middle place. It is exceptionally holy.

THE GENDER BINARY IS A BIG LIE

JEWISH DAYS BEGIN AT NIGHT

This is based on how the biblical creation story describes a day in Genesis 1: "And the evening and the morning were the first day," and then "And the evening and the morning were the second day," and so on.

When is the earliest that night begins? The Jewish scholars said sunset. And when is the latest that night begins? The Jewish scholars said when the third star is visible in the sky. So Jewish holidays begin the night before—even Shabbat, the weekly day of rest, begins at sunset on Friday and ends on Saturday when the third star is visible in the sky.

Rabbi Aron Moss suggests in "Why Do Jewish Holidays Begin at Nightfall?" that defining time in this way says important things about how Jews see life: "That's Jewish time—the comfort in knowing that no matter how dark it may seem, it is light that will have the last word."

In that sermon, Rabbi Zellman reflected that the references to gender diversity in the Mishnah and Talmud reveal that

> our rabbis of ancient times knew that humanity did not fit into two boxes. Just as day and night cannot be clearly divided into two, according to some of our most ancient texts, neither can people. . . . [The Mishnah] goes on to say that people of intermediate sex and gender were not to be harmed; their lives were of equal value to any other person's. . . . Twilight cannot be defined; it can only be sanctified and appreciated. People can't always be defined; they can only be seen and respected.

Here the term references a body's physical characteristics.

Rabbi Zellman continued, **"Like the wide spectrum of sexual identities, gender diversity is a gift to be celebrated. Some transgender experiences are about finding holiness in a journey from one gender to another. Other people choose to sanctify some place in between, or another identity entirely. No one can define twilight, but we all know its power and its beauty. Each human being, no matter what their gender identity, is created in the image of God. God's image transcends all categories."**

And then, on the eve of a new year, Rabbi Zellman gave his congregation a call to action: **"This is the time to throw out last year's fears; to question all the little boxes that tell us what, or where, or who we're 'supposed' to be; to reconsider whatever categories prevent us from exploring or becoming our full authentic selves."**

His words, and the history of gender diversity in Jewish tradition spanning centuries, challenge us to consider the following:

What boxes might you question?

What categories are holding you back?

How might you embrace your full authentic self?

Learning about gender diversity in classical Judaism was especially powerful for me since it is my culture. Is there gender diversity in your culture that might be hiding from you as well?

BROTHERBOYS AND SISTERGIRLS

AUSTRALIA

BEGINNING OF RECORDED TIME TO TODAY

Sistergirls and brotherboys have always been part of First Nations peoples and communities all over the continent called Australia. Brotherboys and sistergirls may identify as male, female, or nonbinary, and may use brotherboy and sistergirl along with other terms—there are many Australian First Nations gender identities beyond the gender binary.

"I'm 18 years old, and I'm a Brotherboy," Kai Clancy explained in a 2014 video interview, "Brotherboys Yarnin' Up—Kai and Dean," posted to YouTube. **"A Brotherboy is an Indigenous transgender or gender diverse person who is assigned female at birth, but inside they have a boy spirit, and they live through that boy spirit, and they take on male roles in society, and community, and they live their lives as a male. And being a Brotherboy encompasses your gender identity as well as your cultural identity."**

But part of the difficult legacy of colonization that suppressed First Nation traditions and imposed the idea that everyone should conform to the gender binary was that people didn't always learn about their cultural legacy of gender diversity. Kai's father, Troy Clancy, is Wulli Wulli, and when Kai came out to him he said, **"I was saddened in a sense, you know, coz I wasn't educated on it."** But in the 2000s a new movement to support and celebrate First Nations gender-diverse people is gaining traction. Clancy said, **"I've got a son now instead of a daughter as the head of my clan, my family and I'm quite happy with that. . . . It was a big weight off his shoulders that this side of his family, his Indigenous side, really gathered and took together . . . that's our tribe; if we got some in the flock that are like that we must nurture them too."**

Sistergirls, First Nations people who were assigned male at birth and have a female spirit and take on female roles in the community have greater visibility in the larger community. In the Tiwi Islands, about 50 miles (80 km) off the north coast of Australia, they are traditionally known as *yimpininni*. In 2017 a group of thirty sistergirls from the Tiwi Islands marched in the LGBTQ+ Mardi Gras in Sydney, part of a celebration of about three hundred thousand people. Sistergirl Jayma Timaepatua said in the *Guardian* that they were marching

"to remember the older sistagirls [sistergirls], who have passed away and who have pain. . . . If not for them I wouldn't be here for now."

Sistergirl Crystal Love Johnson in a video interview for ABC said, **"To go to the Mardi Gras is to showcase our culture and our people, how Tiwi people evolved in this generation and how we became stronger in our community. To show people you can make a change."**

Sistagirl and *brothaboy* are terms of endearment that do not reference a person's gender diversity. *Sistergirl* and *brotherboy* are the terms referencing First Nations gender identities.

The ongoing impact of colonialism—with the gender binary's singular ideas of what a "man" and a "woman" *should* be—was starkly illustrated in a 2020 television interview between Miriam Margolyes and a circle of five sistergirls sitting by the beach on the Tiwi Islands.

"We're Sistergirls, and we're transgender," one of the group tells Miriam.

Miriam doesn't have the vocabulary, and asks, "Are you men becoming women or women becoming men?"

Once Miriam learns they were assigned male at birth and live as women, she gestures to the facial hair on one of the sistergirls and tells her, "But you know, to be a woman, you're going to have to get rid of all that stuff. But I get whiskers on my chin, and I have to pick them out with tweezers. Because that's what women do. Give yourself a chance."

There's so much wrong with how this was asked, but the sistergirls are very gracious. Miriam might have phrased the question, "So your gender is different from the sex you were assigned at birth?"

One sistergirl responded: **"You know, in our culture, we respect a person regardless of the look,"** and here she swept her hand from another sistergirl's head to feet to signify the whole person. **"We don't look on the outside, it's the inside that you have to change."**

Miriam has a moment of understanding, "so my telling you to shave is stupid of me." They laugh, and the sistergirl Miriam had criticized for facial hair smiled and nodded. Miriam continued, "I should know that it's not what you look like outside, it's who you are and how you feel."

"Yes," more than one sistergirl told her.

The sistergirl with facial hair smiled confidently and said, **"It's just like . . . it's there for decoration."**

Lisa, a Worimi sistergirl from New South Wales runs a Facebook group where sistergirls and brotherboys are finding community and support. In an interview in 2017 for the *Star Observer* article "The Reality of Being Black and Trans in Australia," Lisa said, **"Once upon a time, historically, we were very accepted and had a place in the community. I think with the introduction of colonisation and religion and other beliefs, a lot of that stuff has been lost."**

Interviewed for the same article, Taz, a brotherboy from the Kalkadoon and Bwgcolman Nations in Queensland explained that cultural differences distinguish brotherboys from a trans man in the larger community. **"Even though I might be male, I can't just go and play the didge . . . that's still a very big no-no."** Taz added that brotherboys and sistergirls **"face more angles of discrimination. We're not only trans but we're also Aboriginal."** But facing prejudice, Taz said, **"just make[s] me feel even stronger about who I am. . . . We're part of a culture that's been going on for thousands of years. You can't say that's not impressive."**

A state on Australia's southeastern coast

The state just north of New South Wales on Australia's northeastern coast

This is a reference to ceremonial playing of the didgeridoo. Linda Barwick clarifies that "traditionally women have not played the didgeridoo in ceremony," but they do play the instrument informally.

Some First Nations people and communities refer to themselves as Aboriginal people and communities.

In a 2019 article on the Australian website Ygender, Felix (he/him), who identifies as nonbinary, is quoted as saying,

I'm Aboriginal and I still didn't learn that the gender binary was brought to us through colonialism until I was 17. How messed up is that? It's so hard to find info about our traditional gender ideas because the people who invaded our home deliberately erased it like they did with everything else. I wanna see more people, trans people and cis people, binary people and non-binary people, learning about first nations genders. Listen to brotherboys and sistergirls. Listen to us for a change.

Felix is referencing the colonial idea that everyone must fit within the gender binary.

It's inspiring to see that the different generations of gender-diverse First Nations people are looking out for one another. In his fifties, Wiradjuri brotherboy Dean told viewers in the *Brotherboys Yarnin' Up* video recorded with Kai Clancy, **"Be proud of who you are and don't hide it. Don't be ashamed. . . . Shame has no place in our culture."**

CHAPTER 3

HiJRAS

INDIA, PAKISTAN, BANGLADESH, NEPAL

BEGINNING OF RECORDED TIME TO TODAY

WHEN SOMEBODY ASKS ME, "WHO ARE YOU?" I TELL THEM, "I AM THE OLDEST ETHNIC TRANSGENDER COMMUNITY IN THE WORLD, WHICH HAS ITS OWN CULTURE AND OWN RELIGIOUS BELIEFS."

—Laxmi Narayan Tripathi, in a 2015 interview

WHO ARE HIJRAS?

Pronounced "hidjra" for an individual

Laxmi Narayan Tripathi traces her hijra community all the way back to the Manu-smriti, the religious book of codes Hindus believe were formulated at the beginning of the human race. Between 1750 and 500 BCE, hijras were called kinnar and had a high cultural status. In a 2015 interview, Laxmi explained, **"We were very highly regarded people. We were at the court, we were cooks, the keepers of the queen's palace. When the Muslim *nawabs* came, we were the harem keepers, the advisers, responsible for guarding the queens. We were in all the sectors of life, considered special people, nobles, even divine."**

Hijras ask to be referred to with feminine pronouns.

Rulers

The hijra family structure is made up of gurus, who have a mentor/parental role, and their chelas, who are a guru's disciples and have an apprentice/grown child's role. Some chelas will grow with experience and time to become gurus themselves, and take on their own chelas, and so the tradition continues, generation after generation. Gurus are organized into one of seven gharanas,

Anthropologist Serena Nanda describes them as houses, and they've been described by hijras to be like fingers on a hand.

THE GENDER BINARY IS A BIG LIE

each of which has a nayak, or leader. Social rank in the community of hijras, Serena Nanda, professor emeritus of anthropology, says is based on "seniority, judged not by age but by the time of entry into the hijra community."

Laxmi Narayan Tripathi, an Indian hijra, speaking on a 2017 panel at the Melbourne, Australia, Writers Festival on "Gender and the Spaces Between"

Laxmi, a guru with more than fifteen chelas under her wing, says **"The guru's other chelas become the hijra's sisters, the guru's sisters become her aunts or massis, and the guru's guru becomes her nani or grandmother. It is a vast extended family."**

What happened to change hijras' high standing in their culture? Laxmi tells us:

Our status changed after the British came to India. They saw us as a threat to their rule because we were very loyal to the courts and the kingdoms we served. They took away our lands, because they thought inheritance had to be through blood, and they never understood our structure. They didn't allow our land to be inherited by our chelas. Our possessions were taken away from us, and we were left with nothing. . . .

While direct British rule over what today is India and Pakistan lasted from 1858 to 1947 (Queen Victoria gave herself the title Empress of India), British colonialism had started over a hundred years earlier.

After independence, nothing happened. The British mentality was still very deeply rooted in society, and 200 years of British rule had totally discarded our existence. . . . When we started our activism, we had to tell people, "We exist, we are humans. Please give us nothing but our basic dignity." The biggest misery in the world, I believe, is the feeling of being unloved, and that this community faces a lot. You're not even considered to be human.

Nanda wrote *Neither Man nor Woman: The Hijras of India* as an overview of this third, separate, but now less-than-equal gender in Indian culture. Many who might identify as trans, queer, genderqueer, intersex, or other gender-diverse identities or a combination of these have found and still find a place in the hijra community. Nanda says the hijras are "a well-defined, culturally and socially acknowledged, organizationally set apart, ritually specialized, historically continuous, sex/gender variation."

I was really surprised that the very first person Nanda thanked in her book's acknowledgments was John Money—see chapter 7 for more on him.

Hijras self-identify from many different parts of the larger Indian community. Some are Hindu, and some are Muslim. They come from many economic and social classes and varied locations. **"The word 'hij,'"** Laxmi writes, **"refers to the soul, a holy soul. The body in which the holy soul resides is called 'hijra'. The individual is not important here. What is important is the soul and the hijra community [that] possesses it."**

RELIGIOUS POWER AND PLACE

Nanda says, "The hijras, as human beings who are neither men nor women, call into question the basic social categories of gender on which Indian society is built. This makes the hijras objects of fear, abuse, ridicule, and sometimes pity. But hijras are not merely ordinary human beings . . . they are also conceptualized as special, sacred beings, through a ritual transformation."

Hijras hold a special traditional role of performing at and blessing the births of male children and weddings. Taking place a few days or weeks after the birth or wedding, the ceremonies include dancing, singing, drumming, and they have a fertility-blessing component, which is directly related to hijras being physically unable or unwilling to have biological children themselves.

Nanda described one badhai ceremony she attended that took place six weeks after the birth of a male child, Ram, in the courtyard in front of the family's home. **The sound of clapping, drumming, and ankle bells announced that the hijras were arriving. . . . The dancers clapped their hands wildly in the special manner of hijras—with hollow palms—and began to sing and shout and dance.**" At one point the leader of the hijras took the baby and danced with him. "**'Give money to bless this baby,' she demanded of the baby's grandmother. Taking the proffered two-rupee note, Tamasha passed it over the baby's head in a ritualized gesture that is a blessing and that wards off evil spirits. . . . The hijras called on the Indian Mother Goddess, Parvati, and their own special goddess, Bahucharar Mata, to confer**

Back when Nanda witnessed this in the 1980s, two rupees were worth about twenty cents in US money.

fertility, prosperity, and long life on the baby, as the ladies in the audience threw them one- and two-rupee notes."

One hijra told Nanda, "There are other people who imitate us, who dress up in women's clothing and go where a baby is born, but only we have the power of giving it the blessing. This is because we are neither men nor women and have been separated from God, so that God grants our special prayers in every place, to us only. A hijra is born from the stomach of a woman, but can be counted neither among the

HIJRA POWER AND PRECOLONIAL RESPECT ARE ROOTED IN HISTORY

People believe that the blessings of a hijra come true. And the belief originates in no less a source than the Ramayana itself.

—Laxmi Narayan Tripathi

The *Ramayana* is an epic poem likely written around 300 BCE that was "a chronicle of events and characters recorded by Sage Valmiki." In the Indian news outlet the *Pioneer* in 2015, after three years of study, a team of international researchers declared that the *Ramayana* was about real people and things that happened and "not a work of fiction."

men nor the women. **This is why we are called hijras and why we have a right to nothing except singing and dancing."**

RESPECT AND FEAR

The power to bless that hijras are believed to have has a flip side—they are also believed to have the power to curse. Laxmi said, **"People believe that if a hijra curses you, bad things will happen. That God Ram[a] blessed hijras with this power, that our [blessings and] curses will come true. People**

Laxmi summarizes the origin of hijra power as told in the epic poem:

It is said that when Lord Rama began his fourteen-year exile in the forests, the people of Ayodhya accompanied him to the outskirts of the town to bid him farewell. Here, Lord Rama turned to his subjects and said to them, "Oh, all you men and women who love me, please return to your homes. I will complete my exile and be back among you." Among his subjects were hijras too. They were neither men nor women. They couldn't go back to their homes, for he had implored only the men and women to return home. The hijras stayed put at the outskirts of the town for fourteen years until he returned. Lord Rama was moved by the penance of the hijras. He granted them a boon: their blessings and their curses would come true.

give us money because they are scared of our curse. Now that's the only way hijras can survive—by saying 'Give me money, otherwise I'll curse you.' That clap, which scares people, has become our identity. In a way, you use myths and misconceptions for your own survival."

And part of the respect and fear of hijras in Indian society is connected to the changes many hijras make to their bodies.

PHYSICAL ALTERATION OF HIJRA BODIES

Some hijras born with male genitalia go through an initiation ceremony where their male genitalia are removed. For the hijras who go through this type of nirvan (also translated as "nirvana") ritual of rebirth, castration is the removal of the penis and testicles. Other hijras choose not to change their bodies but are still considered hijra by the community. Laxmi explains that **"castration is strictly optional, and every hijra decides for herself whether or not to undergo it. Castration cannot be forced upon a hijra. Though the world believes that a castrated hijra alone is a real hijra, we do not endorse this."**

The nirvan ceremony is not something hijras rush into. Nanda wrote that of the ten hijras she met who had gone through the ceremony, nine of them had been a member of the hijra community for between five to fifteen years before they decided to go through with the ritual themselves.

Salima, one of the hijras who Nanda profiled, was born intersex and had multiple piercings to her nose and ears as the physical aspect of her initiation. Her childhood friends would tell the people who teased her, **"It is not her fault. God made her that way. She doesn't have any masculinity in her; God has made him a woman."**

Renouncing or eliminating the ability to have children of their own is a critical part of a hijra's perceived power. Laxmi shared that among the hijras, **"people get castrated because of peer pressure, because they want to look feminine, because when they go to weddings and beg and people don't give, they can suddenly strip—that's the biggest weapon they have."** It's sad that the weapon being spoken of is hijras' own gender-diverse bodies, seen as so scary by people inside the gender binary that just exposure to a castrated hijra body is interpreted as a threat.

The stigma and fear of hijras extends to the traditional rituals. In describing the hijra ceremony for a wedding, Nanda said that some of the more orthodox Hindu families "do not allow the bride to be present in the courtyard with the hijras . . . believing that the hijras' infertility will contaminate the girl and keep her from having a son."

In the postcolonial world, hijras have been disenfranchised for hundreds of years. They have been dismissed and looked down on by their families of origin and by society. As their opportunity to make a living from the traditional ceremonies for weddings and births of male children diminished, hijras were left with few options. Laxmi said, **"We abuse hijras when they 'harass' us on the streets, without realizing that the things they can do in order to survive can be counted on the fingers of one hand— begging, singing, dancing, and . . . [being physically intimate with other people for money]. Can a hijra in India ever aspire to be a doctor, engineer, teacher, journalist, or business manager? The answer is a resounding NO."**

HiJRAS SELF-IDENTIFY

Nanda notes that "hijras are evidence that the Hindu Indian cultural system not only acknowledges multiple genders, but also incorporates the idea . . . that sex and gender can be changed within an individual's lifetime."

Originally, Laxmi thought she was a young gay man. As Laxmi grew, she realized that **"when I was attracted to a man, I did not think of myself as a man. I thought of myself as a woman."** Finding and joining the hijra community was in some ways a homecoming. Laxmi described it, **"When I became a hijra, a great burden was lifted off my head. I felt relaxed. I was now neither a man nor a woman. I was a hijra. I had my own identity. No longer did I feel like an alien."**

Laxmi acknowledged that joining the hijra has traditionally meant leaving your family of birth for a new family. **"In our community, your parents disown you, your family, friends, everybody disowns you. In the world of being disowned, the guru is the person who gives you shelter, who gives you food, who teaches you how to earn money and live in this world. . . . The guru is the one person who will never question you for the reasons the world questioned you."**

When Laxmi confided in a few friends after joining the hijra community, their reactions ranged from **"Why have you brought this hell on yourself?"** to **"You were, you are, and you will always remain Laxmi for me."** Even other hijras seemed surprised at Laxmi's self-identifying as a hijra and joining the hijra community. Laxmi said, **"To their way of thinking, only the wretched of the earth became hijras. A college-educated boy, who was an accomplished dancer and had the support of his parents, had no need to."** Faced with so many cultural barriers, hijras have been struggling for their rights, respect, and dignity.

HOPE FOR A FUTURE OF DIGNITY FOR HIJRAS

SOME HIJRAS MARRY MEN

Meera, one of the hijras profiled by Nanda, explained how marriage between a hijra and a man worked. **"Among us hijras, if we keep a man as a husband, we must live with him. . . . At this age [middle age] we would like to be more respectable and lead a respectable life. So after some time we fall in love with a man, and eventually we marry him and lead the life of any normal housewife."**

Nanda reflected on how, in contrast to the wider culture's tradition of arranged marriages, "hijras and their husbands freely choose each other as mates."

Marriage to a man was the route taken by Sushila, one of the four hijras featured in Nanda's book. Nanda tells us that in 1981 Sushila "spoke very warmly of her husband and was disconsolate because she could not give him a child. She very much wanted this for him, because she thought it was necessary that he lead 'a normal family life.'" Four years later, Sushila proudly told Nanda that "she was now a mother-in-law and a grandmother! . . . She had adopted her [former] husband as her son and had arranged his marriage with a neighbor's sister. The girl was poor, but respectable, and quite pretty. The couple now had a son, making Sushila a grandmother." As the remarried Sushila told Nanda, **"Now I'm leading the life of a respectable woman with a husband, an adopted son, a daughter-in-law, and a grandson—and running a house. For this we get some respect outside."**

RESPECT

A defining element of contemporary hijra identity seems to be a desire for respectability. Sushila and Laxmi both achieved a measure of respect, Sushila through marriage and forming a traditional-styled family with herself as the matriarch and Laxmi through celebrity and activism on an international stage.

Happily, the lack of employment options for hijras is changing. In her 2015 interview, Laxmi describes hijras who are employed "in social work, the fashion industry, who have PhDs." And in her autobiography, Laxmi mentions a handful of elected hijra politicians! As part of her work as an activist fighting for hijra rights and respect, Laxmi organized a beauty contest for members of the hijra community. Why? **"Hijras are considered to be ugly people. I wanted to reverse that mindset. . . . Our Indian Super Queen contest was being held on a scale as grand as any Miss India or Miss Universe contest."**

Speaking of her own career as a dancer and an activist, Laxmi wrote, **"If the world is a stage, art entertains while activism teaches. . . . If I had to choose between the two, I would choose activism."**

FAMILY

When her parents discovered Laxmi had self-identified as a hijra, her mother said, **"No one in fourteen generations has done such a thing in our family. We are a noble, high-caste Brahman family. Didn't you think of our self-respect? Your sister is married. What will her husband's family think of us?"** Their efforts to pull Laxmi back to the established path for a man included arranging Laxmi's marriage to a young woman.

Laxmi wrote of being **"aghast"** when told of the arrangement. Laxmi was twenty-one years old, and when she refused the wedding, it was the first time she had ever seen her father cry. Looking back, Laxmi says, **"My parents wanted me to lead a normal life. They wanted me to get married and beget children. . . . They were torn between the** demands of society and the love of their son. But how could I let them stifle me?"

Years later, on a popular television show in India, Laxmi's father spoke about Laxmi being a hijra: **"Why should I expel Laxmi from the family? I am his father, he is my responsibility. A hijra can be born to any family. If we spurn them and show them the door, we leave them with no alternative but to become beggars. Driving Laxmi out of the house was out of question."**

Laxmi wrote of her internal conflict: **"I did not want to live in a hijra ghetto. I wanted to be Raju to my parents; Raju, their eldest son. Though my family had reservations about my becoming a hijra, they did not turn into monsters like the families of some other hijras. So I had a duty towards them. . . . If we can be hijras without shaming our families, what's the harm in that?"**

In her autobiography, Laxmi explains how she created a life as a hijra where she embraces the joy and responsibilities of being both the eldest son of her family and a hijra:

> **There's a family I'm related to by blood, and then there are my chelas who are my other family. I need both families and cannot envisage a life without either. And so it is that I live with both these families simultaneously. There are two houses on the same floor in the same building. Only a wall separates them. In one house, my mother, my brother Sashi and his wife, and their son Anshuman live. In the other, I live with my chelas. The doors of both houses are kept open all day. People freely move from one house to the other. . . . My mother gets on well with all my chelas, and they in turn respect her and shower their love on Anshuman.**

MORE GENDER DIVERSITY IN INDIA

There is no single story of gender diversity for a country as vast and varied as India—or any country. Santa Khurai identifies as an Indigenous member of the queer community called Nupi Maanbi and is a spokesperson for the transgender community in Manipur, a state in northeastern India. Thirty different languages are spoken in Manipur, and in Meitei, Khurai explains, **"'Nupi' means 'girl, woman', and 'Maanbi' means 'alike, similar.'"** She spoke about the diversity of her community in a 2020 interview with university student Alessandra Monticelli: **"As a queer person, my identity is challenging, because people question my body. People question queer bodies. People question queer identities, people question my life, my food, and how I sleep with my husband. Beyond me and my personal issues, young queer groups, which we call Nupi-Maanbi, who generally wear female make up and attires, get questioned and attacked."**

Khurai also spoke of other genders in her culture: **"In Manipur, there is a queer community called 'Shumang Lila', which is very visible. They claim cross-dress only for performing, and once off the stage are just cisgender men. That is why they are treated with a sort of privilege. Then we have the 'Nupa Amaibi' transgender shaman peoples, who have a blessed voice. And then the 'Nupi-Maanbi', persons like me, who are far less accepted. . . . There is also a Shuman Lila female group, who, in turn, dress up as men, but people prefer the play performed by the men, accepting this queer identity less."**

In a short documentary on the Nupa Amaibi by Khurai and Siddharth Haobijam posted on YouTube, Yambem Bobby, who identifies as a Nupa Amaibi, shared that **"Nupa Amaibi has been in existence since the earliest time. . . . In fact, knowing their place in the society, the king gave great respect to them."**

Gender diversity in northeastern India is ancient—and threatened. As Khurai explained,

> **Before Christianity spread over the region, as far as I know—for sure in Manipur and Mizoram—there was inclusion of gender plurality and multiplicity in the belief system. . . . There are female and male Shamans in Manipur and researchers always do studies on female shamanism. In the meantime, in the recent years, an organisation has started to threaten them and have instructed them not to wear female attire. So, because of that these people have started going back to the cloister. Male shamans hardly come out. . . . This is a warning to our culture. If we were able to preserve this culture, the male shaman culture, at least this could be another clue for the international community on how different peoples, different queer people, occupy spaces and how the natural behaviour within shamanism is connected to the queer people.**

Another northeastern state of India

Khurai's words on the efforts to eliminate gender diversity are indeed a warning to all cultures.

In Laxmi's 2015 interview, she explained the reason for her activism:

> I wanted my dignity. I wanted to give it back to the society that had tortured my parents, that always said, "Oh, their son is a hijra," and looked down on them. . . . I have become like a role model, and people feel that I must have had a really cool life, my parents accepting me, like a Cinderella story. It's not like a Cinderella story for me. I had to be my own fairy godmother and create myself. . . . Nobody will come and give you your rights. Hijras have got their right. They should know to expand it, should know to demand it.

Laxmi became a celebrity in India, starring in a film about hijras, traveling to international conferences, and in 2012 publishing her autobiography *Me Hijra, Me Laxmi*. She was the plaintiff in the 2014 legal case where the Indian Supreme Court ordered the government to officially acknowledge the existence of a third gender category, saying in their ruling, **"It is the right of every human being to choose their gender."**

Laxmi celebrated the victory, saying, **"Today, I feel a proud citizen of India."**

At the time of the Indian Supreme Court ruling, an estimated two to three million hijras lived in India. In that same 2015 interview, Laxmi said, **"When somebody asks me, 'Who are you?' I tell them, 'I am the oldest ethnic transgender community in the world, which has its own culture and own religious beliefs.' And we are in four countries in South Asia: India, Pakistan, Bangladesh, and the Terai region of Nepal."**

THE GENDER BINARY IS A BIG LIE

Are there insights from the historical heights, the colonial fall, and the current reclaiming of respect for hijra living in India that we can apply to how we see and treat gender-diverse people in our cultures and in our communities?

Are we too quick to dismiss entire categories of people who have few options to support themselves?

How can we offer opportunity and respect to people disenfranchised for any reason—including the authentic expression of their gender?

ZISHU NÜ— SELF-COMBED WOMEN

A.K.A. ZISHUNÜ, GOLDEN ORCHID SOCIETIES, GOLDEN ORCHID SISTERHOODS, MARRIAGE RESISTERS, HEART-TO-HEART FRIENDS

CHINA

UNKNOWN (FIRST SURVIVING RECORD 1644) TO 1950

Dominant culture's stance that everyone is supposed to fit within a gender binary can make it seem as if other cultures line up (and have always lined up) with stereotypes about only one possible role for those assigned male at birth and only one possible role for those assigned female at birth. That's a big lie too. The stories and lives of self-combed women in the Pearl River delta offer us insight into other queer-inclusive paths for people assigned female at birth in China for at least three hundred years—and possibly much longer.

The Pearl River delta area of China was a center of silk production. Somewhat unusual for patriarchal, ◄ preindustrial China, unmarried women as well as men worked outside the home and earned wages.

> A system where men are seen as in charge and women are disenfranchised

Traditionally, daughters were raised to marry men, and when they did, they left their birth family to join their husband's family. This was expensive for the daughter's family, as a dowry had to be paid to the husband's family. In this part of China at that time, unmarried women wore their hair down. As part of the wedding ceremony, the bride's hair was combed and pinned up into the hairstyle of a married woman. Once married, the status of the bride in her new family was seen as very low.

Other paths for people assigned female at birth included those who might today identify as aromantic and/or asexual. Some daughters took vows to *not* marry a man, instead choosing to remain a wage earner contributing to her birth family and enjoy a higher status than she would if married to a man. The ceremony for taking this vow has been described as similar to a wedding ceremony, except without a groom. The daughter would comb and put up her own hair—hence, the Chinese term *zishu nü*, meaning "self-combed woman." The daughter's family would then host a celebration that was comparable to the banquet they would throw for the marriage of a son.

Sometimes the daughter taking the vow was helped in the ceremony by another self-combed woman.

Often self-combed women lived together and shared finances in groupings referred to as golden orchid societies, golden orchid sisterhoods, and heart-to-heart friends. Sometimes there was a romantic element to those relationships, between women who might today identify as lesbians. The 1773 *A Record of the Customs of All China* by Hu Pu'an says, "The practice of the Golden Orchid Oath is known by the common name of 'Heart-to-heart Friends' and also called 'Making Friends.' It is not known when this custom started."

These relationships are described further in the 1935 edition of *The Gazetteer of Chinese Customs*: "Whenever two members . . . developed deep feelings for each other, certain rites of 'marriage' were performed. For such a 'marriage' to be permitted, one partner was designated the 'husband.' The first step consisted of offering to the intended partner a gift of peanut candies, honey, and other sweets. Once this was accepted, a night-long celebration attended by mutual female friends followed. From then on, the couple would live as 'man and wife.' . . . The couple could also adopt female children and these children could inherit the property of their 'parents.'"

All the quote marks around "marriage" and assigning one woman in a lesbian relationship the role of "husband" are probably the biased heteronormative view of the person who wrote about or translated this custom. Early in my twenty-five-plus-year relationship with my husband, multiple people who hadn't met a gay male couple before asked me which one of us was the woman in our relationship. The answer, of course, was neither of us.

Interviewed in 2007, Ying Gu, who was a self-combed woman, said, **"When I was young, I always thought that my aunt's lives were wonderful. They earned money themselves; they enjoyed high status in my family. The best husband could not treat you as well as your brother. My aunts were never forced to do anything, unlike my mother who suffered in the family. . . . Zishu nü did not lose anything but enjoyed their freedom and others' respect. Of course I was keen to choose to be a zishu nü myself."**

The decline of the silk industry in the 1930s and '40s was followed by new marriage laws in 1950 under China's Communist government, which meant that no new daughters

In Shatou Village, Shunde District, Guangdong Province in China's Pearl River delta, money raised by self-combed women built this retirement home for self-combed women known as the Hall of Ice and Jade. Today it is a museum.

of marrying age would become self-combed women. A 2014 article in the *Guardian* interviewed Liang Jieyun (who was eighty-five at the time) and Huang Li-e (who was ninety), both of whom were zishu nü. **"A lot of men chased after me,"** Jieyun said with a shooing motion to illustrate the memory, **"I told them to go away."**

Was zishu nü a different gender? It was certainly a different life path for those assigned female at birth, one that had cultural meaning and respect quite separate from the path of wife and mother.

CHAPTER 4

MĀHŪ

HAWAI'I AND TAHITI

BEGINNING OF RECORDED TIME TO TODAY

A MĀHŪ IS AN INDIVIDUAL THAT STRADDLES SOMEWHERE IN THE MIDDLE OF THE MALE AND FEMALE BINARY.
—Hinaleimoana Wong-Kalu

A PLACE IN THE MIDDLE FOR MĀHŪ

There's a pattern of gender diversity's role in a number of Native and Indigenous communities: honored place to stigmatized during colonization to present-day reclamation and revival. The māhū in Hawaiian and Tahitian culture follow this pattern, and learning about their journey can offer insight into how views of gender diversity were impacted as lands were colonized.

Pronounced "Maw-hoo"

The 2015 short documentary *A Place in the Middle* opens with title cards that explain, **"In the Hawaiian language, *kāne* means 'male' and *wahine* means 'female.' But ancient Hawaiians recognized that some people are not simply one or the other."** Ho'onani Kamai, an eleven-year-old Hawaiian, tells the camera, **"Sometimes kumu says I have more kāne inside than most of the kāne. And some kāne have more wahine than the wahine. Some people don't accept it—they tease about it. But I wouldn't care at all. Because I'm myself, other people are theirselves."**

Kumu is the Hawaiian word for "teacher."

When the documentary was being made, Ho'onani attended Hālau Lōkahi, a public charter school in Honolulu that was **"trying to keep the ancient traditions alive."** Dedicated to native Hawaiian culture, language, and history, the school's focus was the exact subjects that had long been off-limits in Hawai'i's Americanized educational system. The short film was a kid-friendly spin-off of a longer documentary about Ho'onani's teacher, Hinaleimoana Wong-Kalu, called Kumu Hina, and her name is also the name of the documentary. The press materials for the documentary describe Kumu Hina as "a proud and confident māhū, or transgender woman, and an honored and respected kumu, or teacher, cultural practitioner, and community leader." Kumu Hina said, **"A māhū is an individual that straddles somewhere in the middle of the male and female binary. It does not define their sexual preference or gender expression, because gender roles, gender expressions and sexual relationships have all been severely influenced by the changing times. It is dynamic. It is like life."**

While organizing a hulu event for Ho'onani's sixth-grade class, Kumu Hina explained that every student was to get a lei, and kāne would get the yellow leis (while wahine would get the white leis). Kumu Hina asked Ho'onani, "You're happy? You're in boy lei."

A symbol of aloha, a lei is a necklace made of flowers, leaves, shells, or other materials.

Ho'onani answered, "I want to just wear both." Another student responded somewhat jealously, "aww . . . ," as Kumu Hina placed a white lei over Ho'onani's head as well.

Kumu Hina said, "See, you get both cause she's both." Looking up from the yellow and white leis around their neck, Ho'onani smiled.

MĀHŪ PRECOLONIZATION AND TODAY

Kumu Hina described traditional Hawaiian culture, **"Before the coming of foreigners to our islands, we Hawaiians lived in aloha, in harmony with the land and with one another. Every person had their role in society, whether male, female, or _māhū_, those who embrace both the feminine and masculine traits that are embodied within each and every one of us. Māhū were valued and respected as caretakers,** healers, and teachers of ancient traditions. We passed on sacred knowledge from one generation to the next through hula, chant, and other forms of wisdom."

The arrival of American missionaries in the 1800s brought intolerance and the colonial drive to eradicate Native culture—including the existence and role of the māhū. Kuma Hina said, **"They were shocked and infuriated by these practices and did everything they could to abolish them. They condemned our hula and chant as immoral. They outlawed our language, and they imposed their religious strictures across our lands. But we Hawaiians are a steadfast and resilient people. And so, despite 200 years of colonization and repression, we are still here."** Kumu Hina referred to both Native Hawaiians and māhū within Hawaiian culture surviving—and working to thrive.

Restrictions on what people could and could not do

Kumu Hina uses the terms *kāne-wahine* and *wahine-kāne*, **"to address my students whom exude both kāne and wahine. So when the kāne stand up, and when the wahine stand up, they also know that there is a place in the middle for the kāne-wahine, and the wahine-kāne."**

Ho'onani tells us about their teacher, **"Kumu's in the middle too. Everybody knows that. And it's not a secret to everybody. What middle means is . . . a rare person."**

Kumu Hina was given the name Collin Wong and assigned male at birth, and recalls, **"When I was in high school . . . I had a very rough time. I was teased and tormented for being too girlish. But I found refuge in being Hawaiian, being Kanaka Maoli. . . . My purpose in this lifetime is to pass on the true meaning of aloha—love, honor, and respect. It's a responsibility that I take very seriously."**

Native Hawaiian

Kū is the Hawaiian word for male energy. In teaching a group of high school boys a dance that Ho'onani would be part of, Kumu Hina tells them, **"You have a biological wahine, standing over here in front of you, because she has more kū than everybody else around here, even though she lacks the main essential parts of kū."** Here Ho'onani chuckled at the reference to male genitalia. Kumu Hina continued, **"But in her mind and in her heart, she has kū."**

At one point in the documentary, Kumu Hina takes Ho'onani aside and acknowledges that not everyone will honor their being māhū. **"Sometimes I feel like I might be setting you up for some disappointment. I know that you like to go stand with all the boys, and I know that's where you like to go. And Kumu's okay with that. But when you work with other people, they may expect you to stand in the girl's line, okay? So, for as long as you stay a young person, you just roll with it, you know? When you get to be my age, you're not going to have to move for anybody else. Okay?"** It's clearly a hard lesson, and reality, for them both. When Kumu Hina finished saying this, the two hugged.

THE STONES OF LIFE—MĀHŪ HISTORY IN HAWAII AND TAHITI
More than four million people a year visit Waikiki Beach. Just steps from the sand is a monument of four large stones, but the sign doesn't acknowledge that it is to honor and celebrate the contributions of four māhū.

In the *Hawaiian Almanac and Annual for 1907*, Jas. H. Boyd wrote about the "Tradition of the Wizard Stones Ka-Pae-Mahu:

> **From the land of Moaulanuiakea (Tahiti) there came to Hawaii long before the reign of King Kakuihewa [sic], four sooth-sayers from the Court of the Tahitian King. Their names were: Kapaemahu, Kahaloa, Kapuni and**

Kinohi. They were received as became their station, and their tall stature, courteous ways and kindly manners, made them soon loved by the Hawaiian people. The attractiveness of their fine physique and kindly demeanor was overshadowed by their low, soft speech which endeared them to all with whom they came in contact. They were unsexed by nature, and their habits coincided with their feminine appearance, although manly in stature and general bearing. After a long tour of the islands this quartette of favorites of the gods settled at Ulukou, or Kou, W'aikiki, . . .

The wizards or soothsayers proved to be adepts in the science of healing and many wonderful cures by the laying on of hands are reported to have been effected by them so that their fame spread all over this island (Oahu), as the ancients say, "from headland to headland."

In course of time, knowing that their days amongst their Hawaiian friends were drawing to a close, they caused their desire for recognition for past services to be remembered in some tangible form. . . . Four large selected rocks, weighing several tons each, were taken to the beach lot at Ulukou, Waikiki, two of which were placed in the position occupied by their hut and the other two were placed in their bathing place in the sea. The Chief of the wizards, Kapaemahu, had his stone so named, and with incantations and ceremonies transferred his wit[c]hcraft powers thereto, and sacrifice was offered of a lovely, virtuous young

Consider the agenda of the person recording history. Owen Jarus wrote in their Live Science article "25 Cultures That Practiced Human Sacrifice" that it's possible the accounts of human sacrifice in Hawaii "were exaggerated as a way to depict Hawaiian culture as savage and justify desires by Europeans and Americans to control the island."

chiefess, and her body placed beneath the stone. Idols indicating the hermaphrodite sex of the wizards were also placed under each stone and tradition tells that the incantations, prayers and fastings lasted one full moon. Tradition further states—as is related in the old-time meles of that period—that, after the ceremonies which included the transfer of all their powers, by each of the wizards to the stones thus placed, that they vanished, and were seen no more, but the rocks having lately been discovered they have been exhumed from their bed of sand by direction of Governor Cleghorn and have been placed in position in the locality found, as tangible evidence of a Hawaiian tale.

A song, chant, or poem

The stones were recovered around 1906. Colonial disrespect for Indigenous traditions meant that in 1941, when the land where the stones had been placed was leased to build a bowling alley, the stones were used in the building's foundation. When the bowling alley was demolished in 1958, the stones were recovered. They were moved a few times, and in 1997 an effort was made to find a more respectful home for the stones. Manu Boyd, a cultural historian and the great-great-grandson of Archibald Cleghorn, said, "The value and meaning of the stones had faded over time with the changing values and mores of the day. Then, their importance was remembered and embraced by people who wanted to restore them." The final ceremonies installing the stones in their new sacred home, within view of the sea, included a group from Tahiti, who blessed the stones.

Researching the history of the stones in the 1980s, June Gutmanis wrote that in the mid-1800s Princess Miriam Likelike would offer a lei to each of the stones and pray there

The Stones of Life in their current location just off Waikiki Beach, within sight of the ocean waves.

before entering the ocean. Today, two plaques are placed by the stones—one in Hawaiian, the other in English. The English plaque reads:

The Stones of Life
An Pōhaku Ola Kapaemāhu ā Kapunan

Legend says these stones are the living legacy of four powerful Tahitian healers who once resided near this site at a place called Ulukou. From the court of the Tahitian chief, the names of the four were Kapaemāhū, Kapuni, Kinohi and Kahāloa. They came from Moaʻulanuiakea on the island of Raiatea long before the reign of Kākuhihewa, beloved Oʻahu chief during the 1500s.

The fame of the healers spread as they traveled throughout the islands administering their miraculous cures. When it was time to return to Raiatea, they asked that two stones be placed at their Ulukou residence and two at their favorite bathing place in the sea. Four huge stones were quarried from Kaimukī, and

on the night of "Kāne" thousands transported the stones to Ulukou. Incantations, fasting and prayers lasted a full cycle of the moon. The healers then gave their names and *mana* (spiritual power) to the stones before departing for their homeland.

Thousands of people gathered to help move the stones and honor these māhū!

> Pīpī Holo Ka'ao
> (Sprinkled, the tale runs)

In 1997, the stones were raised onto a *paepae* (stone platform), and an *ahu* (altar) and fence were built to honor and protect them. The largest stone was estimated to weigh 7.5 tons [6.8 t]. As part of the project ceremonies, Tahitians from Raiatea presented a stone from the healers' homeland which they named *Ta'ahu Ea* (the life).

These ancient stones are part of the spiritual history of Waikīkī and the native Hawaiian people. They remind us of the need to preserve and honor Hawai'i's unique heritage for generations to come.

> Department of Parks and Recreation
> City and County of Honolulu
> 1997

Dreya Blume points out in the epilogue to *'O Au No Kei: Voices from Hawai'i's Mahu and Transgender Communities* that the plaque doesn't mention that the four honored individuals were māhū. Blume wrote of the irony of the memorial's "conspicuous location," while the true gender diversity of the people it honors "remains deeply buried." Blume connects that injustice to how "many people living on O'ahu, whether of Hawaiian background or not, have little or no understanding of the valuable roles māhū once played in Hawaiian culture."

HIDING MĀHŪ HISTORY IN TAHITI TOO

The presence and role of māhū was also obscured by colonial powers in Tahiti. Captain William Bligh visited Tahiti in 1788 on the British ship HMS *Bounty* with the goal of collecting breadfruit trees to take to the Caribbean where they were to become a food source for the British plantations there. The editors of the Royal Collection Trust, commenting on the copy of Bligh's *A Voyage to the South Sea* in King George III's library at Windsor, said, "During his time on the island, Bligh made several observations on Tahitian culture and society, most notably the Tahitian concept of a third gender, known as māhū (in the middle). Historically only attributed to people who had been designated male at birth with no equivalent for those designated female, māhū held an important role in Tahitian society, serving as teachers and record keepers. Bligh's record, made on 15 January 1789, is included in his log books but is missing from this printed account."

This may be true or just a reflection of the male bias of the people who recorded this history.

It's revealing—and so frustrating—that this record of Native gender diversity was left out of the printed versions of Bligh's testimony. Even the 1979 facsimile edition of Bligh's *A Voyage to the South Sea* that I checked out from the library simply omits the day (and the information about māhū) entirely—with the entry for Wednesday, January 14, being followed directly by Friday, January 16.

Rather famously, some of Bligh's crew mutinied after the ship left Tahiti, but Bligh survived being set adrift with some loyal crew in a small boat. He published the account of his journey—and the mutiny—in 1792.

Amid judgmental comments referring to the physical intimacy of Native people of Tahiti as **"beastly"** and **"polution,"** the missing text includes Bligh's meeting **"a person, who altho I was certain was a Man, had great marks of effeminacy about him."** Bligh reported that on asking someone who the person was, they **"without any hesitation told me he was a friend of hers, and of a class of people common in Otaheite called Mahoo. That the Men had frequent connections with him and that he lived— observed the same ceremonies—and eat as the Women did. . . . The Women treat him as one of their Sex, and he observes every restriction that they do, and is equally respected and esteemed."**

> Europeans called Tahiti this back in the 1790s.

> A phonetic spelling of *māhū*

HAWAIIAN MÅHÜ AND TAHITIAN MÅHÜ

With māhū legacy and presence today in both Hawaiian and Tahitian culture, it is worth looking at the differences between how the two communities are perceived and treated. Aleardo Zanghellini wrote in a 2013 article in the journal *Laws* that while both Hawaiian and Tahitian cultures include people who identify as *māhū*, the term in the 2000s had a more negative meaning and the māhū themselves had a lower social status in Hawai'i as opposed to māhū in Tahiti. Zanghellini suggests that different laws in the two cultures resulted in these different social outcomes.

In Hawai'i, US laws that for generations criminalized physical intimacy between men may have contributed to shifting the cultural celebration of māhū in Hawai'i to an "anti-*māhū* stigma." In the mid-1960s, a law passed by the Honolulu City Council in Hawai'i required trans and māhū people who had been assigned male at birth to wear a badge stating their bodies were male when they were in a particular area of town. Zanghellini wrote, "It seems clear that this requirement, and the police's violent enforcement of it, contributed to anti-*māhū* stigma on O'ahu."

In contrast to the antigay and anti-māhū laws in Hawai'i, the imposition of colonial law in Tahiti under King Pomare II, who was converted to Christianity, in 1819 did *not* include a law criminalizing physical intimacy between men. Some historians think this may have been because Pomare was in a relationship with a person named Toetoe—who was either a māhū or a man themself. The judgmental missionary Reverend William Pascoe Crook described the close relationship between Pomare and Toetoe, saying that together they **"lived in a horrid manner at Matavai."**

Zanghellini says that focusing on physical intimacy between men created a new "modern" gender-diverse identity in Tahiti that was heavily influenced by Western gay and trans identities: the term *rae-rae*. Zanghellini quotes a Tahitian māhū about the difference between māhū and rae-rae in a 2005 article in the French newspaper *Le Monde*, **"Mahu are effeminates in a man's body. I hate the term rae-rae, which appeared in the 1960s, because it makes all that we are turn on the idea of sexuality. For mahu, sexuality is by no means the most important thing. Our role is another: we bring a little sweetness around us, as a woman would do."**

Zanghellini argues that because the term *māhū* in Hawai'i covered both gender diversity *and* intimacy with other people with male bodies, the stigma of antigay laws lowered the social status of māhū in Hawai'i in a way that didn't happen in Tahiti.

There's a terrible historical echo of forcing Jews in Nazi-occupied countries during World War II to wear badges that identified them as Jewish and stigmatizing gay men by forcing them to wear pink triangles.

THE AIKĀNE—A PRECOLONIAL GAY PLACE IN HAWAIIAN SOCIETY

Among the reporting of Europeans and Americans who came to Hawai'i in the first wave of colonization are reports of young Hawaiian men called aikāne. They were part of the court of the chiefs, had intimate relationships with the male chiefs, and held special social and political roles of importance.

Distinct from the māhū, aikāne presented as male. Several aikāne served diplomatic roles in communicating between Captain James Cook's fleet and the Hawaiian rulers. James King, second lieutenant of the ship *Resolution*, wrote in March 1779:

> Indeed these people will fall very short of the Society & Friendly Isles in that very good test of Civilization, the rank & consequence of the Women; they are not only depriv'd of eating with their Lords . . . but what no doubt must be the most grievous of all is the being depriv'd of the natural affections of their Husbands, & seeing this divided by the other sex: the foulest polutions disgrace the Men, & we had no doubt of what an Takaneee [aikāne] meant. Terreeoboo [Kalani'ōpu'u] has five of them, who are men of the first Consequence, indeed all the Chiefs had them.

David Samwell, the ship's surgeon aboard the *Discovery* also documented the aikāne in February of that year. Samwell wrote about an overnight visit to their ship:

> Kamehameha a chief of great consequence & a Relation of Kariopoo [Kalani'ōpu'u], but of a clownish & blackguard appearance, came on board of us

in the afternoon dressed in an elegant feathered Cloak. . . . He with many of his attendants took up his quarters on board the ship for the Night: among them is a **Young Man of whom he seems very fond, which does not in the least surprize us as we have had opportunities before of being acquainted with a detestable part of his Character which he is not in the least anxious to conceal.**

In March 1779, Samwell would tell the story of one of the British/American sailors being asked to be a Hawaiian man's aikāne: **"Karana-toa [Kalanikoa], brother to Teeave [Keawe] by the father's side, being on board the Resolution to day and seeing a handsome young fellow whose appearance he liked much, offered six large Hogs to the Captain [now Clerke] if he would let him stand his Ikany [aikāne] for a little while, such is the strange depravity of these Indians."**

Setting aside the judgments of the Westerners who recorded it, these primary sources offer us a view of precolonial Hawaiian culture and people, and how aikāne (and their relationships with male chiefs) were respected in Hawaiian culture. Robert Morris, in an October 2010 journal article on the aikāne, wrote that their "influence and conduct profoundly affected the course of events at Kealakekua Bay, where Cook was killed in February 1779." Morris said that the gay relationships of the aikāne were "more important that currently accounted for in accepted theories of Hawaiian ethnohistory."

The history of Indigenous and minority people and cultures

GAUGUIN AND MĀHŪ ACROSS THE PACIFIC

In an article for the Tate museum, the Peruvian author Mario Vargas Llosa wrote that when the famous French painter Paul Gauguin arrived in Tahiti in June 1891, his long hair, red fur hat decoration, and flashy clothing had the Indigenous people believe Gauguin was a European māhū!

The colonists, Llosa recounts, told Gauguin that while the māhū had existed from "time immemorial in the cultures of the Pacific" missionaries (both Catholic and Protestant) had "demonized and banned" them. But the māhū survived, resuming their place in the culture when it was safer. Llosa directs us to look at the subjects of Gaugin's paintings from the time Gaugin lived and worked in Tahiti and the Marquesas which include and feature people who appear to combine masculine and feminine traits, people who may be seen as living outside a strict gender binary.

One of Paul Gauguin's 1902 paintings was called *Le Sorcier d'Hiva Oa* in French. It has been translated into English as *The Wizard of Hiva Oa*. Both here and with the Hawaiian Stones of Life—also translated as *Wizard Stones*—the English version attempted to express the magical or spiritual aspects of māhū while at the same time hiding the celebration of gender diversity it was all about.

Paul Gauguin's 1902 painting *Le Sorcier d'Hiva Oa* was variously translated into English as *The Wizard of Hiva Oa*, *The Sorcerer of Hiva Oa*, and sometimes as *Marquesan Man in a Red Cape*. The translations may have been an effort to mask the true gender of the subject.

Hiva Oa is a more than three-hour flight northeast of Tahiti. From there, it's another twenty-plus-hour flight northwest to Hawai'i. The enormous distances traveled by the Pacific Islanders centuries before planes were invented also help us understand that inclusion of māhū as a third gender spanned—and still spans—many cultures across a vast ocean.

RECLAIMING RESPECT FOR MĀHŪ IN HAWAI'I AND BEYOND

The hostile environment around gender diversity in Hawai'i caused many māhū and trans people to drop out of school and be rejected by their families. Dreya Blume wrote in her 2001 book 'O Au No Keia, that "almost all" of the Hawaiian-raised participants at one point or other were physically intimate with other people for money—just so they could survive. The stigma associated with that lowered the status of māhū and trans people in Hawai'i even further.

From a low point where even the term *māhū* was used as a slur, there has been an effort to reclaim respect both by māhū and by Indigenous Hawaiian culture. And those efforts have been supported by allies within and outside of the queer and Indigenous communities. In 2011 Hawai'i was the thirteenth state to pass a law protecting trans people—including māhū—from workplace discrimination.

Books such as Blume's that let māhū and trans people tell their own stories, and documentaries like the two starring Ho'onani and Kumu Hina are making an impact as well. **"It's not easy for a Māhū to find a partner; most men are just too afraid of what other people will say. But I got lucky."** Kumu Hina says of her husband Haemaccelo (Hema) Kalu.

Hema added **"where I come from, it's not accepted to be with a māhū. If a Tongan man is with a māhū, they go** around in secret. But me, I don't care what people say. No one tells me what to do. So when I started going with Hina, I wasn't ashamed." The couple were married in Fiji. After about a year apart, Hema joined Hina in Hawai'i. Hema said that he knew some people would "look down on me for being with a māhū, they might even think I myself was gay. Hawaii is different [then Tonga]. It's okay here for straight people to be with māhū. Everybody mingles with everybody. That gives me strength even more to be with Hina."

Some historians ask if today's māhū are reclaiming ancient traditions or creating new traditions—and perhaps the answer is both. We see some new traditions like Kumu Hina creating terms for her students like *kāne-wahine* and *wahine-kāne*, and there are stories of māhū continuity like Kaua'i Iki shared in Blume's book, *'O Au No Keia*.

KAUA'I IKI

Listening to māhū tell their own stories is a way we can learn and engage with the history—and today's reality—of gender beyond the binary. Born in 1962, Kaua'i Iki told (and edited) their life story in *'O Au No Keia*. Kaua'i Iki wrote:

I was brought up in Kaua'i in a household where it was OK to be *mahu*, unlike a lot of people I know who were ostracized and kicked out of the house; I was loved within my own household. My mom and dad raised me as a *mahu*. I still did all of the tasks a boy would do, but I also did the tasks the girls would do. I was taught everything. . . .

My grandmother would sit me down and tell me stories about this and stories about that, or take me to different places around the island. I thought that everything she told me and the places she showed me, I thought that everybody else knew these things, this family folklore. But it wasn't until her death that I realized that no one else had been told or shown these things. So then I began to think, "Why did she tell me these stories? I don't want to be responsible!" Because with the stories comes responsibility.

For example, she gave me the responsibility of caring for the graves of our ancestors. We have many in the mountains which are difficult to find. If you don't know they are there, you won't know. And we have ancestors buried in caves along areas that are populated now, but where the caves are still protected. If people ever want to develop certain areas, I'll have to say, "You cannot, because my ancestors are buried there!" So one of the things I was charged with was to care for our dead, our ancestors' bones. It's an important responsibility. And for some reason or other my grandmother, who had been their caretaker, had entrusted that to me. . . .

I was also raised by my mom's brother. . . . My uncle took care of me and raised me in the mountains. I lived with him in the mountains of the Na Pali Coast, from Hanalei Valley all the way in. He taught me how to run, fish, jump and hunt. Survival skills are what he gave me. . . . By the time I was in my high school years and I had dropped out of school, that was when he was able to show me and tell me more, give me more. Because I was getting to be a young adult already, going through all those changes. Everybody was looking at me, *"Oh, mahu."* But it didn't bother my uncle one bit.

In fact, the whole time my uncle knew I was *mahu.* People had the nerve to ask him in front of me, "How come you're taking him with you—he's *mahu*." My uncle would turn to them and say, "He's the only one in the family who can handle all of the things that have to be done."

My uncle was also one of the family's caretakers of our ancestors. That's why I was taken to learn about that and learn to fend for myself in the wild. He felt that no matter how I was, it was important that I knew how to survive.

MĀHŪ PAST, PRESENT, AND FUTURE

Kaua'i Iki and Kumu Hina are friends who met at the University of Hawai'i. Kaua'i Iki said in the documentary, **"We were hanging together and she was still Collin Wong. I had a . . . dream vision of her, and in my dream vision of her she was like how you see her now. And so I was the one who told her that she would look and that the holy spirit wanted her to grow her hair. It manifested after a while . . . and what you see is exactly how my dream vision was."**

As part of her work as chair of the O'ahu Island Burial Council, Kuma Hina was present at the trench digging for a rail project. Kumu Hina explained to the forklift operator, **"None of us would want our immediate family dug up. Just because we don't know who these people are and there's no marker . . . does it make it okay?"** The operator agreed with her. And then, Kumu Hina said that **"to turn one's back on one's ancestors is to sever oneself from one's future. And I will do everything that I can to prevent that."** In ways like this Kuma Hina is helping her culture respect māhū traditions and ancestors—which leads to more respect for māhū today.

The winner of *RuPaul's Drag Race*, season 15, Sasha Colby, said in a 2023 interview, **"This renaissance of mahu being** something that you're proud of is really coinciding with the way Hawaiian culture is being exemplified, retaught and trying to save a dying language." Colby remembers the word *māhū* being used against her as a slur, and speaks of her community reclaiming the term: "We also are taking back those words that were used against us by other people who didn't understand it."

Ho'onani cited another sign of progress: "To think about Kumu Hina's perspective, back then, people intimidated her . . . of being *that way*. Nobody respected the middle people, but . . . so yeah, we both are in the middle, and nobody teases us for it."

In the documentary, just before the high school boys' end of year performance (which was about to be led by Ho'onani), Kumu Hina jokingly pointed to Ho'onani and said, "I thought she was a boy, but . . ."

One of the high school boys jumped in to say, "He is."

"He is." Kumu Hina agreed.

"He is." Other boys chorused.

"All right," Kumu Hina said. "Okay, inducted in." And fist-bumped Ho'onani. To all the boys and Ho'onani, Kumu Hina said, "You guys better bring it—bring the house down."

And led by Ho'onani, they did.

Speaking after the performance, Ho'onani's mom said, "When Ho'onani did that number, I was so proud. Love is the biggest thing, you know, that we should always teach our children, is that to love anybody no matter what race, no matter what creed, no matter what sex, no matter what gender. If you love a person for who they are, and let them be who they are, then that's whole circle, right? Love is the surrounding circle of everything that goes around, comes around."

Bretman Rock is a māhū Native Pacific Islander from Hawai'i and a beauty influencer who hosted the red carpet for Miss Universe 2017 in the Philippines as a teenager. Rock said, **"They used to [revere] gay people. It only became a taboo when the Christians came. . . . The word *mahu* quickly became a derogatory term when it never, ever had been. . . . Now that I'm older and wiser, and I know what that word means and what it possesses . . . I'm like, 'Yes, I *am* a *mahu* and you should look up to me!'"**

GIVING RESPECT

Dean Hamer and Joe Wilson, the Hawai'i-based documentary filmmakers behind *Kumu Hina* and the kid-friendly short film *A Place in the Middle* were asked about what surprised them the most in making their films about this third gender role and people in Hawai'i. They said: **"Like many if not most Americans, we tend to think that we have the solution for every problem, and that if other people would just listen to us, all would be well. Wrong! When it comes to gender diversity, Hawaiians have a far more sophisticated understanding than we do, and use that knowledge for the benefit of the entire society. It's a model we would do well to emulate."**

On the *Kumu Hina* film website, there's a Pledge of Aloha that they encourage visitors and those who have seen the documentaries to take. It's a powerful reminder that the fight for recognition and respect is not just for māhū but for Hawaiian and Native cultures as well. Here's the pledge:

Pledge of Aloha

I believe that every person has a role in society, and deserves to be included and treated with respect in their family, school, and community.

I believe that every person should be free to express what is truly in their heart and mind, whether male, female, or in the middle.

I believe that every person should be able to practice their cultural traditions, and to know and perpetuate the wisdom of their ancestors for future generations.

I believe these values are embodied in aloha: love, honor and respect for all.

Therefore, I pledge to live aloha in everything I do, and to inspire people of all ages to do the same.

There's inspiration in knowing the rich history of māhū, determination in confronting the efforts to suppress the role and the people who lived it, and a blossoming of pride for the resurgence and respect māhū are creating for themselves today. The Pledge of Aloha is a way to spread that respect further, including to each of us and our own family, friends, and communities.

Would you consider taking the Pledge of Aloha?

How might living aloha in the way the pledge describes change how you live your life?

DAHOMEY FEMALE WARRIORS

A.K.A. MINO, DAHOMEY AMAZONS
BENIN
1700s TO 1900s CE

The idea that there has always been only one gender path that people born with female bodies can take is shown again and again to be false. In West Africa, what today is the country of Benin was founded in 1625 as the Kingdom of Dahomey. From about 1700, groups of female warriors who fought on the front lines were part of Dahomey's military.

How and why were there female warriors? One theory was that women were conscripted as soldiers due to a shortage of men from both military losses and kidnapping/enslavement by Europeans. Another theory, often referred to as a legend or oral history, says that in the early 1700s Dahomey was briefly ruled by Queen Hangbe, who founded the elite group of female warriors. After the queen was overthrown by her younger brother, all traces of a woman ruling Dahomey were said to have been erased.

Forced to join

While we may not know the exact starting point, the tradition of female warriors stayed and grew. By the 1850s as many as six thousand female warriors were in King Gezo's army—half of the country's armed forces. The female warriors of Dahomey were fierce fighters and were called Amazons by Europeans, after the female warriors of Greek myth. Dahomey female soldiers guarded the palace and royals and fought for the territory of their country. Military campaigns in the 1850s expanded Dahomey to include most of Nigeria. Their weapons included clubs, knives, swords, flintlock muskets, and 3-foot-long (0.9 m) straight razors held with both hands that were reported to be able to slice through a person completely.

Historian Pamela Toler cautions against using "Amazon" to describe these women warriors, saying that in addition to it being a "colonial reference," it reinforces "the idea that they are exceptions, and that no ordinary woman could be larger than life."

One training exercise witnessed in 1861 by Father Francesco Borghero included the barefoot female troops scaling a huge wall of acacia branches bristling with needle-sharp long thorns—a wall that stretched longer than a football field! In Stanley Alpern's book *Amazons of Black Sparta*, at the end of the exercise a female general presented Father Borghero with her commander's baton, about 2 feet (0.6 m) long, that had a carved shark on one end. The female general said that as the shark destroys men, so do the female warriors in battle. Alpern reported that she also said both Europeans and Dahomeans were "rich enough in glory to seek no other conquests but mutual friendship." Other military preparation for the female warriors included hand-to-hand combat, wrestling, executing prisoners, and

Showing they couldn't feel pain was part of the gig.

survival training—being sent into the forest for up to nine days with minimal supplies.

Professor Robin Law doesn't think the existence of Dahomey female warriors means Fon culture viewed males and females as equals. Instead, Law believes that in their culture, the female warriors were thought to "become" men at the moment they killed their first enemy. Other evidence of the female warriors' unique status, position, and gender were recorded by another European traveler in the 1860s, who wrote that when the female warriors left the palace they were accompanied by someone ringing a bell. Alpern said that the sound was a warning to look away—for a man to even touch one of the female warriors was punishable by death. Mike Dash, in an article for *Smithsonian* magazine, added that the female soldiers were all formally married to the king—and because the king was never physically intimate with any of them—the female soldiers were celibate. In 1889, with French colonial troops threatening to take over the country, Dahomey female warriors attacked a village that had been occupied by the French. The village chief had assured the villagers that the French flag would protect them. When the Dahomey female warriors won the fight, their general approached the chief.

Whether the female soldiers had romantic or physical relationships with one another or with other people who were not men outside the military does not seem to have been a possibility on the radar of the mainly male historians writing about them.

Symbolizing the protection of the French military

"So you like this flag?"
The general pointed to the French three-color flag.
"Eh bien, it will serve you."
The general gave a signal, and one of the female warriors swung their sword

and cut off the chief's head. They wrapped the head in the French flag and carried it back to their king.

King Béhanzin, the last king of independent Dahomey

Two wars between the French and the Dahomeans followed, with dozens of battles. The French had more advanced weapons and ultimately won the fight to colonize Dahomey. Dash reported a story told by French fighters that the Dahomey female warriors were the last to surrender—and as prisoners, **"each allowed herself to be seduced by [a] French officer, waited for him to fall asleep, and then cut his throat with his own bayonet."** French soldiers recalled the courage and fighting prowess of the female warriors.

Bern, a French Foreign Legionnaire called them **"warrioresses . . . [who] fight with extreme valor, always ahead of the other troops. They are outstandingly brave . . . well trained for combat and very disciplined."**

A photo of Dahomey female warriors taken around 1890

Henri Morienval, a French Marine, called them **"remarkable for their courage and their ferocity . . . [they] flung themselves on our bayonets with prodigious bravery."**

Dahomey regained its independence in 1960, as the Republic of Dahomey. In 1978 a historian met Nawi, a female warrior who at that time was over one hundred years old. Nawi reported surviving the 1892 war against the French. Female warriors such as Nawi have been called Mino in the local Fon language, which has been translated as both "witch" and "our mothers." They weren't portrayed as maternal, but their example of female empowerment has left a powerful legacy.

In 1975 the country changed its name to Benin.

In a BBC article, Fleur Macdonald writes of the thrill of discovering that the Dora Milaje in the hit 2018 film *Black Panther* had a real-world inspiration—the Dahomey female warriors— and that "the descendants of these women still keep their traditions alive."

Macdonald quotes Professor Leonard Wantchekon, who grew up west of the Dahomey capital in a village that used to be a training camp for female warriors. The villagers remembered an elderly female warrior retiring

A 2010 photo of a contemporary sculpture portraying a Dahomey female warrior—an officer—in Ouidah, Benin. The horns worn on the warrior's head were a symbol of power and sign of military rank.

THE GENDER BINARY IS A BIG LIE

to their village, who was described as "strong, independent and powerful." She was able to challenge the power structures of the village, Wantchekon said, "without any repercussion from the local chief because she was an Amazon." Wantchekon believes that female warrior (as a representative of thousands of female warriors over centuries) served as a role model, inspiring other women in the village—including Wantchekon's mother—to be independent and determined to succeed in whatever they set out to achieve.

CHAPTER 5

SIX MORE PEOPLE WHO LIVED OUTSIDE THE GENDER BINARY

LIVING OUTSIDE THE BOXES

When the society surrounding you insists the gender binary must apply to everyone, a special heroism comes with living your authentic truth outside those boundaries.

Some gender-diverse heroes today have celebrity status, and it's exciting to discover that there have always been gender-diverse people—even in the heart of cultures where the binary was presented as something unchangeable with no exceptions.

> The fancy word for that is immutable.

In this chapter, we'll share the stories of these amazing people:

An intersex soldier and smith, **Daniel Burghammer** lived as a man and gave birth in 1601 in Italy. The child was seen as a miracle.

After thirteen years of marriage to his second wife, **Carl Lapp** died in 1694 in Sweden. Then neighbors discovered Carl had a female body. Even though he was dead, Carl was put on trial.

Julian Eltinge was a male actor famous for impersonating women on stage and screen between the 1900s and the 1930s in the US.

Surrealist artists **Claude Cahun** and **Marcel Moore** were a gender-nonconforming couple from France who resisted the Nazi occupation in the 1940s on Jersey, an island that was part of Britain.

Presenting to the world as a man, **Shi Pei Pu** was a Chinese opera singer who told a male French Embassy worker in China in 1965 that he was secretly a woman. The two had a more than eighteen-year relationship—including a child the embassy worker thought was their son—prompting the embassy worker to become a spy.

> Not that you or your loved ones need to become spies!

In living their genders outside the strict binary their cultures demanded, each of these six people offers a legacy for folks living outside the gender binary today. Let's learn more about them.

DANIEL BURGHAMMER

GAVE BIRTH IN 1601
ITALY

The case of a soldier who lived as a married man and unexpectedly gave birth—with the child hailed as a miracle—was reported in the Fugger newsletters. Fuggerzeitungen in German, these were a vast collection of hand-copied reports and letters from the multinational Fugger business, publicly sold newsletters from German cities called *Neue-Zeitungen*, and accounts from a private subscription news service called Novellanten, all dated between 1568 to 1605. They included news from Europe, North Africa, Asia, and America, and some were printed in a book called *News and Rumor in Renaissance Europe: The Fugger Newsletters*. The collection was named after the two brothers, Octavian Secundus Fugger and Philipp Eduard Fugger, who collected it all.

Here's the Fugger newsletter report on Daniel Burghammer, under the headline: "A Lansquenet Bears a Child":

> The German name for a foot soldier

From Piadena in Italy, the 26th day of May 1601.

A weird happening has occurred in the case of a lansquenet named Daniel Burghammer, of the squadron of Captain Burkhard Laymann zu Liebenau, of the honourable Madrucci Regiment in Piadena, in Italy. When the same was on the point of going to bed one night he complained to his wife, to whom he had been married by the Church seven years ago, that he had great pains in his belly and felt something stirring therein. An hour thereafter he gave birth to

a child, a girl. When his wife was made aware of this, she notified the occurrence at once. Thereupon he was examined and questioned as to how this had come to pass. He then confessed on the spot that he was half man and half woman and that for more than seven years he had served as a soldier in Hungary and the Netherlands; in proof whereof he produced his genuine passport. When he was born he was christened as a boy and given in baptism the name of Daniel. In his youth he learnt the handicraft of a smith, which until this day he had practiced simultaneously with his soldiering. He also stated that while in the Netherlands he only once slept with a Spaniard, and he became pregnant therefrom. This, however, he kept a secret unto himself and also from his wife, with whom he had for seven years lived in wedlock, but he had never been able to get her with child.

The report continues, recounting the church verifying the story and telling us:

Many noted men and women in the nobility as well as five hundred soldiers accompanied the child home again from the christening. The aforesaid soldier is able to suckle the child with his right breast only and not at all on the left side, where he is a man. He has also the natural organs of a man for passing water. Both are well, the child is beautiful, and many towns have already wished to adopt it, which however, has not as yet been arranged. All this has been set down and described by notaries. It is considered in Italy to be a great miracle and is to be recorded in the chronicles. The couple, however, are to be divorced by the clergy.

Super fascinating. Being intersex—and pregnant—is a big secret to keep from the person you're sharing your life with. It makes you wonder what happened to Daniel's child Elizabeth and if the gender diversity of her parentage was shared over the generations of family history—or if the story was covered up to better "fit in" over time.

CARL LAPP

1600s TO 1694
SWEDEN

Traditionally, Indigenous Sámi people lived both nomadically and in villages across a vast area of what became Norway, Sweden, Finland, and Russia. By the mid-1600s, the Kingdom of Sweden worked with the church to force Sámi people within their borders to assimilate to Swedish and Christian culture. Gunlög Fur in "Reading Margins: Colonial Encounters in Sápmi and Lenapehoking in the Seventeenth and Eighteenth Centuries" said that officials of Sweden's church and state "demanded" that Sámi people "participate in church services, catechism lessons, and court sessions." Among the Sámi customs Sweden forbade was traditional burial in the forest, instead insisting that Sámi people who died should receive a Christian burial in religiously consecrated ground. Only a few types of people were deemed so terrible they were unfit for Christian burial—including those who had committed suicide, babies who had been murdered, exiles, and men who were convicted of having been physically intimate with other men.

> Moving from place to place, which some Sámi people did as they herded reindeer

After his first wife and son died, Sámi Carl Lapp walked into Hed Parish in Sweden. He didn't have a beard, and though that was a bit unusual, Carl married his second wife sometime around 1681. About thirteen years later, Carl died. While neighboring women were preparing him for burial, they discovered that Carl's body was female.

The last name Lapp signified Carl was a member of the Sámi people. But like the westernized Lapland, some Sámi in the twenty-first century reject the terms Lapp and Lapland as derogatory. They prefer Sámi for their people and Sápmi for their land.

This was a huge deal. The news went from the women to their local pastor to the cathedral chapter to the provincial governor to the Swedish High Court. Carl, even though he was dead, was put on trial. His second wife—his widow—denied she ever knew Carl's secret, saying he was so old when they married, and she was past childbearing age, so they had never been physically intimate. But what about the first marriage and Carl's son? Fur translated court records that condemned Carl's **"participation in the sin of fornication that the former wife had carried on and kept it silent and hidden it, allowed the child to be baptized and recognized it as his own, and after his former wife's death, continued in his evil intent and grave sin with continued contempt for God's holy order."**

Living as a man with a body that wasn't male, performing only men's tasks, and dressing in men's clothes was seen, Fur said, "as a sin against God and his creation as well as against civil order and thus punishable by death." And Carl had "abused the holy institution of marriage by taking another woman as wife." About twenty years earlier (in the 1670s), the Swedish court had ruled in the case of Lisabetha

Olsdotter, who had a female body but, leaving a husband and children behind, dressed in men's clothes and worked as a soldier and farmhand, and—as a man—married a young woman, Kjerstin Ersdotter. Fur translated the court's sentence against Lisabetha: **"She has thus deliberately mutated sexum, frustrated God and his order . . . she cannot be delivered from the death penalty."**

Latin for "sex" or "gender"

But Carl was already dead. So were his first wife and son. What to do? The Swedish High Court decided that rather than let Carl receive a Christian burial with rites presided over by the pastor, the executioner should bury Carl's body in the forest. It was an ironic punishment—as a Sámi, Carl might have preferred that traditional Sámi resting place.

JULIAN ELTINGE

1881 (OR 1883) TO 1941
USA

Actors sometimes don't want people to know exactly how old they are so they can play younger roles.

Born William Julian Dalton, Julian Eltinge was raised in Butte, Montana. When Julian started performing in drag, his father freaked out and his mother sent Julian to live with her sister in Boston. There, in drag shows with the Boston Bank Officers' Association, Julian got rave reviews, with the *Boston Globe* calling him **"a genius in the impersonation of female characters."** That was the start of his career, and that year, 1904, he moved to New York for his first role on Broadway.

Julian became famous as a drag performer. Nicholas Beyelia, Los Angeles Public Library History and Genealogy Department librarian, wrote that Julian "would spellbind audiences by building the illusion of a gilded age era/belle of the nineties woman, complete with song and dance, only to destroy it in an instant with what became his signature move, campily pulling his wig off at the end of the performance to reveal his male identity." Julian toured the US and Europe, even giving a command performance for King Edward VII of Britain at Windsor Castle. He had his own vaudeville troupe, the Julian Eltinge Players, and starred in New York stage performances and Hollywood movie roles where, for one plot reason or another, he'd be a man compelled to present and pass as a woman. Often the roles involved Julian switching back and forth between presenting as a man and presenting as a woman throughout the story.

1890s

A 1912 photo of Julian presenting as a woman, signed for a fan:
For Sayre
A reminder of
"Eltinge"

Audiences (especially women) loved the magic of the transformation. The comedian W. C. Fields quipped about Julian, **"Women went into ecstasy about him. . . . Men went into the smoking room."**

Julian became one of the highest-paid actors in the world. Elyssa Goodman wrote, "He also had his own magazine, in which he advised women about makeup and promoted his cosmetics line, which was highly regarded for its cold cream. He even had a line of cigars." The cigars were part of the publicity effort to present Julian as a supermasculine man, to make sure no one would think he was gay.

Here again, folks were confusing information about someone's gender and how they presented their gender with information about their romantic and physical attraction. It's an extension of the false belief that there are only two ways to be a human being: people with male bodies who identify as men and who are only attracted to women and people with female bodies who identify as women and who are only attracted to men. But we're seeing that there are many more ways to be and attractions to have (or not have).

Julian had to live in that homophobic culture. To the end of no one suspecting why he was a "lifelong bachelor" who was famous for acting as many different women, Julian fought in staged boxing matches and there was even a story circulated about how when fishing he was almost stabbed by a marlin.

> Coded language for "gay" back when being gay was illegal

> Marlin are fish that can be as big as 14 feet (4 m) long and have an extended, sharp snout like a spear.

Furthering the bad boy image, Julian was arrested at the Canadian border for having liquor during Prohibition and once, in Los Angeles, got into a collision with a police car. Beyelia said about Julian, "When his sexuality was called into question, he responded with a snappy line telling reporters, **'I'm not gay, I just like pearls!'**"

Reviewing Julian's 1912 star performance in *The Fascinating Widow*, the *Los Angeles Times* wrote, **"Most persons balk at the idea of the female impersonator. The Eltinge performance is different from all others in that it cannot possibly arouse distaste. The audience is taken into the complete confidence of the young actor."**

More than fifty years later, the actor Ruth Gordon wrote about Julian, saying, **"Julian Eltinge, as virile as anybody** virile, contributed to the gaiety of nations by playing fascinating widows more fascinatingly than if fascinating real widows played them."

Paramount Pictures advertised their movies starring Julian, saying, **"Unique in the American Theater, Julian Eltinge has won great fame and thousands of followers because he does one thing better than anyone else. As an impersonator of feminine characterizations, he has no equal."** Julian was so famous that in New York City a Times Square movie theater was named after him. When it opened in 1912, the Eltinge 42nd Street Theatre featured a 400-square-foot (37 sq. m) mural of three women dressed as muses with classical fabric gowns flowing around them—and they were likely all Julian in drag.

Julian had a castlelike home built in what became the Silver Lake neighborhood of Los Angeles. Called the Villa Capistrano, it was featured on postcards and in architectural magazines, including a profile in the *Architectural Record*

An ad placed in the movie business newspaper *Variety* aimed at having movie theaters book Julian Eltinge's first three silent films—all of which involved Julian presenting as a woman.

that went out of its way to stress Julian's masculinity. Commenting on the various flights of stairs in the house, the February 1921 article said, "Some women might not like them—but this is not a woman's house!"

Beyelia says, "This last statement only stood to emphasize the fact that, with the exception of his mother, women were noticeably absent from his public and private life. Eltinge never married and was never credibly linked to a relationship with either a woman or a man and he never discussed details of his personal life."

Eventually, Julian's fame faded. In the Great Depression, the New York movie theater wasn't making money and started hosting burlesque, adult-oriented shows. In 1930 the mural of the three muses by the French artist Arthur Brounet was painted over. Laws against cross-dressing and the policing of those laws started to make drag less acceptable in the larger culture. And with the Hays Code in 1934 focused on eliminating any visibility in movies outside het romantic and physical attraction and cis gender expression, Julian didn't get much work as an actor—in or out of drag. His last film in drag was 1931's *Maid to Order*.

See chapter 6 for more about the US laws to create and police the gender binary.

Julian fell on hard times (a bad investment, drinking too much liquor, and trouble finding work), but in his fifties was back in New York doing nightclub appearances. He died in 1941 and has been all but forgotten—even the theater named after him was renamed the Empire Theater in 1954.

But so many primary sources survive that we do know about Julian! And in 2000, the mural thought to be Julian as three female muses was restored, and moviegoers in Times Square can still see it today.

CLAUDE CAHUN AND MARCEL MOORE
1894 TO 1954 AND 1892 TO 1972
FRANCE AND JERSEY (BRITAIN)

Claude Cahun (born Lucy Schwob) and Marcel Moore (born Suzanne Malherbe) met as teenagers. Claude's divorced father married Marcel's mother. Then **"much to the vexation of our families,"** as Claude put it, the stepsiblings fell in love.

Part of the surrealist art movement happening in Paris in the 1920s and '30s, Claude and Marcel were photographers, writers, and artists—often photographing themselves and making photo collages of the images. In 1937 they moved to the island of Jersey (a British crown dependency, 12 miles, or 19 km, off the shore of France) where they lived together and made art.

Bob Le Sueur, a resident of Jersey who was in his late teens when the couple moved there, remembered Claude and Marcel in Barbara Hammer's artistic documentary *Lover Other*, saying **"They both dressed mannishly, which then was unusual, at that time, I mean, women wore trousers . . . only for beach wear and so on before the war. These women seemed to wear them all the time."**

One photo of Claude wearing a face mask in an outfit covered with masks matches well with what they wrote, **"Beneath this mask, another mask. There will be no end to the faces I can peel off."**

The art historian Whitney Chadwick spoke of Claude and Marcel's "theatricalizing of identity" commenting, "identity can only be performed, it can never be revealed." Claude's metaphor of endless masks speaks to that performance of identity.

At one point Claude shaved their own head for a portrait taken by Marcel that Chadwick described as "posed in a way conventionalized in portraits of male intellectuals and writers— often Jewish—inserting herself in another kind of lineage."

It was *their* lineage—
though a tradition reserved
up until then for men. Both
Claude and Marcel were
Jewish, and when the Nazis
occupied Jersey in 1940 the
gender-nonconforming couple
became part of the resistance.
Le Sueur explained, **"We were
not supposed to have radios,
but they did, and they would
listen to the news, write it
down in German—they were**

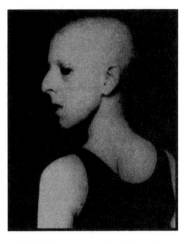

A 1930 photo portrait of Claude
Cahun with their head shaved.

**highly cultivated women—and they would leave these notes
about the day's news under the ashtrays on the tables of the
soldatenheim and even, I'm told, occasionally slip the news in
to the pockets of the soldiers if the soldiers were . . .
standing about and not paying attention."**

The German
soldiers' mess
tent—where
they ate meals

On October 21, 1940, the Nazis ruled that all
Jews on the island had to register—Claude
and Marcel did not. But their ongoing efforts
to circulate leaflets with words and art to
get German soldiers to realize the wrongs of
Nazi ideology and to rise up to overthrow Nazi rule got them
arrested in 1944. On October 28, 1944, the Nazi overseeing
Jersey, Baron von Aufsess, wrote, **"There are very few Jews
in the islands. The two Jewish women who have just been
arrested belong to an unpleasant category. These women had
long been circulating leaflets urging German soldiers to shoot
their officers. At last they were tracked down."**

Tried in the fall of 1944, Claude and Marcel were
sentenced to over six years of "penal servitude"—forced
labor as prisoners—and death. Jersey officials appealed the

death sentences, which the Nazis commuted to life in prison. When World War II ended in Europe, Jersey—and Claude and Marcel—were liberated in May 1945.

Claude and Marcel went back to living together and making art for the rest of their lives. They were surrealists for whom identity was performance art. Today they might identify as lesbians and as people who boldly live outside the gender binary—and so many other cultural expectations as well. Claude died in 1954, and Marcel lived another eighteen years. They are buried under a single headstone that only includes their given names: Lucy Renee Mathilde Schwob and Suzanne Alberte Malherbe. The marker includes this quote from Claude: **"And I saw new heavens and a new earth."**

Known as a couple, as artists, and as part of the resistance to the Nazis during occupation, today Claude and Marcel are honored—with their chosen names—on a street sign in Paris's 6th arrondissement: the **Allée Claude Cahun – Marcel Moore.**

In 1860, Paris, France, was divided into twenty districts, called arrondissements. In 2020 the smallest four at the center of the city were consolidated into a new district called Paris Central, so there are now seventeen arrondissements.

The street sign honoring Claude and Marcel, photographed in 2019

SHI PEI PU

1938 TO 2009
CHINA AND FRANCE

As gender is presented, it makes sense that the size of the audience for that presentation of gender can vary. For Shi Pei Pu, the audience was one. Then a handful. And then the world.

Shi Pei Pu was a Chinese opera singer who spoke fluent French and, by their mid-twenties, was teaching Chinese to French diplomats and their families in 1960s Beijing. At a Christmas party in 1964, Pei Pu—presenting to the world as a man—met Bernard Boursicot, a junior French Embassy accountant who was just twenty years old.

Bernard, who had relationships with other guys while in school, had promised himself he would be straight and was determined to fall in love with a girl . . . but there was something about Pei Pu that compelled him to pursue a friendship. Three months later, Bernard would call Pei Pu his **"best friend."**

Bernard also craved a life of adventure and in March 1965 found out he could join an expedition to the Brazilian jungle. When he told Pei Pu he would be leaving China, Bernard heard the story that would change his life forever. Pei Pu told him that Pei Pu was actually a girl, raised as a boy, living as a man, and outside her parents and the midwife who helped at her birth, no one knew her secret. Joyce Wadler wrote in a 1993 article in the *New York Times Magazine* that it was "far too dangerous, in Mao's China, where men and women are supposed to be equals, to admit." By telling Bernard, Pei Pu was "trusting him with her life."

Bernard believed Pei Pu, who told him she had taken male hormones to look more masculine. And then Bernard realized he was in love with her. Their relationship became

A 1962 photo of Shi Pei Pu dressed for a performance

physical, and just as Bernard was about to leave for Brazil in December 1965, Pei Pu told him she was pregnant. Bernard promised to return.

Bernard did return four years later. In the midst of China's Great Proletarian Cultural Revolution, it was too dangerous for Pei Pu to have any contact with foreigners, but Bernard was obsessed. When they were finally able to talk, Pei Pu told him their son had been born on Bernard's birthday. The child was named Shi Du Du. Bernard would call him Bertrand. Pei Pu showed him a photo, telling him that because of how foreigners were viewed, the child, of mixed heritage, was being raised "far to the west" for safety. Bernard and Pei Pu settled on a routine of once a week sitting on benches on opposite sides of a busy street, staring at each other with longing.

A few months later, Bernard started giving documents from the French Embassy to a Chinese government official in exchange for time with Pei Pu. He had become a spy.

In 1973, on another trip to China, Bernard would meet his son. At this point, Bernard embraced being bi and back in Paris met and started a relationship with another man, Thierry. They lived together, and Thierry even went with Bernard to New Orleans where Bernard worked in the French consulate. In 1975 Bernard told Thierry about Pei Pu and their son and his dream of them all living together as a family.

In 1977 Bernard took a post in Mongolia that had him traveling regularly to Beijing by train to deliver the diplomatic pouch. He started seeing Pei Pu and their son again and made copies of the contents of the pouch to hand over to the same Chinese official. Bernard was a low-level diplomat, and the contents of the pouch included dispatches from the French ambassador including, **"The yak, to the Mongolians, is what the automobile is to the Americans."** Not exactly the stuff of spy thrillers. Bernard used his salary to buy expensive gifts for Pei Pu, including TVs, radios, and Rolex watches.

In October 1982 Bernard finally managed to get Pei Pu and their son to Paris where they moved into Bernard and Thierry's home. Pei Pu continued to live as a man, performing Chinese opera—even appearing on two television shows—as Monsieur Shi. But Thierry and Bernard's family were in on the secret of Pei Pu actually being a woman.

In June 1983, French agents arrested Bernard and Pei Pu. During interrogation, Bernard revealed:

> Bernard: **"I did nothing for money."**
> An Interrogator: **"Who is Shi Pei Pu?"**
> Bernard: **"Pei Pu is a woman."**
> Silence. They are stunned.
> An Interrogator: **"Aaah, that's why she is with her son."**
> Bernard: **"It's my son."**

Bernard was charged with giving secret information to another country. He offered to marry Pei Pu, thinking it might help them. Bernard was in his prison cell when he heard the news on the radio that Pei Pu had a male body. Bernard yelled, **"It's not possible! It's unbelievable. It's a lie!"**

When he had the chance, Bernard confronted Pei Pu, who undressed to show Bernard Pei Pu's male genitals. It was the first time, in a relationship spanning two decades, that Bernard has seen that part of Pei Pu's body. Then, in spring 1984, a paternity test revealed that Shi Du Du/Bertrand was not biologically Bernard's son. Bernard was distraught.

At the 1986 trial, Bernard's lawyer said, **"If this case is anything, it is a crime of passion. The psychiatrists and the police and the investigative judge who has made a study of the proceeding for two years agree that Bernard genuinely believed Pei Pu to be a woman and the mother of his child. But is that truly a crime? Bernard Bouriscot has been accused of supplying intelligence to agents of a foreign power and, in doing so, having done damage to the diplomatic service of France."** The lawyer then shared some of the documents Bernard had access to while stationed in Mongolia, including requests from the ambassador directed to the home office for a cheese tray and a rearview mirror. Bernard's lawyer asked, **"Is this the stuff of espionage? Do you really think what we have here hurt the diplomatic interests of France? This case is absolutely at the bottom of the ladder in the spying world."**

Asked by the trial judge how it all could have happened, Bernard said, **"I was shattered to learn that he is a man, but my conviction remains unshakeable that for me at that time he was really a woman and was the first love of my life. And then, there was the child that I saw, Shi Dudu. He looked like me."** Asked about how their intimate time together didn't cause him to question Pei Pu being a woman, Bernard said, **"He was very shy. I thought it was a Chinese custom."**

> As a baby, Shi Du Du/Bertrand had been adopted by Pei Pu, with an exchange of money, from an Uighur family and wasn't biologically related to either Pei Pu or Bernard.

The jury deliberated for less than an hour. Both Bernard and Pei Pu were sentenced to six years in prison.

Media covered the trial around the world. The *New York Times* headline called it an **"Odd Case of Espionage,"** and the French newspaper *Le Monde*'s headline asked, **"Espion ou Espionne?"**—the French word for "spy" in the masculine and feminine forms, with a question mark.

Both Bernard and Pei Pu were pardoned in 1987. Pei Pu worked as a performer in France and raised Du Du/Bertrand. Bernard continued living with Thierry. Their story inspired an award-winning play, *M. Butterfly*, that was performed on Broadway and around the world. Bernard even attended some performances.

In writing about Shi Pei Pu and Bernard Boursicot in his book *Gay Lives*, Robert Aldrich brings up exoticism and how "Europeans' infatuation for Asians" and "cultural expectations, stereotypes, and a measure of fantasy" all may have played a role in what happened.

Seeing foreign countries, customs, and people as fascinating and attractive

Pei Pu died in 2009 in Paris. When asked about Pei Pu's death, Bernard didn't express sadness. Instead, he reflected on the things Pei Pu had done against him and said that now he, Bernard, was free.

Eight years later, Bernard thought back on it all. **"It was hard for me. If you are in a story like that, I think you are hurt inside. The story was famous, but I think it's important to say what is inside his soul."** Perhaps Bernard was talking of his own soul or Pei Pu's. Either way, clearly, for Bernard, no matter the hurt he felt, no matter Pei Pu's sex/gender, their relationship was the first love of his life.

SIX LIVES OUTSIDE THE BOXES

Daniel Burghammer was seen as the parent of a miracle.

Carl Lapp was seen as a criminal.

Julian Eltinge was seen as a movie star.

Claude Cahun and Marcel Moore were seen as heroes of the resistance to the Nazis.

Shi Pei Pu was seen as a manipulator, duping a low-level diplomat into becoming a spy.

These are just six individuals, but around the world and across time, many people have lived—and are currently living—outside of the gender binary. In the midst of cultures and societies that declare there are only two genders, only two ways to be a human, it's important and empowering to know that gender diversity can still thrive.

Consider people you know who live outside the gender boundaries of your culture or community. Are they ridiculed or celebrated or something in between?

And if we can agree that gender is something each of us performs, does it resonate for you that the first person we perform gender for is ourselves?

TiDAWENA AND NiBORAWENA of THE WARAo

A.K.A. TIDA WENA AND NIBORA WENA
VENEZUELA
BEGINNING OF RECORDED TIME TO TODAY

The Orinoco delta, along the northeastern edge of Venezuela, covers almost 17,000 square miles (44,000 sq. km). For the last eighty-five hundred years, it has been home to the Warao, who describe themselves, according to social anthropologist Christian Sørhaug, as living "on a crust of earth that floats on a large sea." The population estimate is that about thirty thousand or more Warao live in the delta.

In their language, Warao means "people from the . . . soft (marsh) land" as opposed to their term for tourists, Venezuelans, and missionaries—Hotarao—which translates as "people from the . . . hard land."

Between rainy seasons and floods, the ocean tides coming in and the rivers streaming out, the delta is a lush jungle spread across muddy land and water. Warao houses are built on stilts, and the people travel by canoe. Photographer Álvaro Laiz traveled there between 2012 and 2013 for a global project on trans identities. Laiz described the setting, "They are really isolated from the other parts of Venezuela. It was like going to outer space, because you cannot put your feet on solid ground."

The University of Oslo's Museum of Cultural History said that Warao handcrafting skills are passed down through generations and are divided by gender: "Almost all older Warao men can build canoes, and all women can make hammocks." Warao culture also includes two other genders: tidawena and niborawena.

Tidawena has been translated as "twisted woman" and encompasses men who love other men and people with male bodies who live a feminine identity. Tidawena don't make canoes, instead focusing their skills on making hammocks and baskets—tasks otherwise reserved for people with female bodies who identify as women. Jake Naughton in the 2014 *New York Times* article featuring Laiz's photos, "Two Spirits in the Venezuelan Jungle," said tidawena do other tasks normally reserved for women, including childcare, looking after elders, cooking, tending the home, and harvesting crops like ocumo chino. Only women and tidawena wear their hair long, and for Warao men who historically had multiple wives, Naughton reports that tidawena "were sometimes the second or third wives." Some tidawena were also shamans, as they were "thought to possess two spirits, bringing them closer to the ancestor spirits that roam the jungle."

In the book *Worlds in Miniature*, Sorhaug writes of meeting Siri, a tidawena who "would often boast about his abilities in making hau baskets or weaving hammocks, while in the same breath he would say he had no knowledge of how to make a canoe."

Some sources, including the *New York Times*, write it as two words: *tida wena*.

Taro, a tuber that's like a potato but tastes nuttier.

While my instinct would have been to use they/them pronouns for tidawena, both Sorhaug and Laiz met, studied, and photographed these people over time. I've stayed with their usage of he/him pronouns to best respect the individuals discussed here.

Hau is a palm fiber.

Niborawena has been translated as "twisted man," and it is the term for people with female bodies who live a masculine identity and are taught the skill of building canoes—a task otherwise reserved for people with male bodies who identify as men. The Museum of Cultural History says that some niborawena "acquire the knowledge of shamans," meaning that among both tidawena and niborawena, some individuals are seen as providing sacred "function as lines of communication between people and ancestor spirits. The spirits can be good or evil, depending on how they are treated by their living relatives. If they are neglected, they can choose accidents and sickness. If the ancestors are treated reasonably well, then they could provide health and prosperity."

In their time with and study of the Warao, Sorhaug said that in contrast to tidawena, "niborawena is much rarer. In Hobure there was only one niborawena—but it was not talked about." Documentation of Warao who identify as niborawena is very limited—so it's unclear if niborawena was or is an identity that is less claimed, less recorded, or less tolerated through the colonial and patriarchal lens of historians and encroaching Western culture.

Hobure is an area within the Orinoco delta.

Along with modern tools such as chain saws and steel axes and technology such as radio, TV, and DVD players, Catholic missionaries (who arrived in the delta in 1925) have impacted the Warao. But shamanism lives on, as do Warao handicrafts such as hammocks and baskets, and they still make and get around with canoes. The Warao have even adjusted some handicrafts to smaller sizes, so tourists can buy the pieces and then easily fit them in their luggage. Siri gave Sorhaug some miniature baskets as a gift for Sorhaug's mother. As Sorhaug recalls, "He said that my mother could attach these small baskets to her car rear view mirror as decorations. He had recently been to the state capital Tucupita, and there he had seen a taxi driver with something similar hanging from his rear view mirror."

A short film Laiz made of photos and video clips portraying the Warao includes a final title slide that reads: "The existence of ancient animistic rites and the acceptance of transgender people among the warao society could be the last remains of those old pre-Columbian traditions, never photograph[ed] before."

> The idea that all objects, places, and creatures have a spirit

In Laiz's 2014 photo essay featured in the *New York Times*, a number of tidawena are portrayed doing both traditional and more modern tasks, including thirty-nine-year-old Andres Medina, helping his family harvest ocumo chino and posing in a traditional Warao outfit; thirty-eight-year-old Arsenio Beria drying his long hair after swimming in the river; and sixteen-year-old Sanse, combing his long hair after a volleyball match.

It's a reminder that the meaning of "modern" isn't "Western" or "industrialized"—Indigenous cultures can be modern as well. And the gender diversity they embrace—that stretches back thousands of years—can seem more modern than a binary take on gender.

Sanse, a 16-year-old warao tida wena, washed by the river after playing volleyball at Murako's court deep in the Orinoco Delta.

CHAPTER 6

THE COLONIZATION OF GENDER

> **THE WORLD PUT IN PLACE BY COLONIALISTS IS NOT THE ONLY WORLD THAT HAS EVER BEEN. IT IS NOT EVEN NECESSARILY THE ONLY WORLD THAT IS. IT IS MOST ASSUREDLY NOT THE ONLY WORLD THAT CAN BE.**
>
> —Greg Thomas, *The Sexual Demon of Colonial Power*, 2007

IT'S NOT PRETTY—BuT IT'S IMPORTANT To UNDERSTAND

We've seen the pattern: Indigenous cultures embracing and celebrating their gender diversity to colonial rejection and marginalization of genders and people outside the binary to more recent efforts to reclaim both belonging and respect for gender-diverse communities and people. But what were the mechanics of how gender was colonized? What surprising realms did it impact? And since the colonization of gender is still going on, how can we best affirm the naturalness and importance of gender identities beyond the binary? We'll address these questions and more.

THE MECHANICS

First let's look at how they did it. How was gender colonized? There were a lot of tools, and we'll look at five of them: justification; guns, germs, steel . . . and potatoes; racism and eugenics; misogyny; and laws to police fashion and people.

JUSTIFICATION

In Panama in 1513, the Spanish explorer Vasco Núñez de Balboa had some forty Indigenous people with male bodies who dressed and lived as women murdered—by throwing them to his dogs. The Spanish colonizers saw the intimacy these third gender people had with men—which they interpreted as gay intimacy—as a sickness. Reporting on this three years later, the Italian historian Peter Martyr d'Anghiera wrote that the mass murder was greeted with applause by the Indigenous people who witnessed it "for the contagion was confined to the courtiers and had not yet spread to the people." d'Anghiera, a hostile source, had the Indigenous people blaming the third gender folks of their own culture for famine, sickness, and even lightning and thunder.

The Spanish wanted to prove Indigenous men were intimate with other men to justify their colonizing goals. Richard Trexler, professor of history, explained *in Sex and Conquest: Gendered Violence, Political Order, and the European Conquest of the Americas* that people with male bodies dressing as women "was certainly a sin and actionable. However it still did not give the Iberians the right to conquer the natives." In the Spanish legal view of that time, people with male bodies who dressed and lived as women were "not a 'just title of conquest.'" But men being physically intimate with other men "did bestow a right to conquer, if it could be demonstrated that it was widespread and tolerated by the indigenous civil authority."

The Iberian Peninsula includes parts of Spain and Portugal—so this is another way of saying the colonizers.

People with male bodies being intimate with one another, no matter their gender, was a convenient legal excuse for the Europeans. In 1525, when the Bishop Tomás Ortiz (a former missionary) accused the Carib peoples of being men who loved men "more than any other race," King Charles I of Spain condemned the entire nation to slavery.

THE GENDER BINARY IS A BIG LIE

GUNS, GERMS, STEEL . . . AND POTATOES

Sometimes things you wouldn't expect influenced the path of white European colonization since the 1500s.

The National Geographic documentary *Gun, Germs, and Steel*, based on the 1998 Pulitzer Prize–winning book of the same name by Professor Jared Diamond opens with these words: "Modern history has been shaped by conquest. The conquest of the world by Europeans. . . . The conquistadors led the way. A few hundred men who came to the new world and decimated the native population. The secret of their success? Guns, germs, and steel. Ever since, people of European origin have dominated the globe with the same combination of military power, lethal microbes, and advanced technology." Diamond's point, as described in the book's editorial description, was to dismantle "racist theories of human history by revealing the environmental factors actually responsible." Meaning it wasn't something special about the abilities or capabilities of white Europeans that gave them the advantage. It was guns, germs, and steel.

Another influence you might not expect on how the history of colonization unfolded was the potato. Some historians, such as William H. McNeill and Alfred Crosby, say that the turnaround in growth of Europe's population from the 1600s (from decline to boom) was caused by the Spaniards bringing back one crop from South America's Andes to Europe—the potato. Gwynn Guilford in "The Global Dominance of White People Is Thanks to the Potato," a 2017 article in Quartz, said that potatoes were easier to grow than other staples, cheaper than bread (you didn't need to process it like wheat—you just dug it up and cooked it), and were "vastly more nutritious," so much so that the vitamin C in the potatoes "helped end rampant scurvy" across Europe. Summarizing the advantage the potato gave

Potatoes were originally brought to Europe from South America in the 1500s, but it was Frederick the Great of Prussia (*left*) who successfully turned them into a staple food source during wartime in the 1700s.

Europeans, Guilford writes that Europe's population more than doubled (from 126 million in 1750 to 300 million in 1900). "The potato helped prime the economy . . . fuel the Industrial Revolution" and provided Europe with the ability to change the world with their own export: "people."

Including all those guns and steel

And as part of that colonization, racism, misogyny, and a gender binary being applied to everyone were—and still are—intricately connected.

RACISM AND EUGENICS

Racism was also a tool of colonialism to benefit the people in power. Racism is the fear, hatred, and oppression of people whose heritage is different from yours. Maybe a better definition comes from the brilliant author Ta-Nehisi Coates, who writes in *Between the World and Me* that racism is "the need to ascribe bone-deep features to people and then humiliate, reduce, and destroy them."

Racism's connection to colonization has deep roots. In 1886 German doctor—and baron—Richard von Krafft-Ebing wrote in *Psychopathia Sexualis* about primary sexual characteristics (parts of the physical body from birth) and secondary sexual characteristics. He explained that secondary sexual characteristics developed during puberty and happened in the body and in the mind, encompassing thoughts, emotions, and behaviors. He said, "The secondary sexual characteristics differentiate the two sexes: they present the specific male and female types. The higher the anthropological development of the race, the stronger these contrasts between man and woman, and vice versa."

That "anthropological development" von Krafft-Ebing spoke of was the toxic idea that white Europeans were the top of human evolution, and everyone else was backward, on an inevitable journey to "civilize" and catch up. As part of their Instagram series of book reports exploring the history of gender and racism, Alok Vaid-Menon wrote about *The Biopolitics of Feeling* by Kyla Schuller, associate professor of women's, gender, and sexuality studies, and summed up the gendered and racist theory of colonization: "Scientists argued that white people were superior because of their unique ability to display a visual difference between males and females. Black people, Indigenous people, and other people of color (BIPOC) were regarded as sex indistinguishable."

A system set up so people who enslaved other people were in charge

Greg Thomas, professor of Black studies, in his 2007 book *The Sexual Demon of Colonial Power*, wrote that "the slaveocratic order of settler colonialism construes its own as human and its slaves as non-human (or sub-human, if not anti-human). One cannot qualify as human if one is not identified as man or woman, and vice versa, since manhood, womanhood, and humanity are . . . very political notions of empire."

If being a different "race" makes someone unable to be a certain gender, that makes it clear that, like race, gender is a political idea. An idea that defines who can have certain privileges and power, and who cannot.

In an article on President Barack Obama for the *Atlantic*, Ta-Nehisi Coates spoke of "whiteness in America" as "a badge of advantage." And while we like to say that America is a place where a person's abilities and effort are the only things that determine their success (or failure), Coates writes in *Between the World and Me* of the extra burden racism places on Black people in America: "All my life I'd heard people tell their black boys and black girls to 'be twice as good,' which is to say 'accept half as much.' . . . No one told those little white children . . . to be twice as good. I imagined their parents telling them to take twice as much."

Thomas quotes C. A. Diop, who wrote about the manipulation of history to political ends in 1991: "The negation of the history and intellectual accomplishments of Black Africa was cultural, mental murder, which preceded and paved the way for their genocide here and there."

Scientific racism (like measuring brain size and judging people based on their skin color) created coloring-book lines that divided people into categories to privilege rich, white, het, cis, able-bodied, Christian men from Europe and disadvantage everyone else—judging everyone else to be lesser. Less worthy and less able, which, conveniently for those men in power, blamed the lack of those other peoples' success on the members of those disadvantaged minorities themselves rather than on the systems that put them at a disadvantage.

Over centuries, farmers and herders had bred plants and

animals to guide the evolution of a particular species toward a desired goal. Plants were bred for flavor, or shelf life, and animals were bred for things like the color of their wool or how fast they could run. Starting in the early and mid-1900s, a horrible school of thought suggested the same should be done with people. It is called eugenics.

The Nazis in Germany in the 1930s and '40s referred to themselves as a "pure" Aryan race. And they used the idea of racial purity—wanting to create a "master race"—as their excuse to sterilize and murder entire groups

White and of European ancestry

of people who didn't meet their criteria of who deserved to exist in the same world as their supposed superiority. Jews, Roma and Sinti people, and Black people were among their targets. Slavic people (from countries such as Poland and Russia) were also, the Holocaust Memorial Day Trust website says, "considered inferior and were targeted because they lived in areas needed for German expansion. The Nazis wanted to 'improve' the genetic make-up of the population and so persecuted

Many Roma and Sinti people consider the term *gypsy* offensive. The word *gyp* means "to cheat someone," and it's derived from *gypsy*.

people they deemed to be disabled, either mentally or physically, as well as gay people. Political opponents, primarily communists, trade unionists and social democrats, as well as those whose religious beliefs conflicted with Nazi ideology, such as Jehovah's Witnesses, were also targeted for persecution."

It plainly wasn't about race—the Nazis just used that as an excuse to blame problems in society on different minority groups—a cynical strategy still used by too many politicians.

Tragically, eugenics wasn't just a Nazi thing. On Instagram in 2021, Vaid-Menon did a book report on *The Trouble with White Women: A Counterhistory of Feminism* and interviewed the author, Kyla Schuller. Vaid-Menon described eugenics as "a conservative strategy that places blame for instability on marginalized groups instead of systems of inequality like capitalism and colonialism."

Back in 1901 sociologist Edward Ross warned about "race suicide"—that white middle-class women weren't having as many babies as non-white immigrant women and that eventually it would lead to white people being outnumbered.

That fear, according to Schuller, "led eugenicists to seize women's fertility as the best lever for steering the direction of humanity."

Eugenics was practiced as recently as 1970 to 1976 in the US. *Time* magazine reported in November 2019 that during those seven years, "physicians sterilized perhaps 25% of Native American women of childbearing age, and there is evidence suggesting that the numbers were actually even higher. Some of these procedures were performed under pressure or duress, or without the women's knowledge or understanding. . . . [B]lack and Latina women were also targets of coercive sterilization in these years."

MISOGYNY

The battle over control of women's bodies continues. In the debates about a woman's right to choose if she's going to continue a pregnancy or have an abortion, feminist activists say that the goal of the antiabortion movement isn't really to reduce the number of abortions—if it were, those same forces would be promoting birth control. Jill Filipovic wrote in a December 2021 essay in the *New York Times*, "Contraception and abortion are tied together because both offer women the freedom to have sex for pleasure in or outside of marriage, and both allow women greater control over their lives and futures. The 'pro-life' goal isn't an end to abortion. It's to establish another means of controlling women." This, too, is a marker of the gender binary—the rigidly defined roles men and women are "supposed" to play in Western culture. By taking control of their bodies away from women, like the decision to get pregnant, or to have a child, women's opportunities are suppressed.

Not feminists who are white. White feminism is a kind of feminism.

White feminism, which Schuller describes in a 2021 interview with Vaid-Menon, aims to advance white women up the ladder of success—never mind the costs, and often at the expense, of other marginalized groups of people. That means that white feminism reinforces the injustices of the idea that everyone should conform to a gender binary and the injustices of racism. Joan Morgan wrote in the *New York Times* review of Schuller's book of the "centuries-long history of white women, some of them self-declared feminists, colluding with patriarchal white supremacy in an attempt to secure their own rights above those of Black people of any gender." And I'll add above the rights of all people of color, and disabled people, and queer people too.

Many American feminists of the 1800s who have become household names turn out to be white women who believed in white feminism. As examples, Schuller discussed Elizabeth Cady Stanton and Susan B. Anthony. Acknowledging that they were active abolitionists, she shared,

Meaning they fought to end slavery

After the Civil War and Reconstruction and the 15th amendment granted Black men the right to vote, but not any women—and it also inserted the word sex in the constitution for the very first time, by saying people of the male sex can vote—Stanton, especially, and to a lesser degree Anthony, they really drew a line in the sand, and . . . thought that Black men were now the enemy. And Stanton went excessively on speeches and saying things like, "You have let the most uneducated, you know, dirty, unlettered, ignorant, like the most degraded elements of society, you've let them vote. And you're not letting your pure white Mayflower-descendant wives vote."

Frederick Douglass (1818–1895) escaped slavery in 1838 and became an internationally famous speaker, author, and advocate against slavery and for women's rights. In 1852 he gave a speech at a Fourth of July celebration for the city of Rochester, New York, saying, "This Fourth of July is yours, not mine. You may rejoice, I must mourn. . . . What to the American slave is your Fourth of July? . . . a day that reveals to him more than all other days of the year, the gross injustice and cruelty to which he is the constant victim. To him your celebration is a sham . . . your shouts of liberty and equality, hollow mock; your prayers and hymns, your sermons and thanksgivings . . . hypocrisy—a thin veil to cover up crimes which would disgrace a nation of savages."

Frances Ellen Watkins Harper (1825–1911) was also a well-known poet, author, and speaker against slavery and for women's rights. She cofounded the National Association of Colored Women.

Lucretia Mott (1793–1880) was a powerful speaker against the injustice people faced because of their race and/or gender. She was one of the founders of the Philadelphia Female Anti-Slavery Society in 1833.

Schuller acknowledged that for centuries in the US, "sexism as a structural inequality" was "massive." From the early 1800s when "married women, in the North, often couldn't own property" to how "a married woman in the US couldn't have a checking account in her own name until the late 1970s," feminism was the response to these injustices, but it didn't have to be white feminism.

"At that point they declared Black men and immigrant men as the enemy." Schuller continued in that interview with Vaid-Menon, "When it could have been a project of solidarity. Like Frederick Douglass was fighting for, like Frances Harper was fighting for, and . . . like some white women feminists, like Lucretia Mott were fighting for at the time." Thirty-five years into women's suffrage, when Stanton and Anthony wrote a multivolume history of the movement, Schuller said that "they deliberately left Frances Harper out. . . . And when they included Sojourner Truth, they included this completely made up version of her speech, written by a white woman, where she says, 'Ain't I a woman?' . . . She never said 'ain't I a woman?,' and we know that because there is a transcript of her speech published a month after in a Black paper."

Sojourner Truth (1797–1883) escaped slavery in 1827 and became a speaker and author advocating for the end of slavery and for women's rights.

Comparing the speeches side by side is stunning. Leslie Podell, a student at the California College of the Arts in San Francisco, put together a website that does just that. The Sojourner Truth Project shows the original version, transcribed by journalist Marius Robinson who was in the audience at Truth's May 29, 1851, speech. Robinson's version was published on June 21, 1851, in the *Anti-Slavery Bugle*. Truth spoke plainly and from the heart, opening with these lines, **"May I say a few words? I want to say a few words about this matter. I am a woman's rights."**

Twelve years later, Frances Gage created a fictional version of Truth's speech that was published in the April 23, 1863, issue of the *New York Independent*. It starts with, "Well, chillen, whar dar's so much racket dar must be som-ting out o'kilter." Gage gave Truth a dialect that was maybe more like what white people at that time expected a Black woman, emancipated from slavery, to sound like. That **"I am a woman's rights."** became "And ain't I a woman?" and *that* became the famous line Truth said—when she didn't say it at all—is another trick to reshape, rewrite, and yes—colonize—history.

There's a parallel between white feminism and the British Empire's "liberal imperialism." Professor of history Caroline Elkins explained in a 2021 *Publishers Weekly* interview about her book *Legacy of Violence* that "in the 19th and 20th centuries Britain became more democratic at home while ruling an economically exploitive empire of 700 million Black and brown subjects abroad. The philosophy of liberal imperialism reconciled that contradiction with a reformist vision: Black and browns in the Empire would someday become 'British' and civilized, and gain self-government—but 'not quite yet.' Of course, 'not yet' never became 'now.'"

As someone who has always checked "Caucasian" on forms and is Jewish, calling myself "white" seems wrong—like claiming a privilege no one should have over anyone else.

The desire to keep power set the foundation for the construction of race and racial injustice that are still with us. Instead of writing that some people in America are white, Coates wrote of **"Americans who believe that they are white."** Aryans in Nazi-era Germany may have had a skin color that we think of as denoting whiteness in America, but so did many Jews—who were decidedly not seen as Aryan. Again and again, we see that colonialism and the systems it set up are not really about race, or gender, but about political categories of power. Movingly, Coates wrote of being Black in America this way, **"They made us into a race. We made ourselves into a people."**

LAWS TO POLICE FASHION AND PEOPLE

Policing gender norms became a tool of both establishing and reenforcing a strict gender binary for everyone.

In their book *Arresting Dress: Cross-Dressing, Law, and Fascination in Nineteenth-Century San Francisco*, Associate Professor of sociology Clare Sears discusses the significance of the laws passed in forty-five cities between 1848 and 1914 that criminalized a person appearing in public **"wearing a dress not belonging to his or her sex"** or **"wearing the apparel of the other sex."** Sears said growing cities "struggled to develop a system of government that benefited its white, male, merchant elite." So they created "strategies of government . . . restricting who can lay claim to femininity or masculinity and who is permitted to be a woman or man." The laws weren't just about clothing but about who belonged in public spaces and who belonged in the two—and only two—categories of the gender binary.

A police photograph of Geraldine Portica, a Mexican American youth arrested in 1917, as Associate Professor Clare Sears says, "for wearing women's clothes on a body the police classed as male."

EXCLUDING OTHERS TO
GET AHEAD YOURSELF

An uncomfortable echo of white feminism can be found in the history of gay liberation politics in the US. Excluding trans, other gender-nonconforming people, and people of color from progress and politics by white gay and lesbian people actually happened. The idea (or rationalization) was that white, straight-acting, "non-threatening" gays and lesbians could get ahead first and then maybe later help secure rights for the queer people who were less "relatable" to the straight white folks in power.

Randolfe Wicker, a member of the gay rights organization Mattachine Society, participated in what *Time* magazine called the first US picketing protest for gay civil rights in 1964. Wicker spoke in an interview about how he always dressed conservatively when picketing or being interviewed on television as an openly gay man. **"A black suit and tie works wonders**

Activist Marsha P. Johnson (*center left*) at the 1982 Pride March in New York City.

anywhere, because if you wear a black suit and tie people will stop and listen to you and consider what you have to say. . . . It was assumed we were mentally ill; it was considered that we were certainly criminals, and we were also considered to be morally depraved. But people would still sit and listen to you, and that's the beginning of a conversation."

Even well-intentioned representations of the fight for queer rights, like the 2015 movie *Stonewall*, have whitewashed queer history, centering and offering a heroic vision of a fictional white straight-acting gay guy rather than focusing on the trans and gender-nonconforming leaders of that rebellion, like Marsha P. Johnson and Sylvia Rivera.

Marsha P. Johnson (1945–1992) was a renowned drag queen in New York City who fought police at the Stonewall riots in 1969 and was an activist for trans people, gay people, and people with AIDS.

Sylvia Rivera (1951–2022) was a trans activist in New York, who said that while she didn't throw the first Molotov cocktail at police during the Stonewall riots, she threw the second. She was seventeen and was quoted as saying during the six nights of protests, **"I'm not missing a minute of this—it's the revolution!"**

Together, Johnson and Rivera cofounded Street Transvestite Action Revolutionaries in 1970, a shelter and safe space for trans youth and adults.

THE IMPACTS

Imposing a rigid gender binary through colonization had some surprising impacts on beauty, marriage, and even science:

BEAUTY

How has beauty been impacted by colonization?

One powerful example of transformation is shared in *Women with Mustaches and Men without Beards: Gender and Sexual Anxieties of Iranian Modernity* by Afsaneh Najmabadi, professor of history and studies of women, gender, and sexuality.

Najmabadi's book includes the 1877 writings by Carla Serena about Serena's visit to Iran. She described Princess 'Ismat al-Dawlah, **"Over her upper lips she had soft down of a mustache which gave her a manly look."** Serena attended a celebration hosted by the princess and wrote: **"The princess expressed interest in making me up. . . . First she covered my eyebrows across the forehead with mascara and turned each of them into a bow-shape, then she dyed my eyelashes, covered my cheeks with white powder and red blush, and finally made my lips red without forgetting to draw a thin shade of a mustache over my lips, which is apparently considered one of the beauty marks for an Iranian woman's face."**

The Qajar dynasty ruled Iran from 1794 to 1925.

Najmabadi reports that "many Persian-language sources, as well as photographs, from the nineteenth century confirm that Qajar women sported a thin mustache, or more accurately a soft down, as a sign of beauty." In 2001 an Iranian teenager viewed pictures of some of these women from their own culture's history and saw them—in particular, their having mustaches—as **"really ugly."** Najmabadi said, "Over a relatively short period of time . . . this mark of female beauty was transformed to one of ugliness and masculinity."

Najmabadi makes the case that before the 1920s, both women and young men sported these downy mustaches as a sign of beauty that men and the culture at large appreciated. Along with modernity came a cultural "amnesia" denying that men had ever expressed romantic and physical attraction to other men—young men with downy mustaches. Men, as the title of the book says, "without beards." Even though Iran was never technically colonized by European countries, in the late 1800s the United Kingdom controlled the country's tobacco and oil industries. The cultural and financial colonization of Iran came with, as Najmabadi tells it, a cultural shaming and a goal to be "modern" that 1) eliminated gender possibilities outside the binary, 2) made it seem as if there were no other possible romantic and physical attractions besides heterosexual attraction, and 3) changed the expectations of how women's beauty was seen and presented.

Colonization insisted people fit themselves into one of two boxes. This affected who was valued, who could be attracted to whom, and even what it meant to be beautiful.

How much hair we have or don't have, where it's located, and shame about it continues today, and the ideas of what's appropriate when it comes to body and facial hair are very tied to gender. Professor of women and gender studies Breanne Fahs has studied the "social norm" of body hair removal for almost fifteen years and writes that she continually finds it "remarkable that women have been so wholly convinced to adhere to a norm that is purely social and aesthetic, with no notable health or hygiene benefits." Fahs cites studies that show that between 92 to 99 percent of women in the US, UK, Australia, New Zealand, and Western Europe regularly remove hair from their legs and underarms and more than half remove some pubic hair as well. That creates an extra burden of time and money on women in these communities, with one report estimating that women in the US will spend more than ten thousand dollars and more than fifty-eight days removing body hair during their lifetime!

MARRIAGE

Did you know that wearing a white dress for a wedding is also a cultural by-product of colonialism?

In 1840 Queen Victoria wore a white dress for her wedding to Prince Albert. The queen's wedding outfit featured a special kind of lace to support, as the editors of the *Encyclopaedia Britannica* said, "the British lace industry, which was floundering at the time." They didn't have TikTok back then, but the queen's outfit was widely reported and started the trend that in 2020 saturated the $26 billion bridal wear market in the US alone with primarily white dresses.

Marriage was originally a transaction—an exchange made for money or other advantage, such as political alliance. Marrying for love is a relatively new thing. In *Marriage, a History: How Love Conquered Marriage*, historian Stephanie Coontz discusses how "marrying for political and economic advancement was practically universal across the globe for many millennia . . . not until the late eighteenth century, and then only in Western Europe and North America, did the notion of free choice and marriage for love triumph as a cultural ideal."

Even then, the fight over who is allowed to marry whom has been going on for hundreds of years. In the US, during the centuries of slavery, enslaved people weren't allowed by the government or religion to officially marry. After the US Civil War and emancipation, miscegenation laws still prevented people of different heritages from legally marrying each other. And it wasn't until 2015 that the fight for legal gay marriage was won across the US. All these battles were about access to the privilege—the colonially bestowed privilege—of being accepted in this society. That privilege extends to tax laws, Social Security benefits, who inherits what, who can adopt children and be parents, who gets to vote, who is seen as "belonging," and much more. Laws were crafted to steer society in a certain direction, benefiting only certain kinds of people and only certain kinds of relationships. As so we see that marriage comes to us as part of colonization too.

SCIENCE

Even science has been shaped by the strict gender binary imposed by colonization.

Anne Fausto-Sterling writes in *Sexing the Body*, "Scientists do not simply read nature to find truths to apply in the social world. Instead, they use truths taken from our social relationships to structure, read, and interpret the natural." Fausto-Sterling tracks how, beginning around 1918, "hormones, reported on paper as neutral chemical formulae, became major players in modern gender politics."

Fausto-Sterling says that "researchers have learned that testosterone and estrogen affect brain, blood cell formation, the circulatory system, the liver, lipid and carbohydrate metabolism, gastrointestinal function, and gall bladder, muscle, and kidney activities. Yet despite the fact that both hormones seem to pop up in all types of bodies, producing all sorts of different effects, many reporters and researchers continue to consider estrogen the female hormone and testosterone the male hormone."

Even the word *estrogen* is based in misogyny. Fausto-Sterling tells the story of how in the 1930s a bunch of male scientists were drinking in "a place of refreshment" when they chose the root word "estrus (meaning 'gadfly,' 'crazy,' 'wild,' 'insane') as the root on which biochemists [would build] female hormone names." The underlying prejudice of the labeling stuck. She cites the 1961 edition of *Stedman's Medical Dictionary* that said the so-called male hormone androgen "makes a man" while at the same time defining the effects of the so-called female hormone estrogen with these words: "begets mad desire."

Testosterone is a major type of androgen.

Fausto-Sterling says that identity (your body's sex, your gender) is "a cultural phenomenon that becomes woven into the body." Rather than wanting us to think of them as separate things, Fausto-Sterling adds a slash between gender/sex, seeing it as a "developmental, interactive achievement."

Fausto-Sterling credits psychologist Sari van Anders and E. J. Dunn for coming up with the compound word. Van Anders wrote in a 2010 academic paper, "I use gender/sex throughout this paper despite the focus on hormones, because differences cannot knowingly be attributed to biology or gender socialization."

In her book, Fausto-Sterling writes, "The cell, the individual, groups of individuals organized in families, peer groups, cultures, and nations and their histories each provide appropriate locations from which to study the formation and meaning of sexuality and gender." And we shouldn't just study identities outside the binary! She points out that "the mechanism by which cis identity develops remains unexamined." That's another way of saying that no one's looking into gender identity formation when someone fits neatly into the binary boxes.

Professor Joan Roughgarden calls out the **"pathologizing of diversity"** for gender—referring to the medical diagnosis required of trans people in the US before they can take some of the medical steps toward affirming their gender.

In their TEDx talk, Anunnaki Ray Marquez dismisses the notion that the problem is centered on the individual who does not conform to the gender binary—the diagnosis of gender dysphoria. Instead, Marquez puts out a call to **"help us end cultural dysphoria"**—placing the problem on how our culture perceives and treats people outside the binary.

WHAT CAN WE DO?

How do we approach moving forward to a world where gender is expansive, diverse, and free from the policing of the gender binary? First we need to acknowledge that this isn't just historical—the colonization of gender is continuing. And then we'll look at different approaches to healing and affirming every gender beyond the binary.

THE COLONIZING OF GENDER IS ONGOING

How does this limiting view of gender continue, generation after generation?

Fausto-Sterling looks at infant and caregiver interactions as part of the dynamic systems that shape gender identity and how it "acts in a world in which gender, like nitrogen, oxygen, or carbon dioxide, is one of the predominant atmospheric elements." Fausto-Sterling cites multiple studies showing caregivers' gender/sex reinforcement. A father's reaction to his male three-month-old baby's flailing legs accidentally hitting a ball being "Yay! You kicked the ball!" A female seven and then eight months old who "kept stumbling when she tried to crawl because her ankle-length dress got caught under her knees or feet. When her mother noticed and took off the dress, she sped away. Still, months later, she continued to wear long dresses." Fausto-Sterling points to this as an example of how the way cultures approach gender/sex can create differences in motor development and physical abilities. There's heteronormativity built into these interactions too. She cites a male and a female, both six months old, who were playing with a toy phone. "As the girl holds the receiver to her ear, her mother jokingly says, 'No boyfriends calling you yet?' When the boy holds the receiver to his ear, the mother playfully remarks, 'Is that some girl calling you already?'" As Fausto-Sterling says, "Inevitably, gender/sex integrates into each child's body and consciousness."

> Heteronormativity is the expectation that what is "normal" is men only being physically and romantically attracted to women and women only being physically and romantically attracted to men—the societal assumption that everyone is heterosexual, or het.

Look at our world—how so much is designated just for those inside the gender binary. From pronouns to prom, baby clothes to school forms, bathing suits to underarm deodorant, the gender binary idea that only two options apply to everyone is everywhere. It reinforces the inequities of how women are treated, how people of color and Indigenous people are treated, and it marginalizes and pathologizes intersex, trans, genderqueer, gender questioning, gender fluid, nonbinary, and other people who identify as gender diverse.

THE DEBATE

There's debate within many communities that have been traditionally excluded by the systems set up by colonization about what's the best path forward. Do we fight for our right to be included in these systemically unfair structures, or do we fight for new structures?

Or is that choice itself too binary?

Not that everything in Western culture is terrible, but we need to acknowledge that many of the visible structures of society are products of colonial expansion and beliefs—such as racism, heterosexism, and marriage. And that's not a complete list. Professor Thomas wrote in *The Sexual Demon of Colonial Power* that "the world put in place by colonialists is not the only world that has ever been. It is not even necessarily the only world that is. It is most assuredly not the only world that can be."

Knowing the history of gender diversity and how colonization imposed an exclusionary gender binary on much of our world—as a tool of power—is a critical first step. Understanding the mechanics of how they did it and the surprising impacts that a rigid gender binary has had helps us frame questions on how best to move forward. Questions such as

Is America a melting pot, or is it a salad? Should immigrants lose their other identities and be just American, or can they retain their cultural connections *and* be American? Or is that choice also too binary?

Should there be benefits extended to certain people to steer society in a certain direction? Benefits for marriage, for education, for having (or not having) kids, and for participating in things like sports and communities?

What about reparations, affirmative action, and other efforts to compensate and otherwise level a playing field that has been decidedly tilted to benefit some people and disadvantage others?

What do you think?

WHITE DOVES

A.K.A. SKOPT, SKOPTSI, SKOPTSY

RUSSIA

MID-1700s (FIRST RECORD 1771) TO 1900s

> This name in Russian means "the Castrated Ones."

A secret religious group, the White Doves believed angels (God's messengers from heaven) had no physical sex. Many members changed their own bodies to match how they believed an angel would look—by removing physical markers of their body's sex like breasts and testicles. After the physical changes, it's unclear if White Doves saw themselves as inhabiting a new, different gender or if they saw themselves as outside gender entirely or if today they might identify as gender neutral.

> Since they didn't refer to themselves by the terms derived from Skopt, I'll use "White Doves" to be more respectful.

What was behind this expression of their faith? White Doves believed Adam and Eve from the Bible's creation story had bodies with no external markers of sex until the moment of original sin—Adam and Eve eating the off-limits apple. Echoing the shape of that forbidden fruit, Adam's testicles and Eve's breasts were thought to have been placed there by God as both punishment and a sign of their original sin.

The White Doves were inspired by Jesus's counsel from the New Testament, including from Matthew 18:8, 18:9, and 19:12, respectively:

Wherefore if thy hand or thy foot offend thee, cut them off, and cast them from thee: it is better for thee to enter into life halt or maimed, rather than having two hands or two feet to be cast into everlasting fire. . . .

And if thine eye offend thee, pluck it out, and cast it from thee: it is better for thee to enter into life with one eye, rather than having two eyes to be cast into hell fire. . . .

For there are some eunuchs, which were so born from their mother's womb: and there are some eunuchs, which were made eunuchs of men: and there be eunuchs, which have made themselves eunuchs for the kingdom of heaven's sake. He that is able to receive it, let him receive it.

White Doves believed the path to their salvation was "to set the spirit free from the body's desires," as described in 1881 by Anatole Leroy-Beaulieu in *The Empire of the Tsars and the Russians.* So some male White Dove followers would be castrated (sometimes cutting off their testicles and sometimes their testicles and penis) and some female White Dove followers would have their breasts cut off (sometimes their labia and clitoris as well). This transformation toward "the perfection of the individual and the glorification of God," led White Dove followers to see themselves, in the words of one of their hymns, as **"being whiter than driven snow."** Leroy-Beaulieu said that White Doves believed "they are the pure, the saints, who walk untainted through this world of sin."

In a 2017 article in the Awl, Jacob Mikanowski wrote that before the ritual that would change their bodies—a surgical procedure done with no anesthesia—a White Dove prepared for death with these words: **"Farewell sky, farewell earth, farewell sun, farewell moon, farewell lakes, rivers and**

mountains, farewell all earthly elements." Survivors of the surgery would, Mikanowski wrote, "find themselves reborn in a heavenly body."

Because belonging to the White Doves was against the law, with followers put on trial, banished to Siberia, and required to register with the government, the transformation of their bodies and the practice of their religion were done in secret. In a way, this rendered their genderless vision of perfection also a secret.

Kondratii Selivanov, a founder of the White Doves, in a drawing from the early 1800s

An early leader of the White Doves was Kondratii Selivanov. After castrating himself and some followers, he was tried, beaten, and banished to Siberia. Kondratii eventually returned to Saint Petersburg and claimed to be Peter III, both Christ and czar. He was imprisoned in an asylum but then released in 1802. For eighteen years Kondratii lived in the house of a White Dove follower in Saint Petersburg and was the leader of their religious sect. Kondratii was again arrested and this time locked up in a monastery—where he remained until he died in 1832 at the age of one hundred. Throughout, the White Doves grew, with followers from many social classes, including wealthy merchants, peasants, nobles, military and naval officers, civil servants, mechanics, and even priests.

Christ is a title, meaning "the anointed one"—the Hebrew translation is where we get the English word *messiah.* Russian rulers at this time were called tzar, which translates to emperor.

Some White Dove followers became very wealthy and used their money to spread the religion.

White Doves acted as a kind of mutual aid association and had secret ways of communicating, such as revealing themselves to one another by laying a red handkerchief on their lap while talking. They were considered "in daily life, the mildest, most honest of men." Mikanowski wrote, "They lived as model citizens—honest, respectful, and careful not to draw too much attention."

Leroy-Beaulieu recorded that a Russian once told him, **"Were I a banker, I should not want anybody for my cashier but a Skopèts [White Dove]. For a cash box as well as for a harem, there is no safer keeper. At the bottom of every case of defaulting or breach of trust there is a woman. With these people you can sleep soundly and in peace."**

Mikanowski said that White Doves "redirected the passion reserved for children and lovers to the community as a whole—they lived in communes, not families, and held property in common. Their kin were determined by belief, not blood."

Estimates of how many White Doves there were at the height of their membership in the late 1800s vary widely, from less than fifty-five hundred to as many as one hundred thousand. *Encyclopaedia Britannica* editors summarized some of the efforts Russia made to exile and wipe out the White Doves, then wrote, "Repressive measures proving useless, an unsuccessful attempt was made to kill the sect by ridicule: Skoptsi were dressed up in women's clothes and paraded with fools' caps on through the villages."

This effort to humiliate White Doves highlights the patriarchy and misogyny baked into Russian culture.

The *New York Times* reported on October 13, 1910, that "141 adherents of the eunuch sect, including 67 women from 14 to 85 years old" had been put on trial. The article's headline read: "SKOPTSY MEMBERS ON TRIAL: Russia Trying Hard to Suppress an Extraordinary Sect."

The editors of the *Encyclopaedia Britannica* said, "To escape prosecution some of the sect have emigrated, generally to Rumania, where they are known as Lipovans. But though the law is strict—every eunuch being compelled to register—Skoptsism still continues to hold its own in Russia."

And while it's unknown if any White Dove followers are still around (there was one report of a group of one hundred White Doves in the 1970s), both the *Encyclopaedia Britannica* and Leroy-Beaulieu in *The Empire of the Tsars* mention that a "new" (in the 1880s) branch of the sect saw their religious duty as allegorical rather than literal, and so "understood and practiced" what formerly had been castration instead "as chastity."

Chasity means "avoiding physical intimacy."

A 2016 article in Russia Beyond by Oleg Skripnik suggests a religious legacy of the White Doves survives. Mirra, an activist from the anti-sexual movement in Russia, said, **"In Russia there are about 2,000 anti-sexuals and among them are religious ascetics. . . . And a section of them welcomes self-castration."**

An article in Russia Beyond defines anti-sexuals as people who actively reject any physical intimacy even if they feel attracted to other people, distinct from people who identify as asexual, who do not feel physical attraction to other people. Another term used by people who avoid physical intimacy (sometimes for religious reasons) is *celibate*.

Even though the White Doves were altering their bodies to conform to their idea of an idealized gender, I caught myself thinking their practices were so different and

An undated photo of members of the White Doves community

weird. And yet, when I stepped back and considered it, my American culture practices and views two body-altering traditions as completely normal: gender assignment for intersex babies and circumcision for babies with penises. Babies cannot consent to having their physical bodies altered, but the idea of changing bodies to conform to an idealized version of gender isn't so different from something I accepted. But because it's part of *my* culture, I'm used to it.

And it never occurred to me to question it until now.

Intersex people experience this as a violation of their human rights. You can learn more about these medically unnecessary surgeries and the activism to stop them in chapter 7.

CHAPTER 7

INTERSEX ACTIVISM

FIX YOUR HEARTS, NOT OUR PARTS!
—Intersex activists chanting at a July 2018 protest of
medically unnecessary surgery on intersex babies outside of
Lurie Children's Hospital in Chicago, Illinois

THE STANDARD OF CARE

Gender assignment surgery on intersex babies in the US (and beyond) was based on a theory and then on a lie.

In 2017 Human Rights Watch and interACT: Advocates for Intersex Youth released a report and video, "I Want to Be like Nature Made Me: Medically Unnecessary Surgeries on Intersex Children in the US." In it Dr. Susan E. Stred, professor of pediatrics at State University of New York's Upstate Medical University, says, **"For many decades, the standard of care for intersex newborns included surgical procedures to make them look as typically female or typically male as possible."**

Kyle Knight of Human Rights Watch adds, **"But these surgeries can have devastating consequences for the kids that can last a lifetime. We spoke to parents who told us they felt intense pressure from doctors to consent to surgeries even when those operations were medically unnecessary."**

How did this standard of care—operating on babies and children to get them to fit into a strict view of the gender binary needing to apply to everyone—come to be?

The answer is caught up in the debate over how much of our gender identity is biologically determined (nature) vs. how much of our gender identity is shaped by our upbringing (nurture).

Nature vs. nurture

In the mid-1950s, Dr. John Money, based on his study of intersex patients at Johns Hopkins, said that **"behavior and orientation as male or female does not have an innate, instinctive basis . . . psychologically, sexuality is undifferentiated at birth and that it becomes differentiated as masculine or feminine in the course of the various experiences of growing up."**

Here the term refers to gender, or as John Money said, behavior and orientation as male or female, rather than who someone is physically attracted to.

With a PhD from Harvard and a position at the renowned Johns Hopkins Hospital in Baltimore, Maryland, Money's theory and the papers he and his team published were widely embraced. They won the 1955 Hofheimer Prize from the American Psychiatric Association, and Money received large financial grants for decades from the National Institutes of Health. John Colapinto said in his book *As Nature Made Him: The Boy Who Was Raised as a Girl*, "This theory was the foundation on which Money based his recommendation to Johns Hopkins surgeons and endocrinologists that they could surgically and hormonally steer intersexual newborns into whichever sex, boy or girl, they wished." Money was positive about his recommendation as long as it was done before the child was two and a half years old, and the doctors and parents never introduced doubt to the growing child about their assigned (or maybe more accurately, *reassigned*) gender.

Colapinto's book was published in 2000. Today this would probably read "intersex."

Some doctors and scientists disagreed with Money, saying that gender identity was more nature than nurture. One of them, Dr. Milton Diamond, wrote a scientific paper in 1965 that publicly

THE GENDER BINARY IS A BIG LIE

challenged Money's theory. In that paper, Diamond wrote, "We have been presented with no instance of a normal individual appearing as an unequivocal male and being reared successfully as a female."

THE TWINS CASE

In August of that year, twins were born to Janet and Ron Reimer in Winnipeg, Canada. The children both presented physically as male, and the proud parents named them Bruce and Brian. When the boys were seven months old, they were crying when they peed. Their doctor diagnosed it as a condition called phimosis and suggested treating it by having the babies circumcised. They went ahead, but an accident during the circumcision of Bruce destroyed the baby's entire penis. After the accident, the hospital did not go through with the circumcision of Bruce's brother Brian.

Brian's phimosis cleared up by itself before the twins turned one—a harsh reminder to their parents that the circumcision hadn't been necessary after all.

Some of the specialists the distraught parents visited suggested that they consider raising Bruce as a girl and mentioned that a doctor in Baltimore might help them. In February 1967, the twins' parents happened to see Money speaking on TV about the gender affirmation surgeries they were doing at Johns Hopkins in Baltimore. Diane Baransky, a trans woman who had had gender-affirming surgery, was a guest on the program. Asked to compare her life before and after surgery, she said, **"Well, there is a tremendous difference. . . . It's a way of finding yourself. You actually fit into society, you're more accepted in a more normal society."**

The interviewer asked Baransky, **"And now you feel complete as a woman?"**

DON'T CONFUSE TRANS AND INTERSEX IDENTITIES AND LIVES

Looking back, it's frustrating to see that the self-determination of trans people receiving gender-affirming care to have their physical bodies match their internal understanding of their gender was misinterpreted as support for the idea that you could change a person's internal understanding of their gender just by how you raise them. After all, adults like Diane Baransky were raised in the gender that matched their physical bodies and were still trans!

But to Money, trans folks were proof of nurture trumping nature, because he saw them, Colapinto said, as "a person born with apparently normal male biological makeup and genitals whose inner sense of self had differentiated as female—in direct contradiction to his chromosomal, gonadal, hormonal, reproductive, and anatomic sex."

It's tragic that the overarching belief that the gender binary had to include every human had the medical community take the lived experience of trans people as motivation and justification for attempting to erase intersex identities.

Her response? **"Oh, yes, definitely. Yes. Completely—body and mind."**

Baby Bruce's parents met with Money and were convinced they should raise Bruce as a girl. On July 3, 1967, the child underwent surgery to remove his testicles and create genitals that would appear more female. Bruce received a new name, Brenda, and everyone in the child's life was warned the secret had to be kept. There could be no doubt expressed, or it might not work. Janet Reimer told Colapinto what happened the first time she put Brenda in a dress: **"She was ripping at it, trying to tear it off. I remember thinking, Oh my God, she knows she's a boy and she doesn't want girls' clothing. She doesn't want to be a girl. But then I thought, Well, maybe I can *teach* her to want to be a girl. Maybe I can train her so that she wants to be a girl."**

For Money the twins were the perfect experiment. Identical twins born male—one raised as a boy, the other to be raised as a girl. If it worked, it would prove Money's theory that nurture makes all the difference. There was a lot of pressure for the experiment to be a success: 1) The twins' parents (and teachers, guidance counselors, psychologists, family, everyone) being told they were unable to express doubt about Brenda being a girl or risk the child's well-being; 2) the medical community's momentum behind their decision to choose a gender for, and operate on, intersex children; and 3) the famous doctor in charge having his whole career and ego rest on the success of Brenda being happily adjusted to life as a girl. All these resigned the child everyone was calling Brenda to an incredibly painful childhood, which he would later describe as **"psychological warfare."**

Because life as Brenda—as a girl—never quite worked. When remembering their childhood, Brian Reimer commented, **"When I say there was nothing feminine about Brenda,"** Brian laugh[ed], **"I mean there was *nothing* feminine. She walked like a guy. Sat with her legs apart. She talked about guy things, didn't give a crap about cleaning house, getting married, wearing makeup. We both wanted to play with guys, build forts and have snowball fights and play army. She'd get a skipping rope for a gift, and the only thing we'd use *that* for was to tie people up, whip people with it."** Brenda had so many behavioral issues she had to repeat first grade.

Though Money knew about Brenda having trouble adjusting to life and school (he had intervened to keep Brenda from repeating kindergarten), the supposed "success" of the twins case was front and center in his 1972 book and in the speech he gave the day the book was published addressing over a thousand attendees at a conference of the American Association for the Advancement of Science. The supposed triumph of nurture over nature was widely reported in *Time* magazine, the *New York Times Book Review*, and numerous textbooks—which enshrined it for decades as the "truth."

Experts like Dr. Mel Grumbach, who led the University of California San Francisco Department of Pediatrics for twenty years, credited the twins case with, as reporter Colapinto wrote, "the universal acceptance not only of the theory that human beings are psychosexually malleable at birth, but also of sex reassignment surgery as treatment of infants with ambiguous or injured genitalia." Even beyond the US, sex reassignment of intersex babies and babies with injured genitals became the standard of care from the 1970s through today. Intersex advocate Seven Graham points to Sir John Dewhurst as another doctor based in London with a huge impact on spreading the practice of operating on intersex babies globally.

Even without statistical records tracking intersex surgeries on children worldwide, the number of people impacted is staggering. In the US between 1955 and 2020, more than 251 million babies were born. With 1.7 percent of people born with intersex traits, that's over 4,267,000 people. Just in the US. Not that every one of those people had medically unnecessary surgery when they were children, but this clearly impacted *millions* of people around the world for over fifty years.

FEMINISTS TOOK THE SIDE OF NURTURE

Time magazine reported in 1973 about the announced "success" of the twins' case, saying that it "provides strong support for a major contention of women's liberationists: that conventional patterns of masculine and feminine behavior can be altered."

Quoting Money on how babies are born neutral when it comes to gender, Kate Millet wrote in her book *Sexual Politics* (that became a best-selling feminist "bible") that the differences between men and women were not based on biology (nature) but instead on societal expectations and prejudices (nurture). "Psychosexually (for example, in terms of masculine and feminine) there is no differentiation between the sexes at birth. Psychosexual personality is therefore postnatal and learned."

The psychological aspects (mind, emotions, and behaviors) of someone's sexual development

Going back further in history, Mary Wollstonecraft in her 1792 *Vindication of the Rights of Women* pointed to the way high-class British women were raised as the real cause for the differences between women and men. **"Taught from their infancy that beauty is woman's sceptre, the mind shapes itself to the body, and, roaming round its gilt cage, only seeks to adorn its prison."** Wollstonecraft urged her readers, **"Let us then, by being allowed to take the same exercise as boys, not only during infancy, but youth, arrive at perfection of body, that we may know how far the natural superiority extends."**

Women being held back is, indeed, a cultural phenomenon. But, looking back, we can see gender identity was mixed up with gender expression and a culture's rules for what people of different genders were allowed to do—and how they could express themselves.

But the "success" of the twins case was a lie. Seven-year-old Brenda daydreamed of a future self as a young man with a mustache and a sports car—which resulted in the child resisting Money's continued and forceful efforts to have Brenda agree to further genital surgery to make his body more femalelike. Colapinto documents how Brenda learned to tell Money and his team what they wanted to hear, while at the same time any expressions that fell outside Brenda's "girl" identity were dismissed. Money and his coworkers would tell Brenda, **"You shouldn't be ashamed of being a girl,"** and **"That's a typical tomboy thing. . . . You're just a tomboy."**

Pressure to have the surgery from Money and Brenda's parents escalated, and Brenda started to rebel. With the prospect of another annual visit to Money looming, Brenda had **"a nervous breakdown. . . . I remember the summer I turned nine just huddling in a corner and shaking and crying."**

The twins' father recalled, **"I sort of knew it wasn't working after Brenda was seven or something. . . . But what were we going to do?"** The family moved far away from everyone and everything that might connect them to their previous life as a family with two boys. But even in a new school, Brenda was treated as an outcast.

The twins' mother struggled with depression, and their father struggled with alcohol. Brenda tried to be **"more ladylike,"** taking the blame for their parents' marital troubles, **"I thought it was all my fault."**

Meanwhile, Money kept publishing and publicizing the success of the twins case, writing in one paper, **"Her behavior is so normally that of an active little girl, and so clearly different by contrast from the boyish ways of her twin brother."**

Sometimes, primary sources lie.

THE GENDER BINARY IS A BIG LIE

And in his 1976 book *Sexual Signatures*, coauthored with journalist Patricia Tucker, **"At five, the little girl already preferred dresses to pants, enjoyed wearing her hair ribbons, bracelets and frilly blouses, and loved being her daddy's little sweetheart . . . [d]ramatic proof that the gender identity option is open at birth for normal infants."**

One of the few friends Brenda made around the sixth and seventh grade, Heather Legarry, recalled, **"As far as I knew, Brenda was a girl—physically. . . . But from everything that she did and said, she indicated that she didn't want to be a girl."**

An unhappy twelve-year-old Brenda was put on female hormones, and Brenda's body responded by growing breasts. Brenda responded to that by binge eating, to try and hide the physical change. Brenda explained to psychiatrist Dr. Janice Ingimundson about why Brenda wore boys' clothes, saying, **"I like dressing like this. It doesn't feel right to be in a dress, like I shouldn't be in one."**

But Ingimundson didn't see much choice but to follow Money's plan to push Brenda to have surgery so Brenda could fully embrace being female. **"I thought, The decision has been made. . . . If you open up this can of worms now and say, 'Maybe this was the wrong decision'—well, who is going to *do* that?"** Ingimundson urged Brenda's parents to tell their struggling child the truth. And the psychiatrist updated Money, letting him know things weren't going so smoothly.

In May 1978, convinced during a visit with Money that they were about to take Brenda to have the surgery against Brenda's will, Brenda ran away. Colapinto wrote that when Brenda saw their parents later that day at the Baltimore hotel where the family was staying, "Brenda told [her mother] Janet that if ever again forced to see Dr. Money, she would kill herself."

When Brenda was fourteen, a BBC documentary crew reached out to the twins' parents. Brenda's previous psychiatrist, Doreen Moggey, had already spoken to them, telling Colapinto, **"Somebody needed to say that this was not the rosy success story that was presented in the literature."**

The psychiatrist overseeing Brenda's treatment, Dr. Keith Sigmundson, also spoke to the filmmakers on the condition that they keep the family anonymous. Sigmundson told Colapinto, **"By that time there were clear doubts in my mind that this [sex reassignment] ever should have happened. At that point, I think I really wanted the world to know."**

Brenda's parents still thought Money's plan would work. Looking back, Janet Reimer said, **"I had brainwashed myself. I couldn't *afford* to believe anything else."**

When Brenda was fourteen, Ron Reimer finally told his child the truth. Here's how the adult who had been raised as Brenda described it: **"He told me that I was born a boy, and about the accident when they were trying to circumcise me, and how they saw all kinds of specialists, and they took the best advice they had at the time, which was to try to change me over. My dad got very upset. I was *relieved*. . . . Suddenly it all made sense why I felt the way I did. . . . I wasn't crazy."**

Brenda decided to live as a boy as soon as possible and took the name David. He said about choosing his name, **"It reminded me of the guy with the odds stacked against him . . . the guy who was facing up to a giant eight feet [2.4 m] tall. It reminded me of courage."** And a week after he turned fifteen, David made his first appearance at a family event (a wedding) as a boy.

The following years were hard ones for David. At one

point he bought a gun, determined to kill the doctor whose mistake had cost him so much. But when he confronted the doctor and the doctor broke down in tears, David just walked away. When he was about twenty-one, he told a friend that he had **"never felt like a girl."**

David had surgery to construct an artificial penis. And then he met a woman who had three children, and they fell in love. They married when David was twenty-five years old, making him a husband and father.

Even though Janet Reimer had updated Money that Brenda was now David, when asked about the twins, the doctor would say that the case was "lost to follow-up," blaming the intrusions of the media. And even after that (and despite alternative treatments that had become available), he continued to speak and write about how sex reassignment was the only option for baby boys with micropenis, or boys like David Reimer who had lost their penis in an accident. Money continued to be celebrated in the academic and medical communities, including at a 1987 event honoring him as one of four scientists who had received NIH grants for twenty-five years in a row.

THE LIE IS REVEALED

In the early 1990s, David Reimer met Dr. Milton Diamond, who told him how the "success" of David's case was the precedent for thousands of sex reassignments. David recalled Diamond telling him that **"there are people who are going through what you're going through every day and we're trying to stop that."**

"I figured I was the only one. And here Diamond tells me they're doing all these surgeries based on *me*," David said.

This seems like an enormous understatement.

In 1994 Dr. Diamond and Dr. Sigmundson collaborated on a paper that revealed the truth of the twins' case and suggested a new set of guidelines for children born intersex—avoid any surgical intervention until the children are old enough to know and say for themselves what their gender is: **"Rear the child in a consistent gender—but keep away the knife."**

Using the made-up names John/Joan to protect David/Brenda's identity.

Deemed too controversial, the paper wouldn't be published until March 1997. Then the *New York Times* ran a front-page story with the headline, **"SEXUAL IDENTITY NOT PLIABLE AFTER ALL, REPORT SAYS."**

And *Time* magazine reported that **"the experts had it all wrong."**

Tragically, struggling with depression and the impact of everything that had happened to them, just a few years after the book on David's life and the battle between Money and Diamond was published in 2000, both twins would die by their own hands. Colapinto later wrote about the twins' close and fraught relationship, "Brian was jealous of the attention that David had always received because of his medical problems; David was jealous because in his estimation Brian was the lucky one."

No one seems to have been "lucky" in their story. Except once the truth of what happened to the twins was finally known—and Money's theory was shown to be false—change could start to come.

BUT CHANGE IS SLOW

Turning the medical establishment around on a course of care is a daunting task. So many factors must have stood in the way (and probably still stand in the way) of doctors stopping these surgeries; guilt at maybe having done the wrong thing, fear of the possible consequences both financially and to their career if it had been the wrong thing; and ego—the need to have been (and still be) right.

Dr. William Reiner spent eighteen years performing "normalizing" surgeries on intersex children. But in the late 1980s, when he began to believe that nature really did have the larger hand in shaping a person's gender identity, he stopped doing those surgeries. Reiner retrained as a child psychiatrist. Colapinto said Reiner did his own long-term study of "six genetic males who were born without penises and as a result were castrated and raised as girls. Two years into his study, he noted that all six sex-changed boys were closer to males than to females in attitudes and behavior. Two had spontaneously reverted to being boys without being told of their male (XY) chromosome status." Reiner told Colapinto, **"These are children who did not have penises . . . who had been reared as girls and yet knew they were boys. They don't say, 'I wish I was a boy' or 'I'd really rather be a boy' or 'I think I'm a boy.' They say, 'I *am* a boy.'"** Reiner said of the importance of changing the standard of care for intersex children, **"We have to learn to listen to the children themselves."**

Before the 1955 protocol of surgery to assign intersex children to a gender of the doctor/family's choice, one unpublished study reviewed more than 250 cases of intersex people who hadn't had any surgery to change their bodies when they were babies. The author of the study was, Colapinto says, surprised at how well adjusted they were as adults. The study included ten in-depth interviews with intersex people "who received no surgery or hormone treatments until they were old enough to make their own decision. Their lives only strengthened the investigator's impression that the condition of the genitalia plays a strikingly insignificant part in the way a person develops a stable and healthy gender identity, not to mention a secure and confident self-image." And here's the bombshell: The author of that senior dissertation to Harvard University's PhD program in 1951 was Money!

The same Dr. Money!

Acceptance of that paper made him a doctor. And yet his whole career and fame was based on doggedly pursuing and promoting the opposite conclusion. Colapinto said that Money "never explained the shift that occurred in his thinking between the time he finished his Harvard thesis and the time he wrote his first papers on intersexes four years later, and he has never publicly commented on any aspect of his work since the revelations in Diamond and Sigmundson's paper."

After being denied multiple requests for an interview, Colapinto reached Money on the phone in 1997. Colapinto said, **"When I asked Money about Diamond's appeal to delay surgery on intersexual babies until they are old enough to speak for themselves, Money grew angry. Apparently forgetting the conclusions he had reached in his own Harvard thesis review of over two hundred and fifty untreated intersexes, he emphatically rejected the idea that a person could survive a childhood with ambiguous genitalia. 'I've seen the people who were the victim of that. . . . You cannot be an *it*.'"**

It's ironic that Money—who continued to proclaim his theory of treatment for intersex babies based on the lie that Brenda was happily adjusted as a girl—also gets credit for coming up with the term we use so widely today: *gender identity*.

Colapinto's interviews with David Reimer as an adult, twenty years after he stopped living as Brenda, are heartbreaking and powerful. But David didn't blame his parents. **"My parents feel very guilty, as if the whole thing was their fault. . . . But it wasn't like that. They did what they did out of *kindness* and love and desperation. When you're desperate, you don't necessarily do all the right things."** Reflecting on how the medical community treated him, David said,

You know, if I had lost my arms and my legs and wound up in a wheelchair where you're moving everything with a little rod in your mouth—would that make me less of a person? It just seems that they implied that you're nothing if your penis is gone. The second you lose that, you're nothing, and they've got to do surgery and hormones to turn you into something. Like you're a zero. It's like your whole personality, everything about you is all directed—all pinpointed—toward what's between the legs. And to me, that's ignorant. I don't have the kind of education that these scientists and doctors and psychologists have, but to me it's very ignorant. If a woman lost her breasts, do you turn her into a guy? To make her feel 'whole and complete'?

UNNECESSARY SURGERIES ON INTERSEX CHILDREN ARE STILL HAPPENING

In 2017 Human Rights Watch's Kyle Knight said, **"When intersex kids grow up, they may want some of these operations, but that should be their decision to make. . . . Doctors across the US continue to conduct medically unnecessary irreversible surgeries on intersex children when the kids are far too young to consent, and when the operations** could be safely deferred until the kids are old enough to decide for themselves. These surgeries need to stop."

Intersex activist Pidgeon Pagonis, who endured numerous surgeries to change their body as a child, said in that Human Rights Watch and interACT video, **"I wish my parents would've known that I would grow up and not want this to have happened to me. I wish they would've known that when the doctors came to them saying, 'Your kid basically won't be lovable unless we change their vagina, change this, change that, take their clitoris out, et cetera, et cetera,' that they would have let that bounce off and know, 'No.' Like, 'If my daughter's not sick then you're not going to try to change her so that she could be loved. She should be loved for who she is.'"**

Pidgeon Pagonis advocates against unnecessary genital surgery for intersex children.

In 2015 the United Nations High Commissioner for Human Rights, Zeid Ra'ad Al Hussein, spoke about the injustices faced by intersex people, saying, **"Far too few of us are aware of the specific human rights violations faced by millions of intersex people. Because their bodies don't comply with typical definitions of male or female, intersex children and adults are frequently subjected to forced sterilization and other unnecessary and irreversible surgery, and suffer discrimination in schools, workplaces and other settings."** It was (and remains) a call for action to **"end these abuses."**

INTERSEX ACTIVISM

"Fix your hearts, not our parts!" is a protest chant used by members of the Intersex Justice Project, cofounded by Pidgeon Pagonis, Sean Saifa Wall, and Lynnell Stephani Long. Both Pidgeon and Sean had been told they had childhood cancer as an explanation for the multiple surgeries they had as children. Neither of them had cancer.

It's cool to note that back in 1895 a group of intersex people gathered in New York City. Susan Stryker's excellent *Transgender History: The Roots of Today's Revolution* reported that they called their "little club" the Cercle Hermaphroditos, and their aim was "to unite for defense against the world's bitter persecution."

In recent decades, intersex activists and their allies have campaigned to end unnecessary surgeries on intersex children. Founded in 1993 by intersex activist Cheryl Chase, the Intersex Society of North America was **"devoted to systemic change to end shame, secrecy, and unwanted genital surgeries for people born with an anatomy that someone decided is not standard for male or female."** Among the points listed in their mission was that **"intersexuality is primarily a problem of stigma and trauma, not gender."** Chase said she wanted to **"end the idea that it's monstrous to be different."**

Cheryl Chase had been given the name Bonnie Sullivan at birth and as an adult used the names Cheryl Chase and Bo Laurent.

In 2008 the Intersex Society of North America was replaced by interACT: Advocates for Intersex Youth, a nonprofit with **"a focused mission of ending harmful medical interventions on intersex children."** Today its mission is broader. Their website says: **"interACT uses** innovative legal and other strategies, to advocate for the human rights of children born with intersex traits."

The first public protest in North America happened on October 26, 1996, during a conference of the American Academy of Pediatrics in Boston. Members of the Intersex Society of North America and Transexual Menace organized it and used the slogan, "Hermaphrodites with Attitude."

That protest was the inspiration for Intersex Awareness Day—founded in 2004 and celebrated every year on October 26. The website announcing Intersex Awareness Day says: **"Intersex Awareness Day is the (inter)national day of grass-roots action to end shame, secrecy, and unwanted genital cosmetic surgeries on intersex children.**

This all ties back to the false idea that the gender binary includes everyone. Anne Fausto-Sterling wrote in *Sexing the Body* that intersex people have bodies that "do not fall naturally into a binary classification; only a surgical shoehorn can put them there. But why should we care?" Fausto-Sterling provides the medical establishment and

People gather at the ILGA conference in Brussels, Belgium, to honor Intersex Awareness Day on October 26, 2018.

Western culture's answer: "to maintain gender divisions, we must control those bodies that are so unruly as to blur the borders. Since intersexuals quite literally embody both sexes, they weaken claims about sexual difference."

A FEW HOSPITALS DOWN—MANY TO GO

Starting in 2017, for three years intersex activists targeted one hospital in Chicago, organizing a social media, email, and phone call campaign, #EndIntersexSurgery, to get Lurie Children's Hospital of Chicago to become the first US hospital to stop genital surgeries on intersex infants.

And in July 2020, the campaign succeeded. The hospital issued an apology, and a promise, that read in part: **"We recognize the painful history and complex emotions associated with intersex surgery and how, for many years, the medical field has failed these children. Historically care for individuals with intersex traits included an emphasis on early genital surgery to make genitalia appear more typically male or female. As the medical field has advanced, and understanding has grown, we now know this approach was harmful and wrong."** The hospital's announcement acknowledged the evolution of their policies and stated that, moving forward, unless it was medically necessary, **"in intersex individuals . . . irreversible genital procedures . . . should not be performed until patients can participate meaningfully in making the decision for themselves."**

And in July 2021, New York City Health and Hospitals, the largest public health-care system in the United States with over seventy facilities across New York City decided to prohibit the surgeries. Their statement read, in part, **"All medically unnecessary surgery on Intersex [children] should be delayed until the child is of an age to assent/**

consent (adolescence). **If parents are requesting such surgery, the rights of the child to be protected from harm should take precedence over the demands of parents for intervention."**

But there are a lot more hospitals in the US—and around the world—to go. Quoted by the online platform Them about a summer 2021 protest to end surgeries on intersex children at Weill Cornell Medical Center in New York City, Sean Safia Wall, who experienced nonconsensual gender reassignment there during his youth, said,

Part of a different hospital system still doing medically unnecessary surgeries on intersex children

"For nearly three decades, intersex activists have been fighting to interrupt this cycle of harm that continually affects people to this very day. This protest is not only about reconciling our past but embracing a future where people with intersex variations are treated as a whole person and not just genitals, hormones or chromosomes."

AT CORE, THE ISSUE IS THE HUMAN RIGHT TO SELF-DETERMINATION

"I'm sick to death of feeling ashamed of myself. That feeling will never go away. I did nothing wrong, but it's like you're conditioned to feel ashamed of yourself." David Reimer's words feel resonant for children with his experience, as well as for intersex children and every child who doesn't fit the gender binary but is forced into one of the two boxes anyway. David said of his life's journey, from Bruce to Brenda to David, **"Mom and Dad wanted this to work so I'd be happy. That's every parent's dream for their child. But I couldn't be happy for my parents. I had to be happy for me. You can't be something you're not. You have to be *you*."**

THE DARLINGTON STATEMENT ON INTERSEX HUMAN RIGHTS

In March 2017, a group of Australia and Aotearoa/New Zealand intersex community organizations and individual advocates met at a retreat and released "The Darlington Statement." They explain that "it sets out the priorities and call by the intersex human rights movements in our countries." Some highlights:

Preamble A: Intersex people are born with physical or biological sex characteristics (such as sexual anatomy, reproductive organs, hormonal patterns and/or chromosomal patterns) that are more diverse than stereotypical definitions for male or female bodies. For some people these traits are apparent prenatally or at birth, while for others they emerge later in life, often at puberty. . . . We recognise our diverse histories and use the word intersex inclusively, and acknowledging our right to self-determination.

We acknowledge:

1. The Malta Declaration of the Third International Intersex Forum in 2013.
2. That intersex people **exist in all cultures and societies**, throughout history, and that the existence of intersex people is worthy of celebration.
3. The **diversity of our sex characteristics** and bodies, our identities, sexes, genders, and lived experiences. We also acknowledge **intersectionalities** with other populations, including same-sex attracted people, trans and gender diverse people, people with disabilities, women, men, and Indigenous - Aboriginal and Torres Strait Islander, Tangata Whenua - and racialised, migrant and refugee populations.

4. That the word 'intersex', and the intersex human rights movement, **belong equally to all people born with variations of sex characteristics**, irrespective of our gender identities, genders, legal sex classifications and sexual orientations.

5. Our rights to **bodily integrity, physical autonomy and self determination**.

6. Our opposition to pathologising terminology such as "disorders of sex development", not only because such labels are inherently disordering, but also because this promotes the belief that intersex characteristics need to be "fixed".

Human rights and legal reform:

7. We call for the immediate **prohibition as a criminal act** of deferrable medical interventions, including surgical and hormonal interventions, that alter the sex characteristics of infants and children without personal consent. We call for freely-given and fully informed consent by individuals, with individuals and families having mandatory independent access to funded counselling and peer support.

8. Regarding **sex/gender classifications**, sex and gender binaries are upheld by structural violence. Additionally, attempts to classify intersex people as a third sex/gender ← do not respect our diversity or right to self determination. These can inflict wide-ranging harm regardless of whether an intersex person identifies with binary legal sex assigned at birth or not.

> The idea of drawing coloring book lines around the vast diversity of intersex people and calling them a "third gender" is not cool with many intersex people.

Undue emphasis on how to classify intersex people rather than how we are treated is also a form of structural violence. The larger goal is not to seek new classifications but **to end legal classification systems** and the hierarchies that lie behind them. Therefore:

a. As with race or religion, sex/gender should not be a legal category on birth certificates or identification documents for anybody.

b. While sex/gender classifications remain legally required, sex/gender assignments must be regarded as provisional. Given existing social conditions, we do not support the imposition of a third sex classification when births are initially registered.

c. Recognising that any child may grow up to identify with a different sex/gender, and that the decision about the sex of rearing of an intersex child may have been incorrect, sex/gender classifications must be legally correctable through a simple administrative procedure at the request of the individual concerned.

d. Individuals able to consent should be able to choose between female (F), male (M), non-binary, alternative gender markers, or multiple options.

There's much more, and you can check out the full statement online.

The growing support for gender diversity is a hopeful note. In March 2021 the American Psychological Association adopted a resolution opposing efforts to change people's gender identity. The association's president, Dr. Jennifer F. Kelly, is quoted in the press release saying, **"There is a growing body of research that shows that transgender or nonbinary gender identities are normal variations in human expression of gender. . . . Attempts to force people to conform with rigid gender identities can be harmful to their mental health and well-being."**

Another frontier of the fight for self-determination of intersex people is happening before babies are even born. Tests for Differences of Sexual Development (DSD), or as the medical community originally put it, Disorders of Sexual Development, are happening. Prospective parents are then choosing to have a child or not based on the DSD test results. Intersex British creative in Hollywood Seven Graham put it this way: "Doctors are calling us 'disorders' & breeding us out of humanity, before they even understand the magic & gifts that make us us."

It's sobering to learn that surgeries on intersex babies became the standard of care based on a disproved theory and a lie. And it should empower those of us with non-intersex bodies to stand up as allies for the self-determination of intersex people. To end unnecessary surgeries on intersex babies who cannot consent. And to recognize the harm caused by forcing everyone to fit into the gender binary.

Let's end this chapter with two questions from trans activist Pat Califia. Califia asks, "Who would you be . . . if you had never been punished for gender inappropriate behavior?"

And then, with that answer in your mind, Califia challenges us to think about what our culture might be like if "we all helped each other to manifest our most beautiful, sexy, intelligent, creative, and adventurous inner selves, instead of cooperating to suppress them?"

CONCLUSION
HiSTORY, HERSTORY, THEIRSTORY, OURSTORY

My hope is that *The Gender Binary Is a Big Lie: Infinite Identities around the World* is an invitation to see more possibilities. Because even for those of us who identify within the binary, believing that that is all that exists hems us in and limits what we think is appropriate, desirable, and possible. Thinking gender is a strict binary has impacted how we see and treat ourselves and how we see and treat others. We have the opportunity to take this new knowledge about gender diversity and change how we see and treat ourselves, as well as how we see and treat others.

To wrap up this book, we'll look at rainbows one more time (they still hold some surprises for us), explore expressions of gender pride (such as flags and symbols), consider safe spaces for gender diversity (and how to create them), and set our goals for progress: How can we do more than just *acknowledge* the reality that there are many more than two genders? How can we aim higher and *celebrate* the incredible and rich diversity of genders of people across time, around our world, and right where you're reading this, today?

RAINBoWS 2.0

So many more genders exist than we may have been taught by society, just like there are so many more colors of the rainbow. But there are still assumptions about rainbows we make based on our personal experience, the culture we're raised in, and the biases we may not even realize we carry around that effect our understanding.

Take the assumption that rainbows are arcs. When we're standing on the ground, a rainbow appears to be an arc, but it turns out that's not the whole picture. The National Geographic Society explains, "Rainbows are actually full circles. . . . Viewers on the ground can only see the light reflected by raindrops above the horizon."

And while we now understand that rainbows have more than seven colors, another assumption is that rainbows are just the millions of colors we can see. But "visible light is only part of a rainbow. Infrared radiation exists just beyond

A photo of a full-circle rainbow taken from a helicopter near the village of Weggis in Switzerland

visible red light, while ultraviolet is just beyond violet. There are also radio waves (beyond infrared), x-rays (beyond ultraviolet), and gamma radiation (beyond x-rays)." Rainbows have all these additional parts that our human eyes can't register!

At the top, or outside, of the rainbow

At the bottom, or inside, of the rainbow

Just like there's so much we can still learn about rainbows, there's so much more we can still discover about gender. Many and various genders are lived with pride in many and various communities. It's time for all of us to embrace that.

Slowly, progress is being made. As I was writing this book, the US State Department announced on October 27, 2021, that they had issued the very first US passport with an X gender marker for nonbinary, intersex, and gender-nonconforming people. The passport was issued to Dana Zzyym, an intersex and nonbinary activist and US Navy veteran. Lambda Legal said that this was after "a six-year legal battle to get an accurate passport that did not force them to identify as male or female."

Zzyym said: **"I almost burst into tears when I opened the envelope, pulled out my new passport, and saw the 'X' stamped boldly under 'sex,' . . . I'm also ecstatic that other intersex and nonbinary U.S. citizens will soon be able to apply for passports with the correct gender marker . . . to have an accurate passport, one that doesn't force me to identify as male or female but recognizes I am neither, is liberating."**

Let's liberate all of us from seeing the gender binary as the only two possibilities. It's time to celebrate the infinite rainbow colors of gender!

EXPRESSIONS OF GENDER PRIDE

Flags and symbols are some of the ways gender-diverse people signal their identities, communities, and pride.

FLAGS

Just as there are many different pride flags for who someone is (or is not) romantically interested in and/or physically attracted to, there are multiple flags to celebrate and affirm gender identities including trans, intersex, genderqueer, gender fluid, and nonbinary pride.

The colors and shapes have meaning, as do the designs. One popular trans pride flag designed by Monica Helms has five stripes of three colors. Helms explained, **"No matter which way you fly it, it is always correct, signifying us finding correctness in our lives."**

SYMBOLS

Gender symbols have *way* more variety than the binary circle with an arrow off to the top right for men and the circle on top of a plus sign for women.

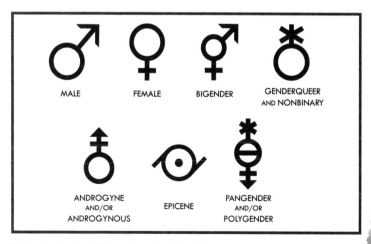

MALE   FEMALE   BIGENDER   GENDERQUEER AND NONBINARY

ANDROGYNE AND/OR ANDROGYNOUS   EPICENE   PANGENDER AND/OR POLYGENDER

Symbols showing different gender identities

A variety of symbols that represent nonbinary people

Twenty-three different gender identity symbols are on the cover of Robyn Ryle's book *She/He/They/Me*. Ryle says that the variety of symbols came from the collaboration of "a group of nonbinary Brazilian artists in 2014." On their website, gender and intersex activist Mx. Anunnaki Ray Marquez has an image from Reddit with thirty gender symbols beyond the binary.

Creating a symbol for the gender you identify as and with is also on the table—for the Brazilian artists Ryle referred to and for each of us. In 2018, a contributor to the Asexual Visibility and Education Network website posted their own invented symbol to represent their **"totally non-binary"** identity, celebrating the freedom for each of us to create a symbol for our own gender and saying, **"it's not like there's some sort of international gender symbol society, right?"** Circles, lines, arrows, asterisks, dots . . . what combinations and configurations have meaning for you? It's not just what you add either. The space you leave blank (negative space) has impact too.

Or a pride flag, if you choose

SAFE SPACES FOR GENDER DIVERSITY

In June 2010, Filipina trans leader Sass Rogando Sasot attended the International Congress on Gender Identity and Human Rights in Barcelona, Spain. In a talk she gave later that year at the University of the Philippines Diliman that was published on *TransGriot*, Sasot recalled what happened: "We had just finished the affairs of the day. I joined the table of a group of transgender women having a lively chat. As I was about to sit, one of them stopped talking and shouted at me *"You are in desperate need of boobs!"* Every one laughed. I felt so embarrassed. I just smiled at her and asked myself, *"How can a transgender rights activist bully and make someone feel bad about her body? Does she really know the point of what she was fighting about?"* I have been harassed, humiliated because I have 'the wrong body.'"

We can all do better.

In that same speech, she said:

> I identify and live my life as a woman, I look at myself in the mirror and I see a penis and a flat chest. How do I convince you that I am a woman? By feeling wrong about it? By hating the genitals I was born with as well as the body my puberty sculpted? By feeling trapped in this body? By transforming this body so that it can resemble the form of your woman? But is this body really wrong? What made it wrong? Who made it wrong? God? Scientists? Politicians? Theorists? Or me?
>
> I am a human being inhabiting a transsexual body. Why am I inhabiting this body is a question that I cannot answer. I know that some dare to answer it by virtue of their whims, religious beliefs, scientific research, or various theoretical discussions. Yet what is the point of subjecting the existence of people like us under the microscope of various opinions? We exist, therefore we are and we do not need to prove and justify why we exist in order to be.
>
> I am a human being who is neither in a wrong

body nor trapped in a wrong body but a human being who is expressing her beingness in one of the various forms of the human body. I am not in a wrong body. I am in this body just like how you are in your body. I am not trapped by my body. I am trapped by your beliefs. And I want to reclaim this body from those who want it to breathe and be fed by their dogmas.

> A rigidly held belief imposed by those in power as a truth you're not supposed to argue with

Sasot offers us a profound insight: we can all be human beings who express our beingness in one of the various forms of the human body. And each of us can respect and celebrate the expressions of beingness in other people in *their* various forms of the human body too.

LOOKING AT THE NUMBERS (EVEN THOUGH IT'S NOT ABOUT THE NUMBERS)

How many people identify outside the gender binary? It's not only who you ask—their age, where they live, and how comfortable they are sharing their truth with the person or organization asking—the answer also depends on *how* you ask the question.

In 2017 one study of high schoolers in the US asked kids if they were transgender and "found that an average of 1.8% of high school students identify as transgender."

> That's eighteen out of one thousand kids.

But in a study published in the June 2021 issue of the journal *Pediatrics*, Dr. Kacie Kidd took a different approach. This time, the researchers asked two questions. First, "What is your sex (the sex you were assigned at birth on your birth certificate?)"

with the options of "female" and "male." Next, they asked "Which of the following best describes you (select all that apply)? With the options of "girl," "boy," "trans girl," "trans boy," "genderqueer," "nonbinary," and "another identity." The idea, Kidd explained, was that by asking **"a more inclusive question about gender identity,"** they would get more accurate results. The study found that **"9.2% of kids consider themselves gender-diverse in some way."** A huge difference!

> Even in this study about physical sex and gender diversity, the researchers didn't offer an "intersex" or "other" possibility that was outside the binary.

> That's ninety-two out of one thousand kids.

In June 2021 the Williams Institute at the UCLA School of Law announced new research on LGBTQ adults between eighteen and sixty that estimated that 1.2 million people in the US identify as nonbinary. And in June 2023 they estimated that 1.6 million people in the US ages thirteen and older identify as trans.

While it's great to see these acknowledgments and representations, we shouldn't fall into the trap of thinking that a disenfranchised group is only worthy of respect, rights, and justice based on their population. Even if it's just one person in a million, or a billion, every human being should be celebrated for being their authentic self. And that absolutely includes intersex, trans, genderqueer, gender questioning, gender fluid, nonbinary, and other gender-diverse people.

For those of us raised within the confines of a gender binary, we need to watch for language and attitudes that may pathologize or treat folks identifying and living outside the binary as if something is wrong with them. There's nothing wrong with them—the issue is the system that defines normal so narrowly. There's inspiration for this from Professor Joan Roughgarden: **"Just as we should speak of 'discovering' a woman to be pregnant, and not of 'diagnosing' her, we should also speak of discovering transgender identity. . . . Coming out as transgendered should be a source of joy and happiness to everyone, just like the birth of an eagerly awaited child."** And that sense of discovery and joy can and should apply to everyone identifying with and living their authentic gender.

While Roughgarden, as a trans person, uses the "ed" here, it's more respectful for those who are not part of the trans community to just use "trans" or "transgender."

COMING OUT

Some gender-diverse people speak of their gender journey as being closeted, of hiding their difference, of living a double life, of coming out, and at last living as their authentic self. That's completely parallel to my own life experience as a gay man—being closeted from the age of eleven, actively hiding my difference, living a double life, and at last coming out at the age of twenty-five and living as my authentic self.

So much of what determines a person's willingness to be authentic is their environment. The question is always, *Is it safe (physically and emotionally) to be my authentic self here/now/ with these people?*

I ask this question every time my husband and I are in public and I want to hold his hand.

The question we should all consider is, *How can we make spaces safe for everyone who is intersex, trans, genderqueer, gender questioning, gender fluid, nonbinary, and other gender-diverse identities?*

THE GENDER BINARY IS A BIG LIE

For every category of identity that is "othered" in our culture, including lesbian, gay, and bi people; women; people of color; Indigenous people; and disabled people: *How can we create safe space for each and every person?*

Because only when people feel safe can they be their authentic selves, in public and with joy.

SETTING OUR GOALS FOR PROGRESS

With all the increased visibility of intersex, trans, genderqueer, gender questioning, gender fluid, nonbinary, and other people who identify as gender diverse, some people who feel their power is invested in the gender binary are pushing back. Anti-trans health-care legislation in the US in the 2020s often uses language about protecting children as justification, but they specifically exempt intersex surgeries on kids and babies without the intersex person's consent. Seven Graham explains, "It's not about protecting children, it's about policing gender." This pushback goes beyond the US too.

One example is the Chinese government targeting their culture's "masculinity crisis," warning that "effeminate" young men were ruining an entire generation. In September 2021, Chinese television banned "sissy men and other abnormal aesthetics" and censors started blurring out male celebrities' earrings.

The famous singer Cai Xukun went from wearing bright eyeshadow and having blond hair on Instagram to sporting dark hair and more "masculine" leather jackets. Writing about this in the *New York Times*, Helen Gao said that "the government's idea of the ideal male reads like an outdated description of 1950s gender norms: muscular, reliable, career-oriented providers."

Commenting on the 2016 election of President Donald Trump and Britain's Brexit vote to leave the European

Union, Juno Dawson in her honest and funny memoir *The Gender Games: The Problem with Men and Women, from Someone Who Has Been Both* offered a theory about the backlash: **"Normal, hardworking people grew tired of the black, immigrant, transgender, homosexual, Muslim 'elite' chomping down on their slice of the pie. 'When is it Straight Pride?' 'What day is International Men's Day?' 'Where are our rights?' cried people who have all the rights already. . . . We aren't after your slice of the pie, we want our own slice, thank you very much."**

Which leads us to these challenges:

- *How can each of us be a better ally to gender-diverse people?*
- *How can we uninvest in the false idea that a gender binary must apply to everyone?*
- *What can we do?*

One idea, suggested by Hida Viloria in their book *Born Both: An Intersex Life*, is **"by saying 'male, female, *and* intersex' or 'man, woman, and intersex person' every time the topic of sex or gender comes up."** If you're filling out a form with only male or female options for "sex," and you have the privilege to and feel safe doing so, comment that there should be another option. And for "gender"—heck, there should be many other options beyond the binary and the respect given to write in your own gender. This is especially powerful if you do fit within the gender binary. Think how much less you risk by bringing it up than someone whose authentic identity is denied by that form, bathroom sign, or conversation.

Including trans, intersex, and other gender-diverse people in popular culture (in movies, TV shows, theater, music, and books) can help everyone outside the gender binary feel seen and celebrated. And that goes for consuming and sharing stories as well as creating them! After all, if being intersex is as common as having red hair (and it is), then how come so many people still think they don't know someone intersex?

WHAT WOULD IT MEAN TO NOT JUST ACKNOWLEDGE BUT CELEBRATE OTHER GENDERS?

I love this story shared by genderqueer activist and radical copyeditor Alex Kapitan about the Family Acceptance Project, an organization in California that works to improve the well-being of LGBTQ youth by decreasing family rejection:

> **In the organization's early years, they were working from a model that there are three kinds of families that a queer or trans youth could come from: rejecting (sometimes violently so), neutral, or tolerant and accepting. What they found over time was that they hadn't accounted for a fourth type of family: actively celebratory. Which is so gorgeous and beautiful!**

I agree with Kapitan! Let's shift our mental model to not just tolerate or accept gender diversity but celebrate gender diversity in all its infinite rainbow colors—every proud culture, every person's role in their culture, and every fellow human being's unique identity.

Doing so will make a better world for us all.

AUTHOR'S NOTE

I wrote this book with a large measure of humility—and some shame too. Being a cis gay kid and teen I worked hard to fit into the neat gender boxes American culture of the 1970s and '80s presented to me: Boys in one box. Girls in another. And I never questioned it.

At thirteen, I forced my voice lower, trying to present as more masculine. At fifteen, I tried not to do anything "girly" (such as skipping as I walked) that might give away my secret: that I liked other guys. At twenty-one, I wished the TV news wouldn't focus on the drag queens when reporting on Gay Pride. I completely fell for the lie about gender being solely binary and the stereotypes about what it meant to be gay—and a man.

> Completely confusing gender and how I expressed my gender with whom I was romantically and physically attracted to

And it took me so long—too long—to see gender with a different lens. To accept my rather high voice. To skip if I want to skip. To cheer on the drag queens. We're so serious about gender in our culture, but we can also see the lines we draw as kind of ridiculous. Do we really need to gender haircuts? Soap? Toys? Clothes? Makeup? Nail polish? The list goes on and on.

What I've tried to bring to this book is respect. Researching and writing this has completely changed how I see and understand gender. I discovered that just as in other realms, the stories that survived the sanitization of history by the people in power are not evenly distributed. Records of gender diversity for people with male bodies vastly outnumber the records of gender diversity for people with female and intersex bodies. Europe and America get much

THE GENDER BINARY IS A BIG LIE

more attention than the rest of the world, and most of it is filtered through a colonial lens.

Across time and around our world, the cultures and people explored here are the beginning—or just a part—of an empowering journey. I hope the true stories in this book will change how you see gender—for others and for yourself too.

Because setting us free from the idea that there are only two possible genders and claiming the legacy of our true gender diversity is what the Queer History Project and *The Gender Binary Is a Big Lie* are all about.

The light in me recognizes and acknowledges the light in you,

Lee

Los Angeles, California

SOURCE NOTES

EPIGRAPH

5: "There are as many genders as there are people in the world.": Alok Vaid-Menon, "Stand Proud: Story 2 of 5; Alok Vaid-Menon, Gender NonConforming Performance Artist and Writer," Squarespace Pride 2019, accessed January 28, 2020, https://pride.squarespace.com/featuredportraits/alok-vaid-menon.

INTRODUCTION: HOW MANY COLORS ARE IN A RAINBOW?

10: Aristotle on the colors in a rainbow: Aristotle, "Meteorology," bk. 3, pt. 2, trans. E. W. Webster, MIT, accessed January 28, 2020, http://classics.mit.edu/Aristotle/meteorology.3.iii.html.

10: Islamic and Chinese scholars on the number of colors in a rainbow: Gemma Tarlach, "20 Things You Didn't Know about Rainbows," *Discover*, April 22, 2019, https://www.discovermagazine.com/planet-earth/20-things-you-didnt-know-about-rainbows.

10: Who saw what colors in a rainbow: Tarlach.

10: Isaac Newton and the apple: Elizabeth Nix, "Did an Apple Really Fall on Isaac Newton's Head?," History.com, updated September 1, 2018, https://www.history.com/news/did-an-apple-really-fall-on-isaac-newtons-head.

10–11: Newton's matching rainbow colors to musical scale: Ashley P. Taylor, "Newton's Color Theory, ca. 1665," *Scientist*, March 1, 2017, https://www.the-scientist.com/foundations/newtons-color-theory-ca-1665-31931.

11: Number of colors in a rainbow: Ethan Siegel, "How Many Colors Are Really in a Rainbow?," *ScienceBlogs*, August 14, 2012, https://scienceblogs.com/startswithabang/2012/08/14/how-many-colors-are-really-in-a-rainbow.

11: Colors in a rainbow: Siegel.

11: "The gradation of color . . . sense of them.": Siegel.

12: "men [oroani], women [makkunrai] . . . equated with priests.": "A Map of Gender-Diverse Cultures," PBS *Independent Lens*, August 12, 2015, https://www.pbs.org/independentlens/content/two-spirits_map-html/.

12–13: "Rani works alongside . . . Rani is calalai.": Sharyn Graham Davies, "Sex, Gender, and Priests in South Sulawesi, Indonesia," *International Institute for Asian Studies Newsletter* 29 (November

2002): 27, https://www.iias.asia/sites/default/files/2020-10
/IIAS_NL29_27.pdf.

13: "the bissu are . . . to confer blessings.": Davies, 27.

14: "There are five genders . . . would become unbalanced.": "Five Genders?
| National Geographic," YouTube video, posted by National
Geographic, October 21, 2008, https://youtu.be/K9VmLJ3niVo
(July 1, 2021) 1:25; Hida Viloria and Maria Nieto, *The Spectrum
of Sex: The Science of Male, Female, and Intersex* (London: Jessica
Kingsley, 2020), 102, accessed online at https://www.google.com
/books/edition/The_Spectrum_of_Sex/Qoq5DwAAQBAJ?hl=en;
it's interesting to note that other sources spell the Bissu High
Priest's name differently, as the *New York Times* did in 2005, where
their name is rendered: Puang Matoa Saidi; Edward Rothstein,
"A Sacred Epic and Its Gods, All Struggling to Survive," *New
York Times*, July 15, 2005, https://www.nytimes.com/2005/07/15
/theater/reviews/a-sacred-epic-and-its-gods-all-struggling-to
-survive.html.

14: Stone Age third gender burial: "The Oldest Gay in the Village:
5,000-Year-Old Is 'Outed' by the Way He Was Buried," *Daily
Mail* (London), April 8, 2011, https://www.dailymail.co.uk
/sciencetech/article-1374060/Gay-caveman-5-000-year-old
-male-skeleton-outed-way-buried.html.

14–15: "We believe this . . . the Czech Republic." and "Gay Caveman":
Phil Gast and Sarah Aarthun, "Scientists Speak Out to
Discredit 'Gay Caveman' Media Reports," CNN, April 11,
2011, http://www.cnn.com/2011/WORLD/europe/04/10
/czech.republic.unusual.burial/index.html.

16: Native nations listed in Roscoe's index: Will Roscoe, *Changing Ones:
Third and Fourth Genders in Native North America* (New York:
St. Martins, 1998) 223–247; Will Roscoe, email message to the
author, October 23, 2016.

17–18: "The Father Missionaries . . . for it was.": Francisco Palóu, *Francisco
Palou's Life and Apostolic Labors of the Venerable Father Junípero
Serra, Founder of the Franciscan Missions of California*, ed., George
Wharton James, trans., C. Scott Williams (Pasadena, CA:
George Wharton James, 1913), 214–215, available at American
Journeys, Wisconsin Historical Society, 1777, electronic
publication, 2003, https://content.wisconsinhistory.org/digital
/collection/aj/id/7538; a somewhat different translation of this
primary source is available online at Gay, Lesbian, Bisexual,
Transgender History Museum, "Item 2 in 'Pioneers!' Display
Case: *Relacion Historia de la Vida y Apostolicas Tareas del Venerable*

Padre Junípero Serra, 1878, translation published as *Life and Apostolic Labors of the Venerable Father Junípero Serra* (San Francisco: GLBT Historical Society, 1913).

19: Joint statement against rash of anti-trans initiatives: statement opposing the rash of anti-transgender initiatives happening in the US: "National Consensus Statement of Anti-Sexual Assault and Domestic Violence Organizations in Support of Full and Equal Access for the Transgender Community," National Task Force to End Sexual and Domestic Violence against Women, updated April 29, 2016, with additional signatories, https://endsexualviolence.org/wp-content/uploads/2017/09/STATEMENT-OF-ANTI-SEXUAL-ASSAULT-AND-DOMESTIC-VIOLENCE-ORGANIZATIONS-IN-SUPPORT-OF-EQUAL-ACCESS-FOR-THE-TRANSGENDER-COMMUNITY.pdf; National Alliance to End Sexual Violence, accessed February 18, 2021, https://endsexualviolence.org/where_we_stand/statement-of-anti-sexual-assault-domestic-violence-organizations-in-support-of-equal-access-for-the-transgender-community/.

19: "trans people . . . 'extraordinary levels' of violence.": "Issues: Anti-Violence," National Center for Transgender Equality, accessed February 18, 2021, https://transequality.org/issues/anti-violence.

20: "punished them both . . . these poor degraded people.": Palou, *Francisco Palou's Life*, 215.

21: Turtle Island definition: Amanda Robinson, "Turtle Island," *The Canadian Encyclopedia*, November 6, 2018, https://www.thecanadianencyclopedia.ca/en/article/turtle-island.

22: "The generally accepted . . . for the girl.": Jeanne Maglaty, "Ask Smithsonian: When Did Girls Start Wearing Pink?," *Smithsonian*, April 7, 2011, https://www.smithsonianmag.com/arts-culture/when-did-girls-start-wearing-pink-1370097/.

22: Viking era: History.com editors, "Vikings," History.com, June 7, 2019, https://www.history.com/topics/exploration/vikings-history#section_6; William R. Short, "Hurstwic," Hurstwic LLC, accessed June 3, 2023, https://www.hurstwic.org/history/articles/society/text/what_happened.htm.

22–23: "a sword, an axe, . . . confirmed by genomics.": Charlotte Hedenstierna-Jonson et al., "A Female Viking Warrior Confirmed by Genomics," *American Journal of Physical Anthropology* 164, no. 4 (December 2017): 853–860, https://www.ncbi.nlm.nih.gov/pmc/articles/PMC5724682/.

INTRODUCTION: ON LABELS AND GENDER

25: AFAB, Affirmed Gender, and AMAB definitions: "PFLAG National Glossary of Terms," PFLAG, updated January 2021, https://pflag.org/glossary.

25: Agender definition: Vera Papisova, "What It Means to Identify as Agender," *Teen Vogue*, January 20, 2016, https://www.teenvogue.com/story/what-is-agender; "Agender," PFLAG, accessed October 21, 2023, https://pflag.org/glossary/.

25: Androgyne definition: "Androgyne," Nonbinary Wiki, accessed August 25, 2021, https://nonbinary.wiki/wiki/Androgyne.

25: Bigender definition: "Gender Expansive, Genderqueer, Gender Nonconforming," It Gets Better, December 13, 2023, https://itgetsbetter.org/glossary/gender-nonconforming/.

26: Demigender definition: "Demigender," MacMillan Dictionary, February 19, 2016, https://www.macmillandictionary.com/us/dictionary/american/demigender.

26: Gender nonconforming definition and usage: Los Angeles LGBT Center trans* lounge ad, "trans* lounge, Keeping the Trans/GNC/ENBY Community Connected," *Vanguard*, Summer 2021, 30.

26: Genderqueer and "a deliberate playing . . . of our culture.": Mary Retta, "What's the Difference between Non-Binary, Genderqueer, and Gender-Nonconforming?," Vice, September 13, 2019, https://www.vice.com/en/article/wjwx8m/whats-the-difference-between-non-binary-genderqueer-and-gender-nonconforming.

26: "more diverse than . . . or female bodies.": Joint consensus statement, "Darlington Statement," March 2017, https://darlington.org.au/statement/. CC BY-NC-ND 3.0 licence.

27: Nonbinary definition and usage: Los Angeles LGBT Center trans* lounge ad, "trans* lounge," *Vanguard*, 30.

27: Polygender definition: "Gender Expansive, Genderqueer, Gender Nonconforming," It Gets Better, December 13, 2023, https://itgetsbetter.org/glossary/gender-nonconforming/.

28: Queer definition and PFLAG recommendation: "Queer," PFLAG.

28: Two-spirit definition: "What Does Two-Spirit Mean?" | InQueery | Them," YouTube video, 0:27 and 6:16, posted by "them," December 11, 2018, https://youtu.be/A4lBibGzUnE.

28: "James Baldwin wrote . . . you to yourself.": James Baldwin, *The Price of the Ticket: Collected Nonfiction 1948–1985* (New York: St. Martin's, 1985), 681.

29: Transsexual definition: Mere Abrams, "Is There a Difference between Being Transgender and Transsexual?," Healthline, accessed September 8, 2021, https://www.healthline.com/health /transgender/difference-between-transgender-and-transsexual.

29: Example of using intersex rather than intersexed: "interACT FAQ," interAct Advocates for Intersex Youth, accessed November 20, 2021, https://interactadvocates.org/faq/.

29: "It's similar to . . . them as Asian.": Johanna Olson-Kennedy, email message to the author, December 28, 2020.

INTRODUCTION: GOOD STUFF TO KNOW

30: "To a biologist, *'male'* . . . Period!": Joan Roughgarden, *Evolution's Rainbow: Diversity, Gender, and Sexuality in Nature and People* (Berkeley: University of California Press, 2013), 23.

30–31: Gametes and male and female: Roughgarden, 23.

31: Egg size compared to sperm size: Roughgarden, 29.

31: "Although the gametes . . . all-egg parts.": Roughgarden, 36.

31: "The key point . . . are social categories.": Roughgarden, 24.

32: "human biological 'sex' . . . secondary sex characters.": Sarah S. Richardson, *Sex Itself: The Search for Male & Female in the Human Genome* (Chicago: University of Chicago Press, 2013), 5–9.

32: "revolution in gender . . . the two sexes.": Richardson, 9.

32: "Gendered assumptions have . . . interpretation of evidence.": Richardson, 202–203.

33: The Human Genome Project: "What Is the Human Genome Project?," National Human Genome Research Institute, October 28, 2018, https://www.genome.gov/human-genome-project/What; "Completing the Human Genome Sequence," National Human Genome Research Institute, August 10, 2021, https:// www.genome.gov/about-genomics/educational-resources /infographics/Completing-the-human-genome-sequence.

33: Danger of repeating mistakes with Human Genome Project: Richardson, *Sex Itself*, 202, 208, 217–224.

34: Cis and trans defined: Jonathan Jarry, "The Word 'Cisgender' Has Scientific Roots," McGill Office for Science and Society, November 13, 2021, https://www.mcgill.ca/oss/article/history -general-science/word-cisgender-has-scientific-roots.

34: "Gender is part . . . through our bodies.": Maya Gonzalez, *The Gender Wheel: A Story about Bodies and Gender for Every Body* (San Francisco: Reflection, 2017), 23.

34: "You're born naked, and the rest is drag": "You Were Born Naked and the Rest Is Drag," YouTube video, 0:01, posted by "luizguilhermejunior6," June 19, 2012, https://youtu.be /bFTheldotb0.

34: Gender Spectrum calls it your "social gender.": "Gender and Young People FAQs," Gender Spectrum, accessed July 7, 2021, https:// www.genderspectrum.org/articles/youth-faqs.

35–36: "They" being word of the year: "Word of the Year: They," Merriam-Webster, accessed May 13, 2021, https://www.merriam-webster .com/words-at-play/word-of-the-year-2019-they/quid-pro-quo.

36: Neopronouns: Ezra Marcus, "A Guide to Neopronouns," *New York Times*, April 8, 2021, https://www.nytimes.com/2021/04/08 /style/neopronouns-nonbinary-explainer.html; "Pronouns," midnightfox452, accessed October 21, 2023, https:// pronouny.xyz/u/midnightfox452; Steven/Jupiter/Juno, "About," midnightfox452, accessed October 21, 2023, https:// midnightfox452.carrd.co/#about.

36: Trevor Project survey of queer youth on pronouns: "Research Brief: Pronouns Usage among LGBTQ Youth," Trevor Project, July 29, 2020, https://www.thetrevorproject.org/2020/07/29 /research-brief-pronouns-usage-among-lgbtq-youth/.

38: The problem with the spectrum metaphor for gender: "Gender 101, Episode 2," YouTube video, 0:47, posted by Lee Wind, March 29, 2011, https://www.youtube.com/watch?v=J3YdHeqhDKI.

38: "a cloud or . . . is really important.": "Gender 101, Episode 2," Lucy, interview.

39: "The medicine wheel represents . . . purpose for us.": Chadwick Moore, "'The Medicine Wheel Represents Men on One Side and Women on the Other, but There's a Space in between That Is for the Two Spirits. We Join the Men and Women and Complete the Circle. That Is Our Place in Life. That Is the Creator's Purpose for Us.' Chadwick Moore Journeys to the Annual Gathering of the Two Spirit Society in Montana," *Out*, October 2015, 68.

40: Maya Gonzalez, "About the Gender Wheel," Gender Wheel/Reflection Press, accessed October 21, 2023, https://www.genderwheel.com /about-the-gender-wheel/#4-circles.

40: "the wheel is alive . . . where someone belongs.": Gonzalez, *The Gender Wheel*, 34.

41: "shifting terrain . . . create for yourself.": Robyn Ryle, *She/He/They/Me: For the Sisters, Misters, and Binary Resisters* (Naperville, IL: Sourcebooks, 2019), 357.

41: Queer theory's idea of queer as a verb: Meg-John Barker and Julia Scheele, *Queer: A Graphic History* (London: Icon Books, 2016), 15.

41: Queer theory includes: Barker and Scheele, 31.

41: "Try to avoid . . . doing, not being.": Barker and Scheele, 171.

41–42: "gender is not . . . in different ways.": "Torah in Transition," TransTorah, 8, accessed October 25, 2021, http://www .transtorah.org/PDFs/Torah-In-Transition.pdf.

42: "Among the Dagara . . . on that basis.": Bert Hoff, "Gays: Guardians of the Gates: An Interview with Malidoma Somé: as in the September 1993 Issue of *M.E.N.* Magazine," MenWeb, September 1993, http://www.menweb.org/somegay.htm.

42: "Any person who . . . gay person gay": Hoff.

42: "as a stable process, not a fixed state.": Anne Fausto-Sterling, *Sexing the Body: Gender Politics and the Construction of Sexuality*, © 2000. Reprinted by permission of Basic Books, an imprint of Hachette Book Group, Inc. (New York: Basic Books, 2020), 272, 290–291.

43: "the frequency of . . . 40 to 80 percent.": Roughgarden, *Evolution's Rainbow*, 36.

43–44: "some individuals are . . . in the afternoon.": Roughgarden, 35.

44: "individuals who begin . . . producing active sperm.": Roughgarden, 31–32.

44–45: "emits a low . . . turning and mating.": Roughgarden, 235.

45: "overlap the home . . . of each other.": Roughgarden, 90–93.

45: "the best documented . . . most feminine category.": Roughgarden, 102–103.

46: "According to Quantum . . . Get over it!": Blair, email message to the author, September 13, 2021.

46: "Our species isn't . . . to social myths.": Roughgarden, 325.

47: "By polarizing human . . . polarized masculine values.": Sandra Lipsitz Bem, *The Lenses of Gender* (New Haven, CT: Yale University Press, 1993), 195.

47: "the twelve-month-old . . . twelve months later.": Bem, 134–135.

47–48: "difference into disadvantage . . . identity and sexuality.": Bem, 189, 198.

48: "Our minds, society . . . malleable, and changeable.": Cordelia Fine, *Delusions of Gender: How Our Minds, Society, and Neurosexism Create Difference* (New York: W. W. Norton, 2010), 239.

48: "Social structure, media . . . masculinity and feminity.": Fine, 216.

48: "If I label my . . . *removing* body parts.": Noreen Giffney and Michael O'Rourke, eds., *The Ashgate Research Companion to Queer Theory* (New York: Routledge Taylor, 2009), 33.

48: "bodies that cannot . . . of intersexed genitals.": Giffney and O'Rourke, eds., 33.

49: "In the everyday . . . to genital inspection.": Giffney and O'Rourke, eds., 45.

49: "non-intersexed anatomies . . . disenfranchises intersexed individuals.": Giffney and O'Rourke, eds., 45.

49: "It is specifically . . . unusual sex anatomies.": Giffney and O'Rourke, eds., 44.

50: Nineteenth Amendment to the US Constitution: "Nineteenth Amendment," Constitution Annotated, Library of Congress, accessed October 21, 2023, https://constitution.congress.gov /constitution/amendment-19/#.

50: Levi Suydam story, and Connecticut official explaining family and locals want to "keep the family name quiet": Anne Fausto-Sterling, "Two Sexes Are Not Enough," *NOVA*, October 2001, https://www.pbs.org/wgbh/nova/gender/fs.html.

51: The character Pat: Dave Itzkoff, "Who Is Julia Sweeney Coming to Terms With? It's Pat," *New York Times*, November 21, 2019, https://www.nytimes.com/2019/11/21/arts/television/julia -sweeney-pat-snl.html.

51: "an all-purpose insult . . . masculinity or femininity." Itzkoff.

51: "was shame embodied . . . not a person.": Itzkoff.

51: "You'd be able . . . would be over": Itzkoff.

CHAPTER 1: EUNUCHS

56: "From which it . . . of all ranks": Ammianus Marcellinus, *The Roman History of Ammianus Marcellinus during the Reigns of the Emperors Constantius, Julian, Jovianus, Valentinian, and Valens*, trans. C. D. Yonge (London: G. Bell and Sons, 1911), 93–94, online at Project Gutenberg, https://www.gutenberg.org /ebooks/28587.

56: "To distinguish . . . gendered identity": Mathew Kuefler, *The Manly Eunuch: Masculinity, Gender Ambiguity, and Christian Ideology in Late Antiquity* (Chicago: University of Chicago, 2001), 29–30.

57: "moral division . . . feminine wickedness.": Kuefler, 29.

57: Genders in Roman culture in Late Antiquity: Kuefler, 29–30.

57: Women who were called infamis: Sarah Bond, "At the Copa: Women, Clothing, and Color Codes in Roman Taverns," History from Below, April 8, 2021, https://sarahemilybond.com/2021/04/08/at -the-copa-women-clothing-and-color-codes-in-roman-taverns/.

57: Sarah Bond origins of the word eunuch: "What 'Game of Thrones' Gets Right and Wrong about Eunuchs and Masculinity," *Forbes*, August 20, 2017, https://www.forbes.com/sites /drsarahbond/2017/08/20/what-game-of-thrones-gets-right -and-wrong-about-eunuchs-and-masculinity/.

57: Pronunciation of ευνούχος: "'ευνούχος' in English," IDM Bab.la Dictionary, accessed October 11, 2021, https://en.bab.la /dictionary/greek-english/%CE%B5%CF%85%CE%BD%CE %BF%CF%8D%CF%87%CE%BF%CF%82.

57–58: Definition of eunuchs by Mark Brustman, a.k.a. Faris Malik: "'Born Eunuchs' Home Page and Library," Mark Brustman, accessed October 17, 2021, https://people.well.com/user/aquarius/.

58: On Ulpian: "Ulpian: Roman Jurist," *Encyclopaedia Britannica*, accessed October 10, 2021, https://www.britannica.com/biography/Ulpian.

58: "those who are . . . kind of eunuchs.": Kuefler, *The Manly Eunuch*, 33.

58: Ulpian on human-made eunuchs: Kuefler, 33.

59–60: "enjoyed the special . . . branches of art.": Cassius Dio, *Dio's Rome: An Historical Narrative Originally Composed in Greek during the Reigns of Septimius Severus, Geta and Caracalla, Macrinus, Elagabalus and Alexander Severus: And Now Presented in English Form by Herbert Baldwin Foster, Fifth Volume: Extant Books 61–76 (A.D. 54–211)*, (1906), the Project Gutenberg e-book of *Dio's Rome*, vol. 5, book 76, 14, https://www.gutenberg.org /cache/epub/10890/pg10890-images.html#b76.

60: Laws against making eunuchs within Roman Empire: Kuefler, *The Manly Eunuch*, 32.

60: "confused legal status" and "could associate . . . reserved to men.": Kuefler, 31, 33.

60: "a third type of human being": Kuefler, 35–36.

60: "In the ancient . . . were her relatives.": Kuefler, 97.

60: "hang down like a mother's paps": Kuefler, 34.

61: "susceptibility to curvature . . . to premature wrinkles.": Kuefler, 34.

61: "He castrated not merely . . . gelded and bearded.": Dio, *Dio's Rome*, book 76, 14.

61: Ammianus Marcellinus wrote about Eutherius: Kuefler, *The Manly Eunuch*, 35; Marcellinus, *The Roman History of Ammianus Marcellinus*, 92–94; 7:1–8.

62: "re-establish the province . . . so formidable an enemy.": Marcellinus, 87–88.

62: Eutherius's heroism: Marcellinus, 92–93, book 16, 7:1–3.

62–63: "Therefore, when he . . . of his greatness": Marcellinus, 92–93.

63: Julian became emperor in 361 CE: "Ancient Rome: The Roman Empire under the 4th Century Successors of Constantine: The Reign of Julian," *Encyclopaedia Britannica*, July 18, 2014, https://www.britannica.com/place/ancient-Rome/The-reign-of-Constantine#ref26703.

63: "The opportunity reminds . . . of gentle disposition.": Marcellinus, *The Roman History of Ammianus Marcellinus*, 93.

64: "[Eutherius was] born . . . men of all ranks": Marcellinus, 93–94.

65: "though men of . . . of the age.": Marcellinus, 94.

65: Claudian's poem trash-talking Eutropius: Kuefler, *The Manly Eunuch*, 66–68.

65–66: "Let the world cease . . . to the year": Claudius Claudianus, *Against Eutropius*, in *Claudian*, trans. Maurice Platnauer (London: William Heinemann, 1922), Project Gutenberg e-book of *Claudian*, vol. 1, https://www.gutenberg.org/cache/epub/51443/pg51443-images.html#EUTROPIUS, 139.

66: Astonied definition: "Astonied," Merriam-Webster Dictionary, accessed October 17, 2021, https://www.merriam-webster.com/dictionary/astonied.

66: "Had a woman . . . a eunuch's rule.": Claudianus, *Against Eutropius*, 163.

66: Fasces definition: "Furniture," United States House of Representatives, accessed October 16, 2021, https://history.house.gov/Exhibitions-and-Publications/House-Chamber/Rostrum/.

66: Fall of Eutropius: Alan Cameron, *Claudian: Poetry and Propaganda at the Court of Honorius* (Oxford: Clarendon, 1970), 134–135.

66: "That name erased . . . Mars' savage work.": Claudianus, *Against Eutropius*, 179.

67: "not fancying her . . . passed her prime": Dio, *Dio's Rome*, book 62, 28.

67: "Sabina also perished . . . celebration of their wedding": Dio, book 62, 27–28.

67: Liberti definition: Tatjana Sandon, review of Rose MacLean, *Freed Slaves and Roman Imperial Culture: Social Integration and the Transformation of Values*. Cambridge; New York: Cambridge University Press, 2018, in *Bryn Mawr Classical Review*, January 27, 2019, https://bmcr.brynmawr.edu/2019/2019.01.27/.

68: "While Nero . . . relieved of great evils": Dio, *Dio's Rome*, book 62, 28.

68: Emperor Nero's death: Dio, book 63, 29.

68: Philetairos and the Attalid dynasty: Donald L. Wasson, "Attalid Dynasty," World History Encyclopedia, October 10, 2016, https://www.worldhistory.org/Attalid_Dynasty/.

69: Greek culture's influence still felt today: Ethel Dilouambaka, "18 Awesome Things Greece Gave the World," Culture Trip, July 11, 2017, https://theculturetrip.com/europe/greece/articles /18-awesome-things-greece-gave-the-world/.

69: Alexander the Great and Hephaestion were in love: Michael Alvear and Vicky A. Shecter, *Alexander the Fabulous: The Man Who Brought the World to Its Knees* (Los Angeles: Advocate Books, 2004), 10–11.

69: "At the capital . . . and kissed him.": Plutarch, "Life of Alexander," in *Plutarch's Lives*, vol. 3, trans. Aubrey Stewart and George Long (London: George Bell and Sons, 1892), Project Gutenberg e-book of *Plutarch's Lives*, vol. 3, https://www.gutenberg.org /cache/epub/14140/pg14140-images.html#LIFE_OF _ALEXANDER, 67.

70: Laws against men having relationships with eunuchs: Kuefler, *The Manly Eunuch*, 100–102.

70: Laws targeting eunuchs were start of Christianity's antigay laws: Mark Brustman, a.k.a. Faris Malik, "'The Historic Origins of Church Condemnation of Homosexuality," Mark Brustman, accessed October 17, 2021, https://people.well.com/user /aquarius/rome.htm.

71: "Though the western . . . 1,000 more years," History.com editors, "Byzantine Empire," History.com, updated August 20, 2019, https://www.history.com/topics/ancient-middle-east /byzantine-empire.

71: The establishment of the Byzantine Empire: "Byzantine Empire."

71: "were attracted . . . domination of women.": Kuefler, *The Manly Eunuch*, 239.

72: "Many of these . . . army and navy.": Kathryn M. Ringrose, "Chapter One: Living in the Shadows: Eunuchs and Gender in Byzantium," in Gilbert Herdt, ed., *Third Sex, Third Gender: Beyond Sexual Dimorphism in Culture and History* (New York: Zone Books, 1994), 94–98.

72–73: "with the head . . . will dramatically increase." Kristina Killgrove, "Skeletons of Two Possible Eunuchs Discovered in Ancient Egypt," *Forbes*, April 28, 2017, https://www.forbes.com/sites /kristinakillgrove/2017/04/28/skeletons-of-two-possible -eunuchs-discovered-in-ancient-egypt/?sh=6c53ed7a1f55.

73: The fall of the Byzantine Empire: History.com editors, "Byzantine Empire."

PROFILE: CASTRATI

74: Castrati overview: Esther Inglis-Arkell, "What Did It Mean to Be a Castrato?," Gizmodo, September 24, 2015, https://gizmodo.com /what-did-it-mean-to-be-a-castrato-1732742399; "Castrato," *Encyclopaedia Britannica*, updated May 9, 2013, https://www .britannica.com/art/castrato; "Farinelli: Italian Singer," *Encyclopaedia Britannica*, updated July 11, 2021, https://www .britannica.com/biography/Farinelli.

74: Castrati vocal training and "Evviva il costello!": John S. Jenkins, "Mozart and the Castrati," *Musical Times* 151, no. 1913 (Winter 2010), online at https://www.jstor.org/stable/25759517?read -now=1&refreqid=excelsior%3A6b9bcc3e8493b837bb279e74f6 9715ae&seq=3#page_scan_tab_contents, 55; "Eviva il coltello" ("Long live the knife!"): "Hear the Only Castrato Ever Recorded Sing 'Ave Maria' and Other Classics (1904)," Open Culture, June 22, 2016, https://www.openculture.com/2016 /06/hear-alessandro-moreschi-the-only-castrato-ever -recorded-sing-ave-maria-and-other-classics-1904.html.

75: Monteverdi opera with four roles for Castrati: Handel writing operas for Castrati: Alan Riding, "In Opera, a Different Kind of Less Is More: 'Handel and the Castrati,'" *New York Times*, April 19, 2006, https://www.nytimes.com/2006/04/19/arts/music/in -opera-a-different-kind-of-less-is-more-handel-and-the.html; a choir of castrati in the Sistine Chapel: Rory Carroll, "Pope Urged to Apologize for Vatican Castrations," *Guardian* (US edition), August 14, 2001, https://www.theguardian.com/world /2001/aug/14/humanities.highereducation.

75–76: Farinelli's fame: "Hear the Only Castrato Ever Recorded," Open Culture; London fans shout: "One God, one Farinelli!": "One God, One Farinelli," International Museum and Library of Music of Bologna, accessed January 16, 2022, http://www.museibologna .it/musicaen/percorsi/65345/luogo/65358/offset/0/id/76217/;

"One God, one Farinelli," credited to a female fan in 1735: Alan Riding, "In Opera, a Different Kind of Less Is More: 'Handel and the Castrati,'" *New York Times*, April 19, 2006, https://www.nytimes.com/2006/04/19/arts/music/in-opera -a-different-kind-of-less-is-more-handel-and-the.html; *Encyclopaedia Britannica* on Farinelli singing to King Philip V of Spain to relieve his "deep-seated melancholia.": "Farinelli: Italian Singer," *Encyclopaedia Britannica*, updated July 11, 2021, https://www.britannica.com/biography/Farinelli.

76: "His voice rose . . . a little candle.": Sam Kean, Mariel Carr, and Rigoberto Hernandez, "The Sinister Angel Singers of Rome," *Distillations*, Science History Institute, episode 293, December 7, 2021, https://www.sciencehistory.org/distillations/podcast /the-sinister-angel-singers-of-rome.

76–77: Famous castrati could be demanding, with the example that Luigi Marchesi would only perform in an opera if appeared on a horse singing, and on how castrati could sell out a theater: Riding, "In Opera."

77: Castrati as romantically and physically desirable: Joseph McLellan, "Sacrificed for the Sound of Seraphim," *Washington Post*, October 3, 1982, https://www.washingtonpost.com/archive /entertainment/books/1982/10/03/sacrificed-for-the-sound -of-seraphim/c195d3f3-500e-43b7-88e1-ba4622d23cf5/; Casanova on seeing a castrato perform: "In a well-made corset . . . earthbound as a German.": Elizabeth Wood, Gary C. Thomas, and Philip Brett, eds., *Queering the Pitch* (New York: Taylor & Francis, 2013), 147–148, online at https:// www.google.com/books/edition/Queering_the_Pitch /yaygBgAAQBAJ?hl=en&gbpv=0.

77: More on Casanova: "Who Was Casanova?," Walks of Italy, February 9, 2012, https://www.walksofitaly.com/blog/art-culture/casanova -the-lover-venice-italy.

77: Poor families gambled on castrating their boys; estimate of number of castrations: Riding, "In Opera."

77: Church prohibition on castration and accepting excuses; end of Castrati era, Domenico Mancini performing for Pope 1939– 1959: Carroll, "Pope Urged to Apologize"; Johannes Kley's edition of the 'Repertorium Rituum' acknowledgment that for church choirs, "women, too, are now generally admitted.": "Women and Girls Were Not Allowed to Be Singers in Church," Wijngaards Institute for Catholic Research, accessed January 17, 2022, https://womenpriests.org/tradition/singers -women-and-girls-were-not-allowed-to-be-singers-in-church/.

CHAPTER 2: THE SIX GENDERS OF CLASSICAL JUDAISM

79: "[An intersex person] . . . men nor women.": "Mishnah Bikkurim 4:2," Sefaria, accessed October 23, 2021, https://www.sefaria.org /Mishnah_Bikkurim.3.12?lang=bi.

79: On the Talmud: Rabbi Jill Jacobs, "Tale of Two Talmuds: Jerusalem and Babylonian," My Jewish Learning, accessed October 23, 2021, https://www.myjewishlearning.com/article/tale-of -two-talmuds/; On the Mishnah: "Jewish Texts: What Is the Mishnah?," My Jewish Learning, accessed October 22, 2021, https://www.myjewishlearning.com/article/mishnah/.

80: Western Wall gender division: in-person visit by the author, September 2, 2023, according to Professor Dalit Shiloni, the area where gender isn't monitored was intended for families to be able to celebrate bar and bat mitzvahs together (men and women) and not as an acknowledgment of gender diversity.

81: "I found a . . . finally came home.": Rabbi Elliot Kukla, "A Created Being of Its Own: Toward a Jewish Liberation Theology for Men, Women and Everyone Else," TransTorah, accessed October 23, 2021, 1, http://www.transtorah.org/PDFs /How_I_Met_the_Tumtum.pdf.

81–82: The six Genders of Judaism from 1–199 CE: Kukla, 1.

82: The eighth gender mentioned in My Jewish Learning is aylonit by human intervention. Someone "identified female at birth but later developing male characteristics through human intervention." It is unclear if this is an acknowledgment of modern gender-affirming human intervention or if this additional category was cited in the Talmud: Rachel Scheinerman, "The Eight Genders in the Talmud," My Jewish Learning, accessed October 31, 2023, https://www.myjewishlearning.com/article/the-eight -genders-in-the-talmud/; Boshes HaBayis, "How Many Genders Are Actually in the Talmud?," Merrimack Valley Havurah: Traditional Egalitarian Torah Study," January 23, 2023, https://merrimackvalleyhavurah.wordpress.com/2023 /01/23/how-many-genders-are-actually-in-the-talmud/.

82: Mamzer definition: "What Is a Mamzer?," My Jewish Learning, accessed October 24, 2021, https://www.myjewishlearning.com /article/the-mamzer-problem/.

82–83: "All are obligated . . . of the community.": Rabbi Elliot Kukla, "Gender Diversity in Halacha (The Way We Walk): Mishna and Tosefta (1st–2nd Centuries C.E.)," TransTorah, accessed October 24, 2021, 1, http://www.transtorah.org/PDFs/Gender _Diversity_In_Halacha.pdf.

83: Intersex people (*androgynos*) definition, mentioned 149 times in the Talmud: Rabbi Elliot Kukla, "Terms for Gender Diversity in Classical Jewish Texts," TransTorah, accessed October 23, 2021, http://www.transtorah.org/PDFs/Classical_Jewish_Terms_for_Gender_Diversity.pdf.

83–84: "[An intersex person] . . . unlike men or women.": "Mishnah Bikkurim 4," Sefaria.

84: "the androgynos he . . . the *androgynos*' identity.": Rabbi Elliot Kukla and Rabbi Reuben Zellman, "Created by the Hand of Heaven: Making Space for Intersex Jews: Commentary on Parshiyot Tazria-Metzora," TransTorah, accessed October 24, 2021, 3, http://www.transtorah.org/PDFs/Making_Space_for_Intersex_Jews.pdf; phrase attributed to Rabbi Meir: Joshua DeMoya, "Androgynos and Tumtum: Reifying or Rejecting Gender Binary?," Sefaria, accessed October 29, 2023, https://www.sefaria.org/sheets/113417?lang=bi.

84: "is a classical . . . its [our] own.": Kukla, "A Created Being," 7.

84–85: "the basis of . . . uniquely created being.": Kukla, 7–8.

85: Tumtum definition, mentioned 181 times in the Talmud: Kukla, "Terms for Gender Diversity in Classical Jewish Texts."

85: "sometimes he is a man and sometimes he is a woman.": "Mishnah Bikkurim 4," Sefaria.

85: "to think of God at all times.": "Tzitzit, the Fringes on the Prayer Shawl," My Jewish Learning, accessed October 29, 2023, https://www.myjewishlearning.com/article/tzitzit/.

85–86: "Women and slaves . . . without a blessing.": "Mishneh Torah, Fringes 3," Sefaria, accessed October 24, 2021, https://www.sefaria.org/Mishneh_Torah%2C_Fringes.3.9?ven=Sefaria_Community_Translation&lang=bi&with=all&lang2=en.

86: Ay'lonit definition, mentioned eighty times in the Talmud: Kukla, "Terms for Gender Diversity in Classical Jewish Texts."

86: "It is anyone . . . or a man.": Yevamot editors of *The William Davidson Talmud*, "Yevamot 80b," Sefaria, accessed October 24, 2021, https://www.sefaria.org/Yevamot.80b.6?ven=William_Davidson_Edition_-_English&lang=bi&with=all&lang2=en.

87: "An aylonit . . . to a ketubah.": Meig Dickson, "9 Kislev 5781," William Davidson digital edition of the Koren Noé Talmud, Sefaria, November 25, 2020, https://www.sefaria.org/sheets/280912.7?lang=bi&with=About&lang2=en.

87: "A common priest . . . marry [an aylnoit].": Yevamot editors of *The William Davidson Talmud*, "Mishnah Yevamot 6," Sefaria,

accessed October 24, 2021, https://www.sefaria.org/Mishnah
_Yevamot.6.5?ven=William_Davidson_Edition_-_English&lang
=bi&with=all&lang2=en.

87: Jewish religious leaders called priests through the 200s–300s CE:
Matthew J. Grey, "Jewish Priests and the Social History of
Post-70 Palestine: A Dissertation Submitted to the Faculty
of the University of North Carolina at Chapel Hill in Partial
Fulfillment of Requirements for the Degree of Doctor
of Philosophy in the Department of Religious Studies,"
University of North Carolina at Chapel Hill, 2011, https://
core.ac.uk/download/pdf/210602023.pdf, 328–330.

87–88: Saris definition, mentioned 156 times in the Talmud: Kukla,
"Terms for Gender Diversity in Classical Jewish Texts."

88: "The Sages taught: . . . his skin is smooth, i.e., hairless." Yevamot
editors of *The William Davidson Talmud*, "Yevamot 80b."

88: "by the hand of Heaven.": Yevamot editors of *The William Davidson
Talmud*.

88: "seris-chammah . . . cannot be healed.": "Mishnah Yevamot 8.4," from
Rabbi Shraga Silverstein, *The Mishna with Obadiah Bartenura*,
trans. Mishnah Yevamot editors, Sefaria, accessed October 24,
2021, https://www.sefaria.org/Mishnah_Yevamot.8.4?ven
=The_Mishna_with_Obadiah_Bartenura_by_Rabbi_Shraga
_Silverstein&lang=bi&with=About&lang2=en.

89: "The interruption of . . . exclusively 'homosexual' men.": Mark
Brustman, "The Ancient Roman and Talmudic Definition of
Natural Eunuchs," Born Eunuchs Home Page and Library, July
27, 1999, https://people.well.com/user/aquarius/cardiff.htm.

89: "No one whose . . . of the Lord." (Devarim 23:2): Eliezer Melamed,
"Peninei Halakhah (Pearls of Jewish Law)," Sefaria, accessed
October 24, 2021, https://www.sefaria.org/Peninei
_Halakhah%2C_Simchat_Habayit_U'Virkhato.7.5.2?ven
=Peninei_Halakhah,_English_ed._Yeshivat_Har_Bracha&lang
=bi&with=About&lang2=en; Levirate Marriage and Halitzah:
Ronald L. Eisenberg, "Levirate Marriage and Halitzah:
Ancient Customs involving a Childless Widow," My Jewish
Learning, accessed October 24, 2021, https://www
.myjewishlearning.com/article/levirate-marriage-and
-halitzah/; On the humiliation of Chalitzah: Tzvi Freeman,
"Why Is Chalitzah So Humiliating?," Chabad, accessed
October 24, 2021, https://www.chabad.org/library/article_cdo
/aid/927557/jewish/Why-is-chalitzah-so-humiliating.htm.

89: Midrash definition: "Midrash Quiz," My Jewish Learning, accessed October 23, 2021, https://www.myjewishlearning.com/quiz/midrash-quiz/.

89–90: References to Gender Diversity in Classical Jewish Texts: Kukla, "Terms for Gender Diversity in Classical Jewish Texts."

90: "who has not . . . not a Barbarian": Eliezer Segal, "Who Has Not Made Me a Woman," My Jewish Learning, accessed January 6, 2024, https://www.myjewishlearning.com/article/who-has-not-made-me-a-woman/.

90: "the cause of . . . pope at Avignon.": Richard Gottheil and Isaac Broydé, "Kalonymus Ben Kalonymus Ben Meïr (Called Maestro Calo)," *Jewish Encyclopedia*, 1906, https://www.jewishencyclopedia.com/articles/9173-kalonymus-ben-kalonymus-ben-meir.

91: "a fair woman": Gottheil and Broydé.

91–93: "What an awful . . . in the ground.": Abby Stein, "(Trans)Gender, Fundamentalism, and Judaism," Sefaria, accessed October 19, 2021, https://www.sefaria.org/sheets/135628.1?lang=bi.

93: "TransTorah is not . . . our identities and gifts.": "About Us," TransTorah, accessed October 19, 2021, http://www.transtorah.org/aboutus.html.

94: "A man's clothes . . . abomination before God.": Rabbis Elliot Kukla and Reuben Zellman, "To Wear Is Human: Parshat Ki Teitze," TransTorah, accessed October 28, 2021, 1, http://www.transtorah.org/PDFs/To_Wear_Is_Human.pdf.

94: Maimonides, called by the Stanford Encyclopedia of Philosophy: "the greatest Jewish philosopher of the medieval period.": Kenneth Seeskin, "Maimonides," Stanford Encyclopedia of Philosophy, ed. Edward N. Zalta, Spring 2021, https://plato.stanford.edu/archives/spr2021/entries/maimonides/.

94: "when it is . . . to cause harm.": Kukla and Zellman, "To Wear Is Human: Parshat Ki Teitze," 1.

95: "a positive *mitzvah* . . . true to ourselves.": Kukla and Zellman, 2.

95: Mitzvah definition: "What Is a Mitzvah?," PJ Library, June 5, 2017, https://pjlibrary.org/mitzvah.

95: "When we cover . . . our Torah prohibits!": Kukla and Zellman, "To Wear Is Human: Parshat Ki Teitze," 2.

96: "although Jewish Sages . . . orderly boxes.": Kukla, "A Created Being," 6.

96: "As to twilight . . . determine its length.": Kukla, 6; a different translation from the Babylonian Talmud: *The William Davidson Talmud* editors, "Shabbat 34b," Sefaria, accessed October 23,

2021, https://www.sefaria.org/Shabbat.34b.3?lang=bi&with
=all&lang2=en.

96: "Our rabbis believed . . . is exceptionally holy.": Rabbi Reuben Zellman,
"The Holiness of Twilight: Delivered at Congregration
Sha'ar Zahav, San Francisco, California, Erev Rosh Hashana
5767/2006," TransTorah and Reuben Zellman, accessed
October 24, 2021, 3, http://www.transtorah.org/PDFs
/Holiness_of_Twilight.pdf.

97: "And the evening . . . the second day.": Anonymous, "Genesis Book
01, Project Gutenberg Ebook the Bible, King James, Book 1:
Genesis," May 2005, https://www.gutenberg.org/cache/epub
/8001/pg8001.html, 01:001:005, 01:001:008.

97: Jewish definition of a day, sunset to next evening's three stars in sky:
"The Jewish Day," Chabad, accessed October 29, 2021, https://
www.chabad.org/library/article_cdo/aid/526873/jewish/The
-Jewish-Day.htm.

97: "That's Jewish time . . . the last word.": Aron Moss, "Why Do Jewish
Holidays Begin at Nightfall?," Chabad, accessed October 29,
2021, https://www.chabad.org/library/article_cdo/aid/160961
/jewish/Why-do-holidays-begin-at-nightfall.htm.

98: "our rabbis of . . . seen and respected.": Zellman, "The Holiness of
Twilight," 4.

98: "Like the wide . . . transcends all categories.": Zellman, 5.

98: "This is the . . . full authentic selves.": Zellman, 6.

PROFILE: BROTHERBOYS AND SISTERGIRLS

100: Brotherboys and sistergirls may identify as male, female, and/or
nonbinary, and may use brotherboy and sistergirl along with
other terms: "Trans Mob," Trans Hub: Health and Gender
Affirmation in NSW [New South Wales, Australia], accessed
January 15, 2022, https://www.transhub.org.au/trans-mob.

100: "I'm 18 years . . . your cultural identity.": "Brotherboys Yarnin' Up—
Kai and Dean," YouTube video, 9:01, posted by Trans Health
Australia, August 23, 2014, https://youtu.be/fTtiYD8GmXQ;
Kai's family name Clancy: Laura Murphy-Oates, "Being
Brotherboys: Coming Out as Transgender," Living Black on
National Indigenous Television, June 8, 2015, https://www.sbs
.com.au/nitv/article/2015/06/08/being-brotherboys-coming
-out-transgender. © SBS.

101: "I was saddened . . . nurture them too.": Murphy-Oates.

101: Sistergirl (and brotherboy) definitions: "Trans Mob," Trans Hub.

101: Tiwi Island sistergirls traditionally known as yimpininni: Allan Clarke, "Meet the Transgender 'Sistergirls' of the Tiwi Islands," BuzzFeed News, August 25, 2015, https://www .buzzfeed.com/allanclarke/sistergirls-of-the-tiwi-islands.

101: "to remember the . . . here for now.": Helen Davidson, "Sydney Gay and Lesbian Mardi Gras: Their First Mardi Gras: A Journey for Tiwi Island Sistagirls Decades in the Making," *Guardian* (US edition), March 3, 2017, https://www.theguardian.com /australia-news/2017/mar/03/their-first-mardi-gras-a-journey -for-tiwi-island-sistagirls-decades-in-the-making.

101: Sistagirls and brothaboys are terms of endearment, as opposed to sistergirls and brotherboys: "Trans Mob," Trans Hub.

101: "To go to . . . make a change.": Davidson, "Sydney Gay and Lesbian Mardi Gras."

102: "We're Sistergirls, and we're transgender,": "Miriam Margolyes Meets the Sistergirls of the Tiwi Islands | Miriam Margolyes: Almost Australian," YouTube video, 2:43, posted by ABC TV & iview, May 25, 2020, https://youtu.be/Fc-WPnNH55c.

102: "Are you men . . . yourself a chance.": "Miriam Margolyes Meets the Sistergirls."

102: Sistergirls talk with Miriam Margolyes: "You know, in . . . have to change.": "Miriam Margolyes Meets the Sistergirls."

102: "so my telling . . . how you feel.": "Miriam Margolyes Meets the Sistergirls."

102: "Yes . . . there for decoration.": "Miriam Margolyes Meets the Sistergirls."

103: "Once upon a time . . . has been lost." Jesse Jones, "The Reality of Being Black and Trans in Australia," *Star Observer*, June 26, 2017, https://www.starobserver.com.au/news/national-news /being-black-trans-australia/159471.

103: "Even though I . . . that's not impressive": Jones.

103: "traditionally women have . . . didgeridoo in ceremony.": Linda Barwick and Judy Skatssoon, "Women and the Didgeridoo: REF: The Didgeridoo, from Arnhem Land to Internet," Perfect Beat Publications / Karl Keuenfeldt / Yidaki Vibes, September 2, 2008, https://web.archive.org/web/20230408092806/https:// yidakivibes.com.au/women-and-the-didgeridoo/.

103: First Nations vs. Aboriginal vs. Indigenous: "First Nations Vocabulary—Using Culturally Appropriate Language and

Terminology," Australian Government: Australian Public Service Commission, July 27, 2022, https://www.apsc.gov.au/working-aps/diversity-and-inclusion/diversity-inclusion-news/first-nations-vocabulary-using-culturally-appropriate-language-and-terminology; "What's the Appropriate Term: Aboriginal. . . . First Nation," Muswellbrook Shire Council, Walking Together Reconciliation Committee, Working with Indigenous Australians, First Nations People, July 2022, http://www.workingwithindigenousaustralians.info/content/Indigenous_Australians_3_Approrpiate_Terms.html#:~:text='Aboriginal'%20and%20'Torres%20Strait%20Islander'%20refer%20to%20different,Australia%2C%20in%20the%20Torres%20Strait.

104: "I'm Aboriginal and . . . for a change.": "Five Non-Binary People Talk about Being Non-Binary," Ygender, July 14, 2019, https://www.ygender.org.au/article/being-non-binary, available at https://web.archive.org/web/20220305144735/https://www.ygender.org.au/article/being-non-binary.

104: "Be proud of . . . in our culture.": "Brotherboys Yarnin' Up," YouTube video, 8:30.

CHAPTER 3: HIJRAS

104: "When somebody asks . . . own religious beliefs.": Shanoor Seervai, "Laxmi Narayan Tripathi: India's Third Gender," Guernica, March 16, 2015, https://www.guernicamag.com/indias-third-gender/.

106: Hijra pronouns: Serena Nanda, *Neither Man nor Woman: The Hijras of India*, 2nd ed. (Belmont, CA: Wadsworth, 1999), iv. Cengage Learning Inc. Reproduced by permission, http://www.cengage.com/permissions.

106: "We were very . . . nobles, even divine.": Seervai "Laxmi Narayan Tripathi"; Manu-smriti: "Manu-smriti," *Encyclopaedia Britannica*, February 4, 2015, https://www.britannica.com/topic/Manu-smriti.

107: "seniority, judged not . . . the hijra community.": Nanda, *Neither Man nor Woman*, 43.

107: "The guru's other . . . vast extended family.": Laxmi Narayan Tripathi, *Me Hijra, Me Laxmi* (New Delhi: Oxford University Press, 2015), 174.

107: British rule over India: "British Raj," *Encyclopaedia Britannica*, September 8, 2020, https://www.britannica.com/event/British-raj.

107–108: "Our status changed . . . to be human.": Seervai, "Laxmi Narayan Tripathi."

108: "a well-defined, culturally . . . sex/gender variation.": Nanda, *Neither Man nor Woman*, 144.

108: "The word 'hij' . . . [that] possesses it.": Tripathi, *Me Hijra*, 39–40.

109: "The hijras, as . . . a ritual transformation.": Nanda, *Neither Man nor Woman*, 23.

109: Hijras's traditional role: Nanda, 1–12.

109: 1980s value of India Rupee: "1 USD to INR from 1947 till Now, Historical Exchange Rates Explained," BookMyForex, March 24, 2021, https://www.bookmyforex.com/blog/1-usd-inr-1947 -till-now/.

109–110: "The sound of . . . and two-rupee notes.": Nanda, *Neither Man nor Woman*, 1–3.

110–111: "There are other . . . singing and dancing.": Nanda, 11.

110: "People believe that . . . the Ramayana itself.": Tripathi, *Me Hijra*, 48.

110: On the Ramayana: "Ramayana: Indian Epic," *Encyclopaedia Britannica*, May 27, 2020, https://www.britannica.com/topic/Ramayana -Indian-epic.

110: "a chronicle of . . . by Sage Valmiki.": Kumar Chellappan, "Ramayana Not a Work of Fiction," *Pioneer*, June 15, 2015, https://www .dailypioneer.com/2015/page1/ramayana-not-a-work-of -fiction.html.

111: "It is said . . . would come true.": Tripathi, *Me Hijra*, 48–49.

111–1112: "People believe that . . . your own survival.": Seervai, "Laxmi Narayan Tripathi."

112: More on the nirvan ritual: Nanda, *Neither Man nor Woman*, 26–29.

112: "castration is strictly . . . not endorse this.": Tripathi, *Me Hijra*, 156.

112: Hijra don't rush to undergo the nirvan ceremony: Nanda, *Neither Man nor Woman*, 118.

112: "It is not . . . him a woman.": Nanda, 100.

113: "people get castrated . . . biggest weapon they have.": Seervai, "Laxmi Narayan Tripathi."

113: "do not allow . . . having a son.": Nanda, *Neither Man nor Woman*, 6.

113: "We abuse hijras . . . a resounding NO.": Tripathi, *Me Hijra*, 110.

113–114: "hijras are evidence . . . an individual's lifetime." Nanda, *Neither Man nor Woman*, 129.

114: "when I was . . . like an alien.": Tripathi, *Me Hijra*, 29, 43.

114: "In our community . . . world questioned you.": Seervai, "Laxmi Narayan Tripathi."

114: "Why have you . . . no need to.": Tripathi, *Me Hijra*, 45.

115: "Among us hijras . . . any normal housewife.": Nanda, *Neither Man nor Woman*, 79.

115: "hijras and their . . . other as mates.": Nanda, 123.

115: "spoke very warmly . . . Sushila a grandmother.": Nanda, 93–94.

115: "Now I'm leading . . . some respect outside.": Nanda, 94.

116: "in social work . . . who have PhDs.": Seervai, "Laxmi Narayan Tripathi."

116: "Hijras are considered . . . reverse that mindset.": Tripathi, *Me Hijra*, 131.

116: "Our Indian Super . . . Miss Universe contest.": Tripathi, 134.

116: "If the world . . . would choose activism.": Tripathi, 104.

116: "No one in fourteen generations . . . think of us?": Tripathi, 47–48.

116: "aghast.": Tripathi, 60.

116–117: "My parents wanted. . . . them stifle me?": Tripathi, 49.

117: "Why should I . . . out of question.": Tripathi, 123.

117: "I did not . . . harm in that?": Tripathi, 73.

117: "There's a family . . . love on Anshuman.": Tripathi, 167–168.

118: "'Nupi' means 'girl, woman', and 'Maanbi' means 'alike, similar.'": Alessandra Monticelli, "Rescuing Traditional Queerness: An Interview with Santa Khurai," Heinrich Böll Stiftung: Regional Office New Delhi, September 4, 2020, https://in.boell.org/en/2020/08/31/rescuing-traditional-queerness-interview-santa-khurai.

118: "As a queer . . . questioned and attacked.": Monticelli.

118: "In Manipur, there . . . queer identity less.": Monticelli.

119: "Nupa Amaibi has . . . respect to them.": "The Unheard Voice," directed by Siddharth Haobijam, YouTube video, 2:32, 4:41, posted by Manipur the Aftermath, November 21, 2014, https://youtu.be/ONA194btLNo.

119: "Before Christianity spread . . . queer people.": Monticelli, "Rescuing Traditional Queerness."

120: "I wanted my . . . to demand it.": Seervai, "Laxmi Narayan Tripathi."

120: India officially recognizes third gender: Zack Beauchamp, "There Is a Third Gender in India, and the Law Finally Recognized

Them," Vox, April 16, 2014, https://www.vox.com/2014/4/16 /5618610/hijras-ruling.

120: "It is the . . . choose their gender.": Seervai, "Laxmi Narayan Tripathi."

120: "Today, I feel a proud citizen of India.": Julie McCarthy, "In India, Landmark Ruling Recognizes Transgender Citizens," National Public Radio, April 15, 2014, https://www.npr.org/sections /thetwo-way/2014/04/15/303408581/in-india-landmark-ruling -recognizes-transgender-citizens.

120: Estimate of two to three million hijra: Beauchamp, "There Is a Third Gender in India, and the Law Finally Recognized Them."

120: "When somebody asks . . . region of Nepal.": Seervai, "Laxmi Narayan Tripathi."

PROFILE: ZISHU NÜ—SELF-COMBED WOMEN

122: Another English term that was sometimes used to describe zishu nü that is seen as misleading is "sworn spinsters": Ziling Ye, "*Zishu Nü:* Dutiful Daughters of the Guangdong Delta," Intersections: Gender and Sexuality in Asia and the Pacific, no. 17 (July 2008): 2, http://intersections.anu.edu.au/issue17/ye.htm.

122–123: Overview of Pearl River delta area silk production, women's roles in China: "Golden Orchid Societies," *Queer as Fact*, podcast, August 15, 2019, https://queerasfact.podbean.com/e/golden -orchid-societies/.

123: Self-combed women including those who might have queer identities; ceremony for self-combed women: "Golden Orchid Societies."

123: "The practice of . . . this custom started.": *A Record of the Customs of All China* by Hu Pu'an, first published in 2 volumes in 1773–1774, as in Chih-Hui Fang and Xiang-Ning Zhang, "Female Romance in Ancient and Modern Chinese Society," Department of Foreign Languages and Literature, Asia University, and Ming Dao High School, accessed January 7, 2022, 41, n114, http://ir.lib.cyut.edu .tw:8080/retrieve/32777/1Fe++maleRomanceinAncientand ModernChineseSociety11-1.pdf.

123–124: Relationships between self-combed women: "Golden Orchid Societies," *Queer as Fact*; individual self-combed women in golden orchid societies, some in lesbian relationships, some not: "The Tradition of Female-Female Unions," Cultural China via the Internet Archive Wayback Machine, October 20, 2012–September 21, 2015, http://traditions.cultural-china.com /en/214T11933T14609.html.

124: "Whenever two members . . . of their 'parents.'": Wayne R. Dynes and Stephen Donaldson, eds., *Asian Homosexuality* (New York: Garland, 1992), 23, accessed online at https://www.google.com /books/edition/Asian_Homosexuality/UgKQ4KNDjsgC?hl=en.

124: "When I was . . . zishu nü myself.": Ziling, *"Zishu Nü,"* 30.

125: The Hall of Ice and Jade retirement home for self-combed women is now a museum: Tania Branigan, "No Regrets, Say the Chinese Women Who Chose Independence over Marriage: The Girls Who Took a Lifelong Vow of Chastity Are Now in Their 80s, the Last Survivors of a Unique Custom," *Guardian* (US edition), July 3, 2014, https://www.theguardian.com/world/2014/jul/03 /survivors-ancient-chinese-custom-self-combed-women.

125: "A lot of . . . to go away.": Branigan.

CHAPTER 4: MĀHŪ

127: "A māhū is . . . and female binary.": "*Kumu Hina* Press Kit," *Kumu Hina*, March 2014, https://kumuhina.com/uploads/websites /590/wysiwyg/Kumu_Hina_Press_Kit_Nov_2014_copySM.pdf.

127: "In the Hawaiian . . . or the other.": *A Place in the Middle*, directed by Dean Hamer and Joe Wilson (Haleiwa, HI: Kanaka Pakipika, 2015), 0:02, https://aplaceinthemiddle.org/.

127: "Sometimes kumu says . . . people are theirselves.": *A Place in the Middle*, 0:25.

127: Information on Hālau Lōkahi public charter school: *Kumu Hina*, Vimeo, directed by Dean Hamer (Haleiwa, HI: Kanaka Pakipika, 2014), 1:13.

127: "trying to keep the ancient traditions alive.": *A Place in the Middle*, 1:13.

128: "A māhū is . . . is like life.": "*Kumu Hina* Press Kit," *Kumu Hina*.

128: "You're happy? You're in boy lei.": *A Place in the Middle*, 1:58.

128: "I want to just wear both.": *A Place in the Middle*, 2:03.

128: "aww . . .": *A Place in the Middle*, 2:10

128: "See, you get both cause she's both.": *A Place in the Middle*, 2:13.

128–129: "Before the coming . . . forms of wisdom": *Kumu Hina*, 2:45.

129: "They were shocked . . . are still here.": *Kumu Hina*, 3:35.

129: "to address my . . . the wahine-kāne.": *A Place in the Middle*, 5:00.

129: "Kumu's in the . . . a rare person.": *Kumu Hina*, 9:35.

129: "When I was . . . take very seriously.": *Kumu Hina*, 6:55.

130: "You have a . . . she has kū." *Kumu Hina*, 16:53.

130: "Sometimes I feel . . . anybody else. Okay?": *A Place in the Middle*, 17:50.

130: More than four million people a year visit Waikīkī Beach: "The Hawaiian Islands: Waikīkī Beach," Hawaiʻi Tourism Authority, accessed November 4, 2023, https://www.gohawaii.com/islands /oahu/things-to-do/beaches/waikiki-beach.

130–132: "From the land . . . a hawaiian tale.": Thos. G. Thrum, comp., *Hawaiian Almanac and Annual for 1907: The Reference Book of Information and Statistics Relating to the Territory of Hawaii, of Value to Merchants, Tourists, and Others* (Honolulu: Thos. G. Thrum, 1906), 139–141, available online at eVols, accessed December 26, 2021, https://evols.library.manoa.hawaii.edu /handle/10524/32457.

131: Was Hawaii human sacrifice exaggerated?: Owen Jarus, "25 Cultures That Practiced Human Sacrifice," Live Science, June 16, 2017, https://www.livescience.com/59514-cultures-that-practiced -human-sacrifice/2.html.

132: Mele definition: "Mele," Ulukau Hawaiian Electronic Library, accessed December 31, 2021, http://wehewehe.org/gsdl2.85/cgi-bin /hdict?a=q&r=1&hs=1&m=-1&o=-1&qto=4&e=d-11000 -00---off-0hdict--00-1----0-10-0---0---0direct-10-ED--4 --textpukuielbert%252ctextmamaka-----0-1l--11-en-Zz-1---Zz -1-home-mele--00-3-1-00-0--4----0-0-11-00-0utfZz-8-00&q =mele&fqv=textpukuielbert%252ctextmamaka&af=1&fqf=ED.

132: "The value and . . . to restore them": Peter T. Young, "Na Pōhaku Ola Kapaemahu A Kapuni—The Healing (Wizard) Stones of Kapaemahu," Images of Old Hawaii, February 6, 2013, https:// imagesofoldhawaii.com/na-pohaku-ola-kapaemahu-a-kapuni -the-healing-wizard-stones-of-kapaemahu/.

132–133: June Gutmanis writing about Princess Likelike and the Stones of Life: Andrew Matzner (Dreya Blume), *O Au No Keia: Voices from Hawaiʻi's Mahu and Transgender Communities* (Bloomington, IN: Xlibris, 2001), 278; Pamela Kelley, ed., "Pohaku: Hawaiian Stories: The Wizard Stones of Waikiki," Pamphlets Polynesia, Brigham Young University–Hawaii Campus, accessed November 4, 2023, https://georgehbalazs.com/wp-content /uploads/2019/04/1980s-HAWAIIAN-STONES.pdf, 33–36.

133–134: Text from the plaque for the Stones of Life, Waikiki Beach: Daniel Ramirez, "The Stones of Life Description: At Waikiki Beach," Wikimedia, March 8, 2015, https://commons.wikimedia.org /wiki/File:The_Stones_of_Life_Description_(16974900081).jpg.

134–135: "conspicuous location . . . in Hawaiian culture.": Matzner, *O Au No Keia*, 279–280.

135: Captain Bligh's "A Voyage to the South Sea" commentary by the editors of the Royal Collection Trust: Vice-Admiral William Bligh (1854–1817), "A Voyage to the South Sea . . . for the Purpose of Conveying the Bread-Fruit Tree to the West Indies . . . Commanded by . . . William Bligh. 1792," Royal Collection Trust, accessed December 26, 2021, https://www.rct.uk/collection/1142197/a-voyage-to-the-south-sea-for-the-purpose-of-conveying-the-bread-fruit-tree-to.

135: The facsimile 1979 edition that deleted the reference to the māhū: Vice-Admiral William Bligh (1854–1817), "A Voyage to the South Sea . . . for the Purpose of Conveying the Bread-Fruit Tree to the West Indies . . . Commanded by . . . William Bligh. 1792," Australiana facsimile editions (Melbourne: Hutchinson of Australia, 1979), 116.

136: "beastly . . . respected and esteemed.": Lieutenant William Bligh, "PRO 412-7269-Public Record Office, Admiralty Records, 1673–1957 [Microform]/Fonds. Records of HM Ships/Series ADM 55/File 151. AJCP Reel No: 1601/Item. Lieutenant William Bligh's Log of the Proceedings of His Majesty's Armed Vessel Bounty," Trove, accessed January 3, 2022, 257–258, https://nla.gov.au/nla.obj-1091409242/view.

136–137: Laws contributing to "anti-*māhū* stigma" in Hawaii: Aleardo Zanghellini, "Sodomy Laws and Gender Variance in Tahiti and Hawai'i," *Laws*, April 9, 2013, https://www.mdpi.com/2075-471X/2/2/51/htm#B54-laws-02-00051.

137: Pink triangles during the Holocaust: Olivia B. Waxman, "How the Nazi Regime's Pink Triangle Symbol Was Repurposed for LGBTQ Pride," *Time*, May 31, 2018, https://time.com/5295476/gay-pride-pink-triangle-history/.

137: Different laws in Tahiti, Tahitian chief Pomare II in relationship with Toetoe—a mahu or man: Douglas L. Oliver, *Ancient Tahitian Society* (Honolulu: University of Hawaii Press, 1974), 372, accessed online at University of Hawai'i Press Open Access, accessed December 28, 2021, https://web.archive.org/web/20220705070255/https://www.hawaiiopen.org/product/ancient-tahitian-society/; Zanghellini, "Sodomy Laws."

137: "Mahu are effeminates . . . woman would do.": Zanghellini.

137: Zanghellini argues why social status of Mahu in Hawaii dropped in a way that didn't happen in Tahiti: Zanghellini.

138: "Indeed these people . . . Chiefs had them.": Robert J. Morris, "*Aikāne*: Accounts of Hawaiian Same-Sex Relationships in the Journals of Captain Cook's Third Voyage (1776–80)," *Journal of Homosexuality* 19, no. 4 (1990), 29.

138–139: "Kamehameha a chief . . . anxious to conceal.": Morris, 33.

139: "Karana-toa [Kalanikoa], brother . . . of these Indians.": Morris, 33.

139: "influence and conduct . . . of Hawaiian ethnohistory.": Morris, 21.

139: Ethnohistory definition: "ASE Mission Statement," American Society for Ethnohistory, accessed December 31, 2021, https://ethnohistory.org/ase-mission-statement/.

140: When Gauguin arrived in Tahiti, he was seen as a European mahu: Mario Vargas Llosa, "The Men-Women of the Pacific," Tate, Autumn 2010, https://www.tate.org.uk/tate-etc/issue-20-autumn-2010/men-women-pacific.

140: "time immemorial in . . . demonized and banned": Llosa.

140: Gauguin's Le Sorcier de Hiva Oa translated as "Marquesan Man in a Red Cape.": "Paul Gauguin, Le Sorcier d'Hiva Oa, (Marquesan Man in a Red Cape), 1902," Alamy Stock Photo, March 19, 2011, https://www.alamy.com/stock-photo-paul-gauguin-le-sorcier-dhiva-oa-marquesan-man-in-a-red-cape-1902-175121286.html; translated as "The Wizard of Hiva Oa": Paul Gauguin: "The Wizard of Hiva-Oa," Paul Gauguin: The Complete Works, accessed December 29, 2021, https://www.paul-gauguin.net/The-Wizard-Of-Hiva-Oa.html; translatated as "The Sorcerer of Hiva Oa": Casey Hoke, "Paul Gauguin—The Sorcerer of Hiva Oa (1902)," Queer Art History, August 7, 2017, https://www.queerarthistory.com/uncategorized/paul-gauguin-1848-1903/.

141: Mahu in cultures at great physical distances from each other: "Māhū," Spectrum Map Project, accessed December 29, 2021, https://spectrummapproject.wordpress.com/mahu/; distance in flight time from Tahiti to Hiva Oa and then to Hawaii: Google Maps searches, accessed December 29, 2021, https://www.google.com maps/dir/Hawaii/Hiva+Oa,+French+Polynesia/@5.0079552,-156.3726834,5z/data=!3m1!4b1!4m14!4m13!1m5!1m1!1s0x7bffdb064f79e005:0x4b7782d274cc8628!2m2!1d-155.5827818!2d19.8967662!1m5!1m1!1s0x7637213df916acbf:0x5d6e61d74d5943c5!2m2!1d-139.0211225!2d-9.7546726!3e4; https://www.google.com/maps/dir/Hiva+Oa,+French+Polynesia/Tahiti,+French+Polynesia/@-13.6619846,-148.7321934,6z/data=!3m1!4b1!4m14!4m13!1m5!1m1!1s0x7637213df916acbf:0x5d6e61d74d5943c5!2m2!1d-139.0211225!2d-9.7546726!1m5!1m1!1s0x769bb353982d1e65:0x413cf43a8988a3fa!2m2!1d-149.4260421!2d-17.6509195!3e4.

141: "almost all": Matzner, *O Au No Keia*, 283.

141: 'Māhū' used as a slur: "Māhū," Spectrum Map Project; Hawaii passes law offering trans workplace protection: "Hawaii Governor Signs Transgender Workplace Protections Bill into Law," LGBTQ Nation, May 6, 2011, https://www.lgbtqnation.com /2011/05/hawaii-governor-signs-transgender-workplace -protections-bill-into-law/.

141: "It's not easy . . . I got lucky.": *Kumu Hina*, 10:14.

141–142: "Where I come . . . be with Hina.": *Kumu Hina*, 11:06, 59:54.

142–144: Kaua'i Iki tells part of their life story: Matzner, *O Au No Keia*, 23–30.

144: "We were hanging . . . dream vision was.": *Kumu Hina*, 56:15.

144: "None of us . . . to prevent that." *Kumu Hina*, 1:03:53.

144–145: Sasha Colby on reclaiming 'māhū: Dino-Ray Ramos, "'Drag Race' Winner Sasha Colby Talks How Her Hawaiian Culture, Queer Journey, and Grief Shaped Her Art and Life," *Diaspora*, April 21, 2023, https://thediasporatimes.com/2023/04/21/drag -race-winner-sasha-colby-talks-how-her-hawaiian-culture -queer-journey-and-grief-shaped-her-art-and-life/.

145: "To think about . . . us for it." *Kumu Hina*, 9:20, 1:02:50.

145: "I thought she was a boy, but . . . ": *Kumu Hina*, 1:07:00.

145: "He is.": *Kumu Hina*, 1:07:00.

145: "He is.": *Kumu Hina*, 1:07:00.

145: "He is.": *Kumu Hina*, 1:07:00.

145: "All right, . . . the house down." *Kumu Hina*, 1:07:00.

145: "When Ho'onani did . . . around, comes around.": *Kumu Hina*, 1:09:57.

146: "They used to . . . up to me!": David Artavia, "Move Over, Kylie: This Out Hawaiian Teen Has a Global Following and Flourishing Makeup Line," *Advocate*, August/September 2018, 32.

146: "Like many if . . . well to emulate.": Craig Philips, "Telling the Story of Kumu Hina," PBS, May 4, 2015, https://www.pbs.org /independentlens/blog/telling-the-story-of-kumu-hina.

146–147: "I believe that . . . do the same.": Pledge of Aloha, *Kumu Hina*, accessed March 16, 2024, https://kumuhina.com/.

PROFILE: DAHOMEY FEMALE WARRIORS

148: Dahomey/Benin history and history of the female warriors of Dahomey: "A History of Female Empowerment: The Mino of Benin," Culture Trip, September 28, 2016,

https://theculturetrip.com/africa/benin/articles/a-history-of
-female-empowerment-the-mino-of-benin/.

148: Theories about the female warriors coming to be, military losses
and kidnapping/enslavement of men: Mike Dash, "Dahomey's
Women Warriors," *Smithsonian*, September 23, 2011, https://
www.smithsonianmag.com/history/dahomeys-women-warriors
-88286072/.

148: Theories about the female warriors coming to be, Queen Hangbe:
Fleur Macdonald, "The Legend of Benin's Fearless Female
Warriors," BBC Travel, August 27, 2018, https://www.bbc.com
/travel/article/20180826-the-legend-of-benins-fearless-female
-warriors.

148–149: Dahomey military expansion included most of Nigeria and their
being called "Amazons" by Europeans: "A History of Female
Empowerment," Culture Trip.

149: "colonial reference . . . larger than life": Rachel Jones, "The Warriors
of This West African Kingdom Were Formidable—and
Female," *National Geographic*, September 14, 2022, https://
www.nationalgeographic.com/history/article/the-true-story
-of-the-women-warriors-of-dahomey.

149: Dahomey female warriors numbers and types of weapons: Dash,
"Dahomey's Women Warriors."

149: Another description of the female warrior weapons and the training
exercise witnessed by Father Francesco Borghero: Stanley
B. Alpern, *Amazons of Black Sparta: The Women Warriors of
Dahomey* (New York: New York University Press, 2011), 13–15.

149: "rich enough in glory . . . but mutual friendship.": Alpern, 15.

149–150: Father Francesco Borghero witnessing Dahomey female warrior
training, and other training: Dash, "Dahomey's Women
Warriors."

150: Professor Robin Law on Dahomey female warriors, and Sir Richard
Burton: Dash.

150: "So you like this flag?": Dash.

150: "Eh bien, it will serve you.": Dash.

151: "each allowed herself . . . his own bayonet.": Dash.

151: "warrioresses . . . and very disciplined.": Dash.

152: "remarkable for their . . . with prodigious bravery.": Dash.

152: Dahomey independence in 1960, female warrior Nawi: Dash;
translated as "our mothers" and alternately by Professor

Leonard Wantchekon as "witch": Macdonald, "The Legend of Benin's Fearless Female Warriors."

152: "the descendants of . . . their traditions alive.": Macdonald.

152: Horns worn as symbol of power and sign of rank: Francesca Piqué and Leslie H. Rainer, *Palace Sculptures of Abomey: History Told on Walls* (Los Angeles: Getty Conservation Institute and J. Paul Getty Museum, 1999), available online at http://d2aohiyo3d3idm.cloudfront.net/publications/virtuallibrary/0892365692.pdf, 14.

153: "strong, independent and . . . was an Amazon.": Macdonald, "The Legend of Benin's Fearless Female Warriors."

CHAPTER 5: SIX MORE PEOPLE WHO LIVED OUTSIDE THE GENDER BINARY

Daniel Burghamer

156: About the Fugger Newsletters: "About the Fugger Newsletters," Die Fuggerzeitungen, accessed November 26, 2021, https://fuggerzeitungen.univie.ac.at/en/about-fugger-newsletters.

156: Lansquenet definition: "Lansquenet," Merriam-Webster Dictionary, accessed January 22, 2022, https://www.merriam-webster.com/dictionary/lansquenet.

156–157: "From Piadena . . . her with child.": George T. Matthews, ed., *News and Rumor in Renaissance Europe (The Fugger Newsletters)*, (New York: Capricorn Books, 1959), 247–248, section 259.

157: "Many noted men . . . by the clergy.": Matthews, ed., 247–248, section 259.

Carl Lapp

158: Some Sami lived nomadically and herded reindeer: "Sami: People," *Encyclopaedia Britannica*, October 5, 2021, https://www.britannica.com/topic/Sami.

158: "demanded . . . and court sessions.": Gunlög Fur, "Reading Margins: Colonial Encounters in Sápmi and Lenapehoking in the Seventeenth and Eighteenth Centuries," *Feminist Studies* 32, no. 3 (Fall 2006): 495–496, 498–499.

159: Carl Lapp's name signifying he was a member of the Sámi: Fur, 497.

159: Lapp and Lappland seen as derogatory, Sámi prefer Sámi and Sapmi: Catherine Stein, "Samis Don't Want to Be 'Lapps': The

Norwegian Indigenous People Officially Known as Sami Are Upset about the Use of What They Call the 'Derogatory' Terms Lapp and Lappland," Aftenposten via the Internet Archive Wayback Machine, February 8, 2008, https://web .archive.org/web/20080929001926/http://www.aftenposten.no /english/local/article2246107.ece.

159: Carl Lapp's life, death, and what happened next: Fur, "Reading Margins," 495–498.

159: "participation in the . . . God's holy order.": Fur, 495–496.

159–160: "as a sin . . . the death penalty.": Fur, 496–497.

160: Sexum is Latin for 'gender': Google Translate, Latin to English, accessed January 8, 2022, https://translate.google.com/?sl =la&tl=en&text=sexum&op=translate&hl=en.

160: Irony of Carl buried in forest as punishment, a Sami practice: Fur, "Reading Margins," 498.

Julian Eltinge

160: Julian raised in Montana and going to Boston and starting his career in drag: Elyssa Goodman, "Drag Herstory: This Drag Queen Was Once the Highest Paid Actor in the World," Them, April 6, 2018, https://www.them.us/story/julian-eltinge-drag-queen -history.

160: "a genius in the impersonation of female characters.": Nicholas Beyelia, "The King of (Drag) Queens: The "Fascinating" Julian Eltinge," *Los Angeles Public Library Blog*, June 19, 2018, https://www.lapl.org/collections-resources/blogs/lapl/king -drag-queens-fascinating-julian-eltinge.

160–161: Julian's fame: Goodman, "Drag Herstory."; Beyelia, "The King of (Drag) Queens."; John Holusha, "A Theater's Muses, Rescued; Mural Figures Recall Celebrity of a (Well-Painted) Face," *New York Times*, March 24, 2000, https://www.nytimes .com/2000/03/24/nyregion/a-theater-s-muses-rescued-mural -figures-recall-celebrity-of-a-well-painted-face.html.

161: "Women went into . . . the smoking room.": Holusha.

161: "He also had . . . line of cigars.": Goodman, "Drag Herstory."

161: Julian's super masculine image: Holusha, "A Theater's Muses."

162: Marlin fish information: "Blue Marlin," *National Geographic*, accessed December 19, 2021, https://www.nationalgeographic.com /animals/fish/facts/blue-marlin.

162: "When his sexuality . . . just like pearls!'": Beyelia, "The King of (Drag) Queens."

162: "Most persons balk . . . the young actor.": Beyelia.

162–163: "Julian Eltinge, as . . . widows played them.": Holusha, "A Theater's Muses."

163: "Unique in the . . . he has no equal.": Beyelia, "The King of (Drag) Queens."

163: New York movie theater named after Julian and the mural showing him as three different female muses: Holusha, "A Theater's Muses."; Michael Padwee, "Bits and Pieces: Two "E"s—Eltinge and Elks, and More about Jean Nison," *Architectural Tiles, Glass and Ornamentation in New York* (blog), August 1, 2014, https://tilesinnewyork.blogspot.com/2014/08/.

164: "some women might . . . a woman's house!," Beyelia, "The King of (Drag) Queens."

164: "This last statement . . . his personal life.": Beyelia.

164: Times changing and Julian's fame fading: Beyelia.

164: An overview of Hollywood's Hays Code: Maria Lewis, "Early Hollywood and the Hays Code," ACMI (formerly Australian Center for the Moving Image), January 14, 2021, https://www.acmi.net.au/stories-and-ideas/early-hollywood-and-hays-code/.

164: Hard times for Julian, nightclubs in his fifties, dying in 1941: Beyelia, "The King of (Drag) Queens."

164: Movie theater history and mural restoration: Holusha, "A Theater's Muses."

Claude Cahun and Marcel Moore

165: "much to the vexation of our families.": *Lover Other*, DVD, directed by Barbara Hammer (New York: Barbara Hammer, 2006), 0:37, 0:50.

165: "They both dressed . . . all the time.": *Lover Other*, 16:56.

165: "Beneath this mask . . . can peel off.": *Lover Other*, 19:10.

165: "theatricalizing of identity . . . never be revealed.": *Lover Other*, 18:48.

165: "posed in a . . . kind of lineage.": *Lover Other*, 22:57.

166: On both Claude and Marcel being Jewish—their gravestone in Jersey shows two stars of David above each birth name: "Claude Cahun and Marcel Moore's gravestone, Jersey," Flickr, August 14,

2013, https://www.flickr.com/photos/erincatherinemackenzie/9586417084/in/photostream/; Chandni Bhatt, "Art ahead of Its Time: The Distinctive Work of Claude Cahun and Marcel Moore," Arts Help, accessed November 4, 2023, https://www.artshelp.com/art-ahead-of-its-time-the-distinctive-work-of-claude-cahun-and-marcel-moore/.

166: "We were not . . . not paying attention.": *Lover Other*, 29:30.

166: Jersey Isle Jews had to register: *Lover Other*, 33:55.

166: "There are very . . . were tracked down.": *Lover Other*, 35:15.

167: Liberation of Jersey Isle: "The Liberation of the Channel Islands," Liberation Route Europe, accessed December 18, 2021, https://www.liberationroute.com/stories/195/the-liberation-of-the-channel-islands; Claude and Marcel sentenced, reprieved, liberated: *Lover Other*, 43:01, 45:40, 48:00.

167: "And I saw new heavens and a new earth.": *Lover Other*, 52:26.

167: Paris had twenty arrondissements, now it has seventeen: "The Paris Arrondissements—A Guide to the Neighborhoods," Paris Insiders Guide, accessed November 5, 2023, https://www.parisinsidersguide.com/paris-arrondissements.html.

Shi Pei Pu

168: Shi Pei Pu and Bernard Bouriscot meet: Joyce Wadler, "The True Story of *M. Butterfly*; The Spy Who Fell in Love with a Shadow," *New York Times Magazine*, August 15, 1993, https://www.nytimes.com/1993/08/15/magazine/the-true-story-of-m-butterfly-the-spy-who-fell-in-love-with-a-shadow.html?pagewanted=all.

168: Bernard's past relationships and determination to fall in love with a woman, friendship with Pei Pu, and calling Pei Pu his "best friend": Wadler.

168: "far too dangerous . . . with her life.": Wadler.

168–169: Pei Pu tells Bernard that she has taken male hormones and that she is pregnant: Wadler.

169: Bernard back in China, staring at Pei Pu across the street: Wadler.

169: Pei Pu and Bernard's child and Bernard becomes a spy: Wadler.

169: Bernard meets his son and relationship with Thierry: Wadler.

170: Bernard spying during his post in Mongolia and gifts for Pei Pu; the French ambassador in Mongolia: Wadler.

170: "The yak, to . . . to the Americans.": Wadler.

170: Pei Pu and Du Du/Bertrand come to Paris: Wadler.

170: "I did nothing . . . It's my son.": Wadler.

170: "It's not possible! . . . It's a lie!": Wadler.

170–171: Bernard confronts Pei Pu, survives suicide attempt: Wadler.

171: "If this case . . . the spying world.": Wadler.

171: "I was shattered . . . a Chinese custom.": Richard Bernstein, "France Jails 2 in Odd Case of Espionage," *New York Times*, May 11, 1986, https://www.nytimes.com/1986/05/11/world/france-jails -2-in-odd-case-of-espionage.html.

172: Jury deliberation, sentencing: Wadler, "The True Story of *M. Butterfly*."

172: Media coverage of Shi Pei Pu and Bernard Bouriscot trial: Bernstein, "France Jails 2 in Odd Case of Espionage."; Le Monde headline "Espion ou Espionne?": Wadler, "The True Story of *M. Butterfly*."

172: Pei Pu and Bernard pardoned: Wadler.

172: Pei Pu living in France after the trial, Bernard continuing to live with Thierry: Robert Aldrich, *Gay Lives* (New York: Thames & Hudson, 2012), 283–286; T. Rees Shapiro, "Shi Pei Pu Dies at 70; Chinese Opera Singer Inspired *M. Butterfly*," *Los Angeles Times*, July 6, 2009, https://www.latimes.com/local/obituaries /la-me-shi-pei-pu6-2009jul06-story.html.

172: *M. Butterfly*, with Bernard attending performances: Nelson Pressley, "By Chance, Meeting the Disgraced 'M. Butterfly' Diplomat Whose Lover Misled Him," *Washington Post*, August 11, 2017, https://www.washingtonpost.com/entertainment/theater_dance /by-chance-meeting-the-disgraced-m-butterfly-diplomat -whose-lover-misled-him/2017/08/11/7fb44744-77c1-11e7 -9eac-d56bd5568db8_story.html.

172: "'Europeans' infatuation for . . . measure of fantasy.": Aldrich, *Gay Lives*, 286.

172: Pei Pu dies in 2009: Shapiro, "Shi Pei Pu Dies at 70."

172: Bernard on Pei Pu's dying: Laramie Mok, "Who Was Shi Peipu, a Chinese Spy and Opera Star Who Cross-Dressed as a Woman and Had a Long-Term Sexual Relationship with a French Diplomat?," *South China Morning Post*, June 30, 2019, https:// www.scmp.com/magazines/style/article/3016474/who-shi-peipu -chinese-singer-and-spy-who-masqueraded-woman-and-had.

172: "It was hard . . . inside his soul.": Pressley, "By Chance."

172: Pei Pu being the first love of Bernard's life: Bernstein, "France Jails 2 in Odd Case of Espionage."

174: "on a crust of earth that floats on a large sea,": "The Warao," University of Oslo Museum of Cultural History, December 11, 2020, https://www.historiskmuseum.no/english/exhibitions /exhibitions-archive/america-present-past-identity/south -america/the-warao/.

174: A much higher (forty-eight thousand people) estimate of Warao population: "Support to Indigenous People from Venezuela and Host Communities in Brazil," International Organization for Migration, May 2020, https://brazil.iom.int/sites/g/files /tmzbdl1496/files/documents/OIM%2520Brasil%2520Informe %2520Ind%25C3%25ADgena%2520-%2520Final_0.pdf.

174: "people from the . . . soft (marsh) land" and "people from the . . . hard land.": "Support to Indigenous People."

174: "They are really . . . on solid ground.": Jake Naughton, "LENS: Two Spirits in the Venezuelan Jungle," *New York Times*, September 5, 2014, https://lens.blogs.nytimes.com/2014/09/05/two-spirits -in-the-venezuelan-jungle/.

175: "Almost all older . . . can make hammocks,": "The Warao," University of Oslo Museum of Cultural History.

175: Tidawena translation, tasks: "The Warao."

175: Tida Wena vs. tidewena: Naughton, "LENS."

175: "were sometimes the . . . roam the jungle.": Naughton.

175: "would often boast . . . make a canoe.": Christian Sørhaug, "Composing Warao Indigeneity and Miniatures," in Charlotte Dixon and Jack Davy, eds., *Worlds in Miniature: Contemplating Miniaturisation in Global Material Culture* (London: UCL Press, 2019), 123, available online at https://www.google.com /books/edition/Worlds_in_Miniature/Mb-kDwAAQBAJ?hl =en&gbpv=1&bsq=.

176: "acquire the knowledge . . . health and prosperity.": "The Warao" University of Oslo Museum of Cultural History.

176: "niborawena is much . . . not talked about.": Christian Sørhaug, "The Domestication and Indigenization of Global Forces through Consumption," *Material World* (blog), August 7, 2009, https:// materialworldblog.com/2009/08/the-domestication-and -indigenization-of-global-forces-through-consumption/.

176: Hobure, an area within the Orinoco delta cited here: H. Dieter Heinen and Kenneth Ruddle, "Ecology, Ritual, and Economic Organization in the Distribution of Palm Starch among the Warao of the Orinoco Delta," *Journal of Anthropological Research* 30, no. 2 (1974): 118, fig. 1, accessed online at http://www.jstor.org/stable/3629642.

176: Modern tools, technology, impact of Catholic missionaries, Shamanism and handcrafts live on: "The Warao," University of Oslo Museum of Cultural History.

176–177: "He said that . . . rear view mirror,": Sørhaug, "Composing Warao Indigeneity," 122–123.

177: "The existence of . . . never photograph[ed] before.": "Wonderland," directed by Álvaro Laiz (Bristol, UK: IC Visual Lab, 2013), available online at Vimeo, https://vimeo.com/77139160, 4:26.

177: Animistic definition: "Animism," Merriam-Webster Dictionary, accessed January 22, 2022, https://www.merriam-webster.com/dictionary/animistic.

177: Tidawena Andres Medina, Arsenio Beria, and Sanse featured in the photo gallery in the *New York Times*: Naughton, "LENS."; many of the same photos are at Álvaro's website: Álvaro Laiz, "Wonderland," Álvaro Laiz, accessed January 18, 2022, http://www.alvarolaiz.com/wonderland.

CHAPTER 6: THE COLONIZATION OF GENDER

179: "The world put . . . that can be.": Greg Thomas, *The Sexual Demon of Colonial Power: Pan-African Embodiment and Erotic Schemes of Empire* (Bloomington: Indiana University Press, 2007), 154.

180: "for the contagion . . . to the people.": Richard Trexler, *Sex and Conquest: Gendered Violence, Political Order, and the European Conquest of the Americas* (Ithaca, NY: Cornell University Press, 1995), 82.

180: "was certainly a . . . indigenous civil authority": Trexler, 82–84.

180: "more than any other race.": Will Roscoe, *The Zuni Man-Woman* (Albuquerque: University of New Mexico Press, 1991), 171.

181: "Modern history has . . . and advanced technology.": "Guns, Germs, and Steel: 1 of 3 Official," YouTube video, 1:03:01, posted by Stella M. Shannon, National Geographic Society, October 7, 2015, https://www.youtube.com/watch?v=dgGw8kZnJxE.

181–182: "vastly more nutritious . . . people.": Gwynn Guilford, "The Global Dominance of White People Is Thanks to the Potato," Quartz, December 8, 2017, https://qz.com/quartzy/1148452/potato2.

182: "the need to . . . and destroy them.": Ta-Nehisi Coates, *Between the World and Me* (New York: Spiegel & Grau, 2015), 7.

183: Richard was a baron: "Richard, Baron von Krafft-Ebing: German Psychologist," *Encyclopaedia Britannica*, August 10, 2021, https://www.britannica.com/biography/Richard-Freiherr-von -Krafft-Ebing.

183: "The secondary sexual characteristics . . . and vice versa.": R. von Krafft-Ebing, *Psychopathia Sexualis with Especial Reference to the Antipathic Sexual Instinct: A Medico-Forensic Study*, translated by F. J. Rebman (London: William Heinemann, 1931), available online at Wellcome Collection, https://iiif.wellcomecollection .org/pdf/b31362254, 42/PDF 63.

183: "Scientists argued that . . . as sex indistinguishable.": Alok Vaid-Menon, "The Racist History of the Sex Binary," Instagram, October 3, 2021, https://www.instagram.com/p/CUkka3pLoe9/.

183–184: "the slaveocratic order . . . notions of empire.": Thomas, *Sexual Demon*, 28.

184: "whiteness in America . . . badge of advantage.": Ta-Nehisi Coates, "My President Was Black: A History of the First African American White House—and of What Came Next," *Atlantic*, January/February 2017, https://www.theatlantic.com /magazine/archive/2017/01/my-president-was-black/508793/.

184: "All my life . . . twice as much.": Coates, *Between the World*, 90–91.

184: "The negation of . . . here and there.": Thomas, *Sexual Demon*, 15–16.

184: Measuring brain size first as tool of racism and then of misogyny: Fausto-Sterling, *Sexing the Body*, 124.

185: Nazi racism, wanting to create a "master race": "Nazi Racism," United States Holocaust Memorial Museum, accessed November 13, 2021, https://encyclopedia.ushmm.org/content/en/article /nazi-racism.

185: Nazi mass sterilizations and murder: "Nazi Racial Science," United States Holocaust Memorial Museum, accessed November 15, 2021, https://www.ushmm.org/collections/bibliography/nazi -racial-science.

185: "considered inferior and . . . targeted for persecution.": "Nazi Persecution: 1933–1945," Holocaust Memorial Day Trust, accessed March 18, 2024, https://www.hmd.org.uk/learn -about-the-holocaust-and-genocides/nazi-persecution/.

186: "a conservative strategy . . . capitalism and colonialism.": Alok Vaid-Menon, "Book Report: *The Trouble with White Women:*

A Counterhistory of Feminism by Kyla Schuller. Foreword by Brittney Cooper (New York: Bold Type Books, 2021)," "a conservative strategy . . . ," @alokvmenon, Instagram, November 4, 2021, https://www.instagram.com/p /CVx7mrTgZ-d/.

186: "race suicide": Schuller, *The Trouble with White Women*, 127.

186: "led eugenicists to . . . direction of humanity.": Schuller, 127.

186: "physicians sterilized perhaps . . . in these years.": Brianna Theobald, "A 1970 Law Led to the Mass Sterilization of Native American Women. That History Still Matters" *Time*, November 28, 2019, https://time.com/5737080/native-american-sterilization -history/.

186–187: "Contraception and abortion . . . of controlling women.": Jill Filipovic, "Opinion: Guest Essay: The Anti-Abortion Movement Could Reduce Abortions If It Wanted To," *New York Times*, December 14, 2021, https://www.nytimes.com /2021/12/14/opinion/abortion-contraception-pregnancy.html.

187: Alok Vaid-Menon and Kyla Schuller Instagram live, "White Feminism in the US," Instagram interview between Alok Vaid-Menon and Kyla Schuller about *The Trouble with White Women: A Counterhistory of Feminism*, November 2, 2021, https://www .instagram.com/p/CVx7mrTgZ-d/, 4:00.

187: "centuries-long history . . . of any gender.": Joan Morgan, "How White Feminism Threw Its Black Counterpart Under the Bus," *New York Times*, October 5, 2021, https://www.nytimes.com/2021 /10/05/books/review/kyla-schuller-the-trouble-with-white -women-a-counterhistory-of-feminism.html.

187–188: "After the Civil War . . . Mayflower-descendant wives vote.": Instagram interview between Alok Vaid-Menon and Kyla Schuller about *The Trouble with White Women*, 14:42.

188: Frederick Douglass: Noell Trent, "Frederick Douglass: United States Official and Diplomat," *Encyclopaedia Britannica*, updated November 3, 2023, https://www.britannica.com/biography /Frederick-Douglass.

188: Frederick's speech, "This Fourth of . . . nation of savages.": "Frederick Douglass: Our American Story," National Museum of African American History & Culture, Smithsonian, accessed November 5, 2023, https://nmaahc.si.edu/explore/stories /frederick-douglass.

188: Frances Ellen Watkins Harper: Kerri Lee Alexander, "Frances Ellen Watkins Harper (1825–1911)," National Women's History

Museum, accessed November 5, 2023, https://www
.womenshistory.org/education-resources/biographies/frances
-ellen-watkins-harper.

188: Lucretia Mott: Debra Michals, ed., "Lucretia Mott (1793–1880)," National Women's History Museum, accessed November 5, 2023, https://www.womenshistory.org/education-resources /biographies/lucretia-mott.

189: "sexism as a . . . late 1970s.": Instagram interview between Alok Vaid-Menon and Kyla Schuller about *The Trouble with White Women*, 6:00.

189: "At that point . . . a Black paper.": Instagram interview, 16:22.

189: Sojourner Truth: Debra Michals, "Sojourner Truth (1797–1883)," National Women's History Museum, accessed November 5, 2023, https://www.womenshistory.org/education-resources /biographies/sojourner-truth.

189–190: Marius Robinson's transcription of Sojourner Truth's speech as published in the *Anti-Slavery Bugle*, June 21, 1851: Marius Robinson, "Women's Rights Convention: Sojourner Truth," Library of Congress: Ohio History Connection Columbus, Ohio, *Anti-Slavery Bugle* (New Lisbon, OH), June 21, 1851, Library of Congress, accessed November 20, 2021, https:// chroniclingamerica.loc.gov/lccn/sn83035487/1851-06-21/ed-1 /seq-4/, 160, image 4.

190: Sojourner Truth speech: Marius Robinson's transcription versus Frances Gage's fictionalized version: Leslie Podell, "Compare the Two Speeches," Sojourner Truth Project, accessed November 20, 2021, https://www.thesojournertruthproject.com /compare-the-speeches.

190: "in the 19th and 20th . . . never became 'now.'": Will Boisvert, "Bloody Britain: 'PW' Talks with Caroline Elkins," *Publishers Weekly*, November 5, 2021, https://www.publishersweekly.com /pw/by-topic/authors/interviews/article/87818-bloody-britain -pw-talks-with-caroline-elkins.html. Copyright © PWxyz, LLC. Used by permission.

190: "Americans who believe that they are white.": Coates, *Between the World*, 6.

191: "They made us . . . into a people.": Coates, 149.

191: "wearing a dress . . . woman or man.": Clare Sears, *Arresting Dress: Cross Dressing, Law, and Fascination in Nineteenth-Century San Francisco* (Durham, NC: Duke University Press, 2015), 2–6.

191: "for wearing women's . . . classed as male.": Sears, 87.

192–193: "A black suit . . . of a conversation.": Jess McHugh, "'The Beginning of a Conversation': What It Was Like to Be an LGBTQ Activist before Stonewall," *Time*, June 25, 2019, https://time.com/longform/mattachine-society/.

193: The movie *Stonewall* centering a straight-acting white gay man: Nigel M Smith, "Gay Rights Activists Give Their Verdict on *Stonewall*: 'This Film Is No Credit to the History It Purports to Portray,'" *Guardian* (US edition), September 25, 2015, https://www.theguardian.com/film/2015/sep/25/stonewall -film-gay-rights-activists-give-their-verdict.

193: Marsha P. Johnson and Sylvia Rivera: "Marsha P. Johnson: 2017 Icon," LGBT History Month, accessed November 5, 2023, https:// lgbthistorymonth.com/marsha-p-johnson?tab=biography; Emma Rothberg, "Marsha P. Johnson (1945–1992)," National Women's History Museum, accessed November 5, 2023, https://www.womenshistory.org/education-resources /biographies/marsha-p-johnson.

193: "I'm not missing . . . it's the revolution!": Emma Rothberg, "Sylvia Rivera (1951–2022)," National Women's History Museum, accessed November 5, 2023, https://www.womenshistory.org /education-resources/biographies/sylvia-rivera.

194: "Over her upper . . . Iranian woman's face.": Afrsaneh Najmabadi, *Women with Mustaches and Men without Beards* (Berkeley: University of California Press, 2005), 232–233.

194: "many Persian-language sources . . . ugliness and masculinity.": Najmabadi, 233.

194: Qajar dynasty: "Qājār Dynasty: Iranian Dynasty," *Encyclopaedia Britannica*, February 7, 2017, https://www.britannica.com /topic/Qajar-dynasty.

195: "amnesia": Najmabadi, *Women with Mustaches*, 2–4, 232–237.

195: A financial colonization of Iran: Shahram Akbarzadeh, "The Long History of Iranian Distrust of the West," Conversation, December 1, 2011, https://theconversation.com/the-long -history-of-iranian-distrust-of-the-west-4480.

195: "social norm . . . or hygiene benefits.": Breanne Fahs "Can Everyday Body Hair Practices Have Revolutionary Implications?," June 15, 2022, University of Washington Press Blog, https:// uwpressblog.com/2022/06/15/can-everyday-body-hair -practices-have-revolutionary-implications/#_ftn1.

195–196: Amount of time and money US women spend removing body hair: "Women Spend Up to $23,000 to Remove Hair," UPI

Heath News, June 24, 2008, https://www.upi.com/Health
_News/2008/06/24/Women-spend-up-to-23000-to-remove
-hair/64771214351618/.

196: Queen Victoria and brides wearing white: "Why Do Brides Wear
White?," *Encyclopaedia Britannica*, accessed October 12, 2021,
https://www.britannica.com/story/why-do-wear-white;
"Global Bridal Wear Industry (2021 to 2027)—Social Media
and e-Commerce in Weddings Continues to Grow—
ResearchAndMarkets.com," Business Wire, November 10, 2021,
https://www.businesswire.com/news/home/20211110005713
/en/Global-Bridal-Wear-Industry-2021-to-2027---Social
-Media-and-e-Commerce-in-Weddings-Continues-to-Grow
---ResearchAndMarkets.com.

196: "marrying for political . . . a cultural ideal.": Stephanie Coontz,
Marriage, a History: How Love Conquered Marriage (New York:
Penguin Books, 2006), 6–7.

196: Enslaved people's marriages were not legally binding or sanctified by the
church: Tera W. Hunter, "Enslaved Couples Faced Wrenching
Separations, or Even Choosing Family over Freedom,"
History.com, September 20, 2019, https://www.history.com
/news/african-american-slavery-marriage-family-separation.

197: "Scientists do not . . . modern gender politics.": Fausto-Sterling,
Sexing the Body, 118, 178.

197: "researchers have learned . . . the male hormone.": Fausto-Sterling, 185.

197–198: "a place of . . . begets mad desire.": Fausto-Sterling, 196, 427 n84.

198: Testosterone is an androgen: "Androgens," Cleveland Clinic, October
24, 2021, https://my.clevelandclinic.org/health/articles/22002
-androgens.

198: "a cultural phenomenon . . . into the body.": Fausto-Sterling, *Sexing
the Body*, 272.

198: "developmental, interactive achievement.": Fausto-Sterling, 285.

198: "I use gender/sex . . . or gender socialization.": Sari van Anders,
"Chewing Gum Has Large Effects on Salivary Testosterone,
Estradiol, and Secretory Immunoglobulin A Assays in Women
and Men," *Psychoneuroendocrinology* 35, no. 2 (February 2010):
305, available online at ScienceDirect, https://www.sciencedirect
.com/science/article/abs/pii/S030645300900198X.

198: "The cell, the individual, . . . sexuality and gender.": Fausto-Sterling,
Sexing the Body, 266.

198: "the mechanism by . . . develops remains unexamined.": Fausto-Sterling, 278.

198: "pathologizing of diversity.": Roughgarden, *Evolution's Rainbow*, 299.

199: "help us end cultural dysphoria": Anunnaki Ray Marquez, "Born Intersex: We Are Human!," TEDxJacksonville, October 2018, 7:28, https://www.ted.com/talks/mx_anunnaki_ray_marquez_born_intersex_we_are_human.

199: "acts in a . . . predominant atmospheric elements.": Fausto-Sterling, *Sexing the Body*, 309.

199: "Yay! You kicked the ball!": Fausto-Sterling, 291–292.

199: "kept stumbling when . . . wear long dresses.": Fausto-Sterling, 274.

200: "As the girl holds . . . calling you already?'": Fausto-Sterling, 296.

200: "Inevitably, gender/sex integrates . . . body and consciousness.": Fausto-Sterling, 309.

201: "the world put . . . that can be.": Thomas, *Sexual Demon*, 158.

PROFILE: WHITE DOVES

202: Skopt in Russian means "the Castrated Ones.": Jacob Mikanowski, "The Wheel and the Knife," Awl, March 17, 2017, https://www.theawl.com/2017/03/the-wheel-and-the-knife/.

202: White Dove belief that angels had no physical sex: Anatole Leroy-Beaulieu, *The Empire of the Tsars and the Russians*, vol. 3 (London: G. P. Putnam's Sons, 1896), 422–423, accessed online at Google Books, https://www.google.com/books/edition/The_Empire_of_the_Tsars_and_the_Russians/w8LOAAAAMAAJ?hl=en&gbpv=0.

202: White Dove belief that Adam and Eve had no physical sex until original sin: Mikanowski, "The Wheel and the Knife."

202: White Dove belief that male and female genitalia represent the forbidden fruit: Romeo Vitelli, "The White Doves," Providentia: A Biased Look at Psychology in the World, December 11, 2015, https://drvitelli.typepad.com/providentia/2015/12/the_skoptzy.html.

203: New Testament passages Matthew 18:8, 18:9, and 19:12: "Wherefore if thy . . . let him receive it.": "Matthew 18:8, 18:9, and 19:12; King James Version," Bible Gateway, accessed January 9, 2022, https://www.biblegateway.com/passage/?search=Matthew%2018&version=NIV;KJV.

203: "to set the . . . this world of sin.": Leroy-Beaulieu, *The Empire of the Tsars and the Russians*, 422–423.

203: White Dove castration of women and men including breasts and sometimes the labia and clitoris: "The White Doves," Providentia; Leroy-Beaulieu, *The Empire of the Tsars and the Russians*, 422–423.

203–204: "Farewell sky, farewell . . . a heavenly body.": Mikanowski, "The Wheel and the Knife."

204: White Dove secret: "Skoptsi," *Encyclopaedia Britannica*, accessed January 9, 2022, https://en.wikisource.org/wiki/1911_Encyclop%C3%A6dia_Britannica/Skoptsi; Leroy-Beaulieu, *The Empire of the Tsars and the Russians*, 422–423.

204: Life of Kondratii Selivanov and various followers of White Dove: Leroy-Beaulieu, 422–423; "Skoptsi," *Encyclopaedia Britannica*.

204: Christ is a title: Jaroslav Jan Pelikan, E. P. Sanders et al., "Jesus," *Encyclopedia Britannica*, updated November 5, 2023, https://www.britannica.com/biography/Jesus.

204: *Czar* means "emperor": "Czar," Merriam-Webster Dictionary, accessed January 9, 2022, https://www.merriam-webster.com/dictionary/czar.

205: "in daily life . . . too much attention": Mikanowski, "The Wheel and the Knife."

205: "Were I a banker, . . . and in peace.": Leroy-Beaulieu, *The Empire of the Tsars and the Russians*, 422–423.

205: "redirected the passion . . . belief, not blood." Mikanowski, "The Wheel and the Knife."

205: "Repressive measures proving . . . through the villages.": "Skoptsi," *Encyclopaedia Britannica*.

205: White Dove estimated at height to be one hundred thousand: Mikanowski, "The Wheel and the Knife."

205–206: "141 adherents of . . . an Extraordinary Sect.": "Skoptsy Members on Trial: Russia Trying Hard to Suppress an Extraordinary Sect," *New York Times*, October 13, 1910, https://timesmachine.nytimes.com/timesmachine/1910/10/13/105095186.html?pageNumber=6.

206: "To escape prosecution . . . own in Russia.": "Skoptsi," *Encyclopaedia Britannica*.

206: 1970s reference to one hundred White Doves: Vitelli, "The White Doves."

206: Chastity definition: "Chastity," Merriam-Webster Dictionary, accessed November 11, 2023, https://www.merriam-webster.com /dictionary/chastity.

206: Russia Beyond article on "anti-sexuals": Nikolay Shevchenko, "No Sex Please! Meet the People Crusading against the 'Filthy Deed,'" Russia Beyond, August 17, 2018, https://www.rbth.com /lifestyle/328986-sex-russian-antisexual-asexual.

206: Asexuality defined and explored: "Asexuality Archive: Welcome to the Asexuality Archive!," Asexuality Archive, accessed January 10, 2022, https://www.asexualityarchive.com/.

206: Celibate defined: "Celibate," *Encyclopaedia Britannica*, accessed November 11, 2023, https://www.britannica.com/dictionary /celibate.

206: "In Russia there . . . welcomes self-castration.": Oleg Skripnik, "The Skoptsy: The Story of the Russian Sect That Maimed for Its Beliefs," Russia Beyond, August 25, 2016, https://www.rbth.com /politics_and_society/2016/08/25/the-skoptsy-the-story-of -the-russian-sect-that-maimed-for-its-beliefs_624175.

CHAPTER 7: INTERSEX ACTIVISM

209: "Fix your hearts, not our parts!": Jenji Learn, "Fix Your Hearts, Not Their Parts," BioEthics.net, July 27, 2018, http://www .bioethics.net/2018/07/fix-your-hearts-not-their-parts/.

209: "For many decades . . . as male as possible.": "Human Rights Watch and interACT Intersex Feature Video (English Subtitles)," YouTube video, 6:00, posted by interACT, August 29, 2017, https://youtu.be/c6JFw_gD97I.

209: "But these surgeries . . . were medically unnecessary,": "Human Rights Watch."

210: Money's theory: John Colapinto, *As Nature Made Him: The Boy Who Was Raised as a Girl* (New York: Harper Collins, 2000), 32–40.

210–211: Dr. Milton Diamond challenging Money's theory: Colapinto, 40–48.

211: Bruce and Brian born and accident during circumcision: Colapinto, 9–15.

211: Brian's phimosis clears up by itself: Colapinto, 17.

211: "Well, there is . . . more normal society.": Colapinto, 21–22.

211: "And now you feel complete as a woman?": Colapinto, 22.

212: Money and Diane Baransky on TV: Colapinto, 18–23.

212: Money saw Christine Jorgensen and other trans lives as proof of nurture being more important than nature: Colapinto, 35–36.

212: "Oh, yes, definitely. Yes. Completely—body and mind.": Colapinto, 22.

213: "She was ripping at it. . . . be a girl.": Colapinto, 56.

213: "psychological warfare.": Colapinto, xiii.

213: "When I say . . . people with it.": Colapinto, 57.

214: Money proclaims success of twins case: Colapinto, 65–70.

214: Dr. Gumbach bio: Nina Bai, "Melvin Malcolm Grumbach, Renowned Pediatric Endocrinologist, Dies at 90: Grumbach Led the Department of Pediatrics for 20 Years," University of California San Francisco, October 7, 2016, https://www.ucsf.edu/news /2016/10/404501/melvin-malcolm-grumbach-renowned -pediatric-endocrinologist-dies-90.

214: "the universal acceptance . . . ambiguous or injured genitalia.": Colapinto, *As Nature Made Him*, 75.

214: Dewhurst training doctors around the world to operate on intersex children: Seven Graham, email correspondence with the author, February 4, 2024.

214: Twins case changes standard of care worldwide: Colapinto, 75–76.

214: 1.7 percent of population born intersex: "Its Intersex Awareness Day—Here Are 5 Myths We Need to Shatter," Amnesty International, October 26, 2018, https://www.amnesty.org/en /latest/news/2018/10/its-intersex-awareness-day-here-are-5 -myths-we-need-to-shatter/.

214: US births 1955–2020: "Chart: Number of Births in the United States from 1990 to 2019 (in Millions)," Statista.com, March 2021, https://www.statista.com/statistics/195908/number-of-births -in-the-united-states-since-1990/.

215: The "success" of the twins' case "provides strong support . . . behavior can be altered.": "The Sexes: Biological Imperitives," *Time*, January 8, 1973, https://content.time.com/time/subscriber /article/0,33009,910514,00.html.

215: "Psychosexually . . . postnatal and learned.": Kate Millett, *Sexual Politics* (New York: Touchstone, 1990), 30–31.

215: Pyschosexual definition: "Psychosexual," Merriam-Webster Dictionary, accessed November 11, 2023, https://www.merriam-webster.com /dictionary/psychosexual; Sam N., "Psychosexual," Psychology Dictionary, April 28, 2013, https://psychologydictionary.org /psychosexual/.

215: "Taught from their . . . natural superiority extends.": Sharon Ruston, "Mary Wollstonecraft, Feminism, and the Nature v Nurture Debate," *Guardian* (US edition), November 12, 2013, https://www.theguardian.com/science/the-h-word/2013/nov/12/mary-wollstonecraft-gbbo-feminism-nature-nurture.

216: "You shouldn't be . . . just a tomboy": Colapinto, *As Nature Made Him*, 80, 92–93.

216: "a nervous breakdown . . . shaking and crying.": Colapinto, 99–107.

216: "*I* sort of knew . . . going to do?": Colapinto, 99.

216: "more ladylike" and "I thought it was all my fault.": Colapinto, 107.

216: "Her behavior is . . . her twin brother.": Colapinto, 104.

217 "At five, the . . . for normal infants.": Colapinto, 104–105.

217: "As far as . . . be a girl.": Colapinto, 125.

217: Hormones, and Dr. Ingimundson's interactions with Brenda: Colapinto, 129–133.

217: "I like dressing . . . be in one.": Colapinto, 122.

217: "I thought, The decision . . . going to *do* that?": Colapinto, 122.

217: "Brenda told [her mother] Janet . . . would kill herself.": Colapinto, 179.

218: "Somebody needed to . . . in the literature.": Colapinto, 179.

218: "By that time . . . world to know.": Colapinto, 179.

218: "I had brainwashed . . . believe anything else.": Colapinto, 180.

218: Brenda's dad tells the truth: Colapinto, 179–180.

218: "He told me . . . I wasn't crazy.": Colapinto, 179–180.

218: The name David and living as a boy: Colapinto, 181–183.

218: "It reminded me . . . me of courage.": Colapinto, 181–183.

218–219: Hard years for David: Colapinto, 183–190.

219: "never felt like a girl.": Colapinto, 190.

219: David rebuilds his life: Colapinto, 190–195.

219: Money continues to push his theory and sex reassignment: Colapinto, 202–204.

219: "there are people . . . to stop that.": Colapinto, 208–209.

219: "I figured I . . . based on me.": Colapinto, 209.

220: Diamond and Sigmundson writing paper to reveal the truth: Colapinto, 205–211.

220: "Rear the child . . . away the knife.": Colapinto, 210.

220: "Sexual identity not pliable after all.": Colapinto, 214.

220: "the experts had it all wrong.": Colapinto, 215.

220: Diamond and Sigmundson's paper revealing twins case was not a success: Colapinto, 211–215.

220: Death of the twins: "David Reimer: A Tragic Update," in Colapinto, About the Book, 10–13.

220: "Brian was jealous . . . the lucky one.": "David Reimer: A Tragic Update," in Colapinto, About the Book, 12.

221: Rise of medical malpractice lawsuits in the 1960s: "Medical Malpractice Law: Ancient History to Recent Controversies," Reiter & Walsh, accessed October 6, 2021, https://www.abclawcenters.com/resources/medical-malpractice-overview/.

221: Dr. William Reiner stopping surgeries: Colapinto, *As Nature Made Him*, 211–214.

221: "Six genetic males . . . the children themselves.": Colapinto, 213.

221–222: "who received no . . . confident self-image.": Colapinto, 234.

222: Money's PhD thesis: Colapinto, 233–237.

222: "never explained the . . . and Sigmundson's paper." Colapinto, 237.

222: Colapinto interviews Money: Colapinto, 245–248.

222: "When I asked . . . cannot be an *it*.'": Colapinto, 247–248.

222: Gender identity term: "John Money, Ph.D.," Kinsey Institute, Indiana University, accessed October 2, 2021, https://web.archive.org/web/20220319172837/https://kinseyinstitute.org/about/profiles/john-money.php; Colapinto, *As Nature Made Him*, 25.

222–223: David reflects on the surgery: Colapinto, *As Nature Made Him*, xiii, 262.

223: "My parents feel . . . the right things.": Colapinto, xvii.

223: "You know, if . . . 'whole and complete'?": Colapinto, 262.

223–224: "When intersex kids . . . need to stop.": Human Rights Watch "Human Rights Watch and interACT Intersex Feature Video," YouTube video, 3:36.

224: "I wish my . . . who she is.": Human Rights Watch and interACT, 5:30.

224: "Far too few . . . end these abuses.": Morgan Carpenter, "Statement on Intersex by UN High Commissioner for Human Rights," Intersex Human Rights Australia, September 15, 2015, https://ihra.org.au/29966/statement-hrc30-intersex/.

225: "Fix your hearts, not our parts!": Learn, "Fix Your Hearts, Not Their Parts."

225: Pidgeon and Sean told they had cancer: Kate Sosen, "After Years of Protest, a Top Hospital Ended Intersex Surgeries. For Activists, It Took a Deep Toll," The 19th, August 5, 2020, https://19thnews.org/2020/08/intersex-youth-surgeries-top -hospital-ended-intersex-activists/.

225: The Cercle Hermaphroditos: Susan Stryker, *Transgender History: The Roots of Today's Revolution* (New York: Seal, 2017), 57.

225: Info on Cheryl Chase: "Cheryl Chase," Queer Bio.com, June 16, 2020, https://queerbio.com/wiki/index.php?title=Cheryl_Chase.

225: ISNA mission: "Our Mission," Intersex Society of North America, accessed October 2, 2021, https://isna.org/.

225: "End the idea that it's monstrous to be different.": Colapinto, *As Nature Made Him*, 220.

225–226: "a focused mission . . . with intersex traits.": "Organizational History," interACT, accessed November 20, 2021, https:// interactadvocates.org/about-us/mission-history/.

226: "Hermaphrodites with Attitude.": Morgan Holmes, "When Max Beck and Morgan Holmes went to Boston," Intersex Day, October 17, 2015, https://intersexday.org/en/max-beck -morgan-holmes-boston-1996/.

226: Intersex Awareness Day: Tyler Austin, "Today in Gay History: First Public Demonstration by Intersex People in North America," *Out*, October 26, 2016, https://www.out.com/today-gay -history/2016/10/26/today-gay-history-first-public -demonstration-intersex-people-north-america.

226: "Intersex Awareness Day . . . on intersex children.": Betsy Driver, "The origins of Intersex Awareness Day," Intersex Day, October 14, 2015, http://intersexday.org/en/origin-intersex-awareness-day/.

226–227: "do not fall . . . about sexual difference.": Fausto-Sterling, *Sexing the Body*, 9.

227: Pidgeon's protest videos for #EndIntersexSurgery: Pidgeon, "5 Ways You Can End Intersex Surgery," YouTube video, 8:25, posted by pidge pagonis, August 29, 2018, https://youtu.be/1YcbCAMZpjk.

227: Intersex Justice Project's and interACT: Activists for Intersex Youth's press release, "Targeted by Intersex Justice Project's#endintersexsurgery Campaign, First U.S. Hospital Promises Action to Stop Genital Surgeries on Intersex Infants—Advocacy Groups Call for Further Change," July 28, 2020, https://www.intersexjusticeproject.org/uploads/1 /1/7/4/117454019/press-release-intersex-justice-projects -endintersexsurgery-victory.pdf.

227: The hospital's statement on ending unnecessary surgery on intersex children, "We recognize the . . . decision for themselves.": Dr. Thomas Shanley, president and CEO et al., "Intersex Care at Lurie Children's and Our Sex Development Clinic," Ann & Robert H. Lurie Children's Hospital of Chicago, June 28, 2020, https://www.luriechildrens.org/en/blog/intersex-care-at -lurie-childrens-and-our-sex-development-clinic/.

227–228: New York City Health + Hospitals statement, "All medically unnecessary . . . parents for intervention.": "New York City Health and Hospitals Prohibits Intersex Surgery," interACT, July 7, 2021, https://interactadvocates.org/new-york-city -health-and-hospitals-prohibit-intersex-surgery/.

228: "For nearly three . . . hormones or chromosomes": Oliver Haug, "Activists Plan to Protest Nonconsensual Intersex Surgeries at New York Hospital," Them, August 6, 2021, https://www .them.us/story/activists-plan-protest-nonconsensual-intersex -surgeries-new-york-hospital.

228: "I'm sick to . . . to be *you*." Colapinto, *As Nature Made Him*, 265.

229–231: Darlington Statement on Intersex Human Rights: "Darlington Statement," Intersex Human Rights Australia and Intersex Peer Support Australia, March 2017, https://darlington.org.au /statement/.

232: "There is a . . . and well-being.": "APA Adopts Resolution Opposing Biased or Coercive Efforts to Change Individuals' Gender Identity," APA, March 2, 2021, https://www.apa.org/news /press/releases/2021/03/change-gender-identity.

232: "Doctors are calling . . . make us us.": Seven Graham, email.

233: "Who would you . . . gender inappropriate behavior": Kukla, "A Created Being," 3.

233: "we all helped . . . to suppress them": Kukla, 3.

CONCLUSION

234: Regarding the title for the conclusion, I first heard the term *theystory* in this Instagram post by Lambda Legal: Lambda Legal, "This week, one of our clients made theystory. Dana Zzyym received the first gender-neutral U.S. passport. We have so much more work to do, but this is a big moment in our fight for equal rights," Instagram, October 30, 2021, https://www.instagram.com/p /CVqKbiApHVy/.

235: "Rainbows are actually . . . above the horizon.": Jeannie Evers and Emdash Editing, "Resource Library: Encyclopedic Entry: Rainbow," National Geographic Society, accessed February 11, 2021, https://www.nationalgeographic.org/encyclopedia/rainbow/.

235–236: "visible light is . . . gamma radiation (beyond x-rays).": Evers and Emdash Editing.

236: First US Passport with X gender marker: US State Department press release: Ned Price, State Department Spokesperson, "Issuance of the First U.S. Passport with an X Gender Marker: Press Statement," United States Department of State, October 27, 2021, https://www.state.gov/issuance-of-the-first-u-s-passport-with-an-x-gender-marker/.

236: "a six-year . . . male or female": "BREAKING: Lambda Legal Client Dana Zzyym Receives First U.S. Passport with an X Gender Marker," Lambda Legal, October 27, 2021, http://support.lambdalegal.org/site/MessageViewer?em_id=51542.0&dlv_id=51641.

236: "I almost burst . . . is liberating.": Lambda Legal, email to the author, October 29, 2021.

237: "No matter which . . . in our lives.": Rachel Alatalo and Matthew Solomon, "Flags of the LGBTIQ Community," Outright International, September 20, 2021, https://outrightinternational.org/content/flags-lgbtiq-community.

237–238: Alternative gender symbols: Dawning, "A Symbol for the Totally Non-Binary," Asexuality.org, July 10, 2018, https://www.asexuality.org/en/topic/173699-a-symbol-for-the-totally-non-binary/.

238: Gender diversity symbols: Ryle, *She/He/They/Me*, cover and "Note on the Cover."; Mx. Anunnaki Ray Marquez, "All the Gender Symbols," Anunnakiray.com, accessed October 30, 2021, https://anunnakiray.com/all-the-gender-symbols/.

238: "totally non-binary . . . symbol society, right?": Dawning, "A Symbol for the Totally Non-Binary."

239: "We had just . . . 'the wrong body.'": Sass Rogando Sasot, "Reclaiming the Wronged Body," *TransGriot* (blog), October 6, 2010, https://transgriot.blogspot.com/2010/10/reclaiming-wronged-body.html.

239–240: "I identify and . . . by their dogmas.": Sasot.

240: Study of trans student population in high school just asking if kids were trans: Michelle M. Johns et al., "Transgender Identity and Experiences of Violence Victimization, Substance Use, Suicide Risk, and Sexual Risk Behaviors among High School Students—19 States and Large Urban School Districts, 2017," *Morbidity and Mortality Weekly Report* 68, no. 3 (January 24, 2019): 67–71, https://www.cdc.gov/mmwr/volumes/68/wr/mm6803a3.htm.

240–241: Study of high school gender diversity with different questions: Lisa Selin Davis, "High Schoolers May Be More Gender-Diverse Than Previously Thought, New Study Says," CNN, May 18, 2021, https://www.cnn.com/2021/05/18/health/gender-diverse-high-school-study-wellness/index.html.

241: Williams Institute announces 1.2 million US adults identify as nonbinary: Williams Institute, "Press Release: 1.2 Million LGBTQ Adults in the US Identify as Nonbinary," UCLA School of Law, Williams Institute, June 22, 2021, https://williamsinstitute.law.ucla.edu/press/lgbtq-nonbinary-press-release/.

242: "Just as we . . . eagerly awaited child.": Roughgarden, *Evolution's Rainbow*, 299.

243: 2021 had a record number of anti-trans and anti-LGBTQ+ state laws introduced: Wyatt Ronan, "As 2022 State Legislative Sessions Begin, a Review of 2021's Record-Breaking Anti-LGBTQ+ Sessions," Human Rights Campaign press release from January 13, 2021, as posted at *Erie Gay News*, https://www.eriegaynews.com/news/article.php?recordid=202202hrc2021legisreview.

243: "It's not about . . . about policing gender.": Graham, conversation with author, February 5, 2024.

243: "masculinity crisis," "effeminate" and "sissy men and other abnormal aesthetics": Helen Gao, "Guest Essay: China's Ban on 'Sissy Men' Is Bound to Backfire," *New York Times*, December 31, 2022, https://www.nytimes.com/2021/12/31/opinion/china-masculinity.html.

243: Cai Xukun's Instagram wearing eyeshadow and blond hair: Cai Xukun (KUN) "Canada I'm coming for you! Tickets on sale 10am May 13 Monday Eastern Time. I can't wait to see you all," Instagram, May 10, 2019, https://www.instagram.com/p/BxSN_ChH3w2/; Cai Xukun (KUN), December 25, 2020, https://www.instagram.com/p/CJOFslkHdPt/.

243: Cai Xukun's Instagram with dark hair and leather jackets: Cai Xukun (KUN), Instagram, December 10, 2022, https://www.instagram.com/p/CXTg3-5lbrI/; Cai Xukun (KUN), "Phenomenon," Instagram, January 10, 2022, https://www.instagram.com/p/CYk-wLEL2en/.

243: "the government's idea . . . career-oriented providers": Gao, "China's Ban on 'Sissy Men' Is Bound to Backfire."

244: "Normal, hardworking people . . . you very much": Juno Dawson, *The Gender Games* (London: Two Roads, 2017), 341–342.

244: "by saying . . . gender comes up.": Hida Viloria, *Born Both: An Intersex Life* (New York: Hachette Book Group, 2017), 307.

245: "In the organization's . . . gorgeous and beautiful!": Tomo Hillbo, "Ministry of Language: Interview with Alex Kapitan," Meadville Lombard Theological School, accessed November 14, 2021, https://www.meadville.edu/ml-commons/details/ministry-of-language-interview-with-alex-kapitan/.

RECOMMENDED RESOURCES

IF YOU'RE IN CRISIS

Trevor Project
https://www.thetrevorproject.org/

ON GENDER

Bailar, Schuyler. Instagram
https://www.instagram.com/pinkmantaray/

Bem, Sandra Lipsitz. *The Lenses of Gender: Transforming the Debate on Sexual Inequality*. New Haven, CT: Yale University, 1993.

Bornstein, Kate. *My Gender Workbook: How to Become a Real Man, a Real Woman, the Real You, or Something Else Entirely*. New York: Routledge, 1998.

Fausto-Sterling, Anne. *Sexing the Body: Gender Politics and the Construction of Sexuality*. New York: Hachette Book Group, 2020.

Gonzalez, Maya. *The Gender and Infinity Book for Kids: A Gender Wheel Book*. San Francisco: Reflection, 2023.

———. *The Gender Wheel: A Story about Bodies and Gender for Every Body*. San Francisco: Reflection, 2017.

"A Map of Gender-Diverse Cultures." PBS *Independent Lens*. https://www.pbs.org/independentlens/content/two-spirits_map-html/

Roscoe, Will. *Changing Ones: Third and Fourth Genders in Native North America*. New York: St. Martins, 1998.

Ryle, Robyn. *She/He/They/Me: For the Sisters, Misters, and Binary Resisters*. Naperville, IL: Sourcebooks, 2019.

Stryker, Susan. *Transgender History: The Roots of Today's Revolution*. New York: Hachette Book Group, 2017.

Vaid-Menon, Alok. *Beyond the Gender Binary*. New York: Penguin Workshop, 2020.

———. Instagram
https://www.instagram.com/alokvmenon/

"What Does 'Two-Spirit' Mean? | InQueery." YouTube video, 6:16. Presented by Geo Neptune. Posted by Them, December 11, 2018. https://www.youtube.com/watch?v=A4lBibGzUnE&t=46s.

ON GENDER DIVERSITY IN NATURE

Roughgarden, Joan. *Evolution's Rainbow: Diversity, Gender, and Sexuality in Nature and People*. Berkeley: University of California, 2013.

Schrefer, Eliot. *Queer Ducks (and Other Animals): The Natural World of Animal Sexuality*. Illustrated by Jules Zuckerberg. New York: HarperCollins, 2023.

ON THE LGBTQIA2+ COMMUNITY

LGBT History Month Icons: Icons from All Years
https://lgbthistorymonth.com/icon_search/all

Prager, Sarah. *A Child's Introduction to PRIDE: The Inspirational History and Culture of the LGBTQIA+ Community*. Illustrated by Caitlin O'Dwyer, New York: Black Dog & Leventhal, 2023.

ON EUNUCHS

Kuefler, Mathew. *The Manly Eunuch: Masculinity, Gender Ambiguity, and Christian Ideology in Late Antiquity*. Chicago: University of Chicago, 2001.

ON CASTRAI

"Alessandro Moreschi Sings Ave Maria (no scratch)." YouTube video, 3:15. Posted by Javier Medina, December 26, 2011. https://www.youtube.com/watch?v=KLjvfqnD0ws.

ON THE SIX GENDERS OF CLASSICAL JUDAISM

TransTorah
http://www.transtorah.org/

ON BROTHERBOYS AND SISTERGIRLS

"Brotherboys Yarnin' Up—Kai and Dean." YouTube video, 9:01. Posted by Trans Health Australia, August 23, 2014. https://www.youtube.com/watch?v=fTtiYD8GmXQ.

"Miriam Margolyes Meets the Sistergirls of the Tiwi Islands | Miriam Margolyes: Almost Australian," YouTube video, 2:43. Posted by ABC TV & iview, May 25, 2020. https://youtu.be/Fc-WPnNH55c.

ON HIJRAS

Nanda, Serena. *Gender Diversity: Crosscultural Variations*. Long Grove, IL: Waveland, 2000.

———. *Neither Man nor Woman: The Hijras of India*. Belmont, CA: Wadsworth, 1999.

Tripathi, Laxmi Narayan, translated from the Marathi original by R. Raj Rao and P. G. Joshi. *Me Hijra, Me Laxmi*. New Delhi: Oxford University, 2015.

ON MĀHŪ

Kumu Hina. Video. Produced by Connie M. Florez, Dean Hamer, Joe Wilson. Directed by Dean Hamer & Joe Wilson. Haleiwa, HI: Qwaves, 2014. https://kumuhina.com/.

Matzner, Andrew (now Dreya Blume). *'O Au No Keia: Voices from Hawai'i's Mahu and Transgender Communities*. Self-published, Xlibris, 2001.

A Place in the Middle. Video. Produced by Joe Wilson. Directed by Dean Hamer and Joe Wilson. Haleiwa, HI: Qwaves, 2014. https://aplaceinthemiddle.org/.

Wenke, Joe. *The Human Agenda: Conversations about Sexual Orientation & Gender Identity*. Stamford, CT: Trans Über, 2015.

ON DAHOMEY FEMALE WARRIORS

Alpern, Stanley B. *Amazons of Black Sparta: The Women Warriors of Dahomey*. New York: New York University, 2011.

Dash, Mike. "Dahomey's Women Warriors," *Smithsonian*, September 23, 2011. https://www.smithsonianmag.com/history/dahomeys-women-warriors-88286072.

ON CLAUDE CAHUN AND MARCEL MOORE

Lover Other. DVD, Produced and directed by Barbara Hammer. New York: Barbara Hammer, 2006.

ON SHI PEI PU AND BERNARD BOURISCOT

Wadler, Joyce. "The True Story of *M. Butterfly*; The Spy Who Fell in Love with a Shadow." *New York Times Magazine*, August 15, 1993. https://www.nytimes.com/1993/08/15/magazine/the-true-story-of-m-butterfly-the-spy-who-fell-in-love-with-a-shadow.html.

ON TIDAWENA AND NIBORAWENA OF THE WARAO

Naughton, Jake. "LENS: Two Spirits in the Venezuelan Jungle." *New York Times*, September 5, 2014. https://lens.blogs.nytimes.com/2014/09/05/two-spirits-in-the-venezuelan-jungle/.

"The Warao," University of Oslo Museum of Cultural History, December 11, 2020. https://www.historiskmuseum.no/english/exhibitions/exhibitions-archive/america-present-past-identity/south-america/the-warao/.

INDEX

PHOTO ACKNOWLEDGMENTS

Image credits: Sahara Prince/Shutterstock, p. 12; INDRA ABRIYANTO/ AFP/Getty Images, p. 13; Eddie Gerald/Alamy, p. 15; SuperStock/Alamy, p. 18; Geo Neptune/flickr, p. 21; Wikimedia Commons (Public Domain), pp. 23, 68, 151, 163; Aseo neutral/Wikimedia Commons (Public Domain), p. 24; KMazur/WireImage/Getty Images, p. 35 (left); Amanda Edwards/ Getty Images, p. 35 (right); The Gender Wheel symbol was created by Maya Gonzalez. Gender Wheel® is a registered trademark owned by Reflection Press, p. 40; © Bridgeman Images, p. 59; PHGCOM/ Wikimedia Commons (Public Domain), p. 68; National Gallery of Art/ Wikimedia Commons (Public Domain), p. 70; Wikimedia Commons (CC0 1.0 DEED), p. 71; Rijksmuseum/Wikimedia Commons (public domain), p. 72; Wikimedia Commons (Public Domain), p. 76; Antonina Reshef/Wikimedia Commons (CC BY-SA 3.0), p. 80; Timothy Herbert/ Wikimedia Commons (Public Domain), p. 107; Tania Branigan/ Guardian/eyevine/Redux, p. 125; Daniel Ramirez f/Wikimedia Commons (CC BY 2.0 DEED), p. 133; Paul Hermans/Wikimedia Commons (Public Domain), p. 140; Adam Jones, Ph.D/Wikimedia Commons (Public Domain), p. 152; Willis Sayre Collection of Theatrical Photographs/ University of Washington: Special Collections/Wikimedia Commons (Public Domain), p. 161; lightsgoingon/flickr (CC BY 2.0), p. 166; Celette/ Wikimedia Commons (CC BY-SA 4.0), p. 167; Danvis Collection/Alamy, p. 169; Álvaro Laiz García, p. 177; www.dhm.de/Wikimedia Commons (Public Domain), p. 182; UC Berkeley, Bancroft Library/Wikimedia Commons (Public Domain), p. 191; Barbara Alper/Getty Images, p. 192; Unknown/Wikimedia Commons (Public Domain), p. 204; Chronicle/ Alamy, p. 207; AP Photo/M. Spencer Green, p. 224; Sparrow/Wikimedia Commons (CC BY-SA 4.0), p. 226; Valentin Gubanov/Alamy, p. 235; Design element: pashabo/Shutterstock; Marina Santiaga/Shutterstock; Alexander Yurkevich/Shutterstock; aomvector/Shutterstock.

ACKNOWLEDGMENTS

This book is so queer, the fact that it got published is a cause for celebration!

Anne Lamont, in her amazing book on writing, *Bird by Bird*, talks about how lighthouses don't run all over an island looking for boats to save. They just stand there and shine.

I take a lot of inspiration from that—from imagining each book I get out in the world; each talk to students, teachers, or librarians; and each social media and blog post as turning on another light in my lighthouse. I'm not trying to convince anyone that I'm right and they're wrong about queer history and gender. I'm just shining a light on all these cool things I learned that would have totally changed my life had I known them back when I was a kid and teen. And with this book, I'm focused on holding space for all these amazing voices of gender diversity and letting them shine bright.

As part of the celebration of you holding *The Gender Binary Is a Big Lie* in your hands, my lighthouse is also shining with a rainbow of gratitude for the following:

Lucy, thank you for your honesty in sharing your gender truth, your enthusiasm to record the Gender 101 videos with me, and for introducing me to some of your amazing gender-diverse friends.

Michael, thank you for your advice that approaching this book as an invitation might lead to more understanding. You were right.

Seven Graham, thank you for your passionate advocacy for intersex people, your careful review of this manuscript, and your excellent suggestions and contributions. This book—and me as a human—are better for it.

Alok Vaid-Menon, while I don't know you personally, I want to thank you for leading and teaching and responding to adversity with love. It's inspiring.

My brilliant editor Shaina Olmanson, thank you for helping me craft the best and most powerful version this book could be. And thanks to the rest of the Zest Books/ Lerner team too, for taking this manuscript and making it such a beautiful book—special shout-outs to Andy Cummings, Rachel Zugschwert and the PR/marketing team, Annie Zheng for help with permissions, production designer Erica Johnson, and L. Whitt and Danielle Carnito for the design that makes this nonfiction book less medicine and more chocolate. It's beautiful!

My agent, Marietta Zacker, thank you for believing that my books are important and deserve a spot in the marketplace of ideas. Most of all, thanks for believing in me as a writer.

My SCBWI, IBPA, KidLit, and Queer KidLit Creators communities, thank you for being my colleagues, my friends, and for cheering me on.

My husband, Mark, and our incredible daughter, Gavi, thank you for letting me love you so fiercely, and thank you for the love radiating back. It makes everything possible.

And thank you to all the librarians, teachers, and booksellers who are getting this book into the hands of the very readers who need it most.

Most importantly, thank you for reading this. I hope the queer history—and today's reality—of gender that includes and goes beyond the binary helps you shine with rainbow light too.

ABOUT THE AUTHOR

Lee Wind (he/him) has a superpower: stories. Stories—true and fictional—that center marginalized kids and teens and celebrate their power to change the world. Closeted until his twenties, Wind writes the books that would have changed his life as a young gay Jewish kid. His master's degree from Harvard didn't include blueprints for a time machine to go back and tell these stories to himself, so he pays it forward with a popular blog that has over four million page views (*I'm Here. I'm Queer. What The Hell Do I Read?*) and books for kids and teens.

Wind is the award-winning author of the nonfiction *No Way, They Were Gay? Hidden Lives and Secret Loves,* the first book in the Queer History Project series, which won the International Literacy Association Book Awards, Young Adult Nonfiction Award, 2022; the Chicago Public Library Best of the Best Books, Winner, 2021; was named a Junior Library Guild Gold Standard Selection; and was acknowledged for "Outstanding Merit" by the Children's Book Committee of the Bank Street College of Education "Best Books of the Year" 2021. *No Way, They Were Gay?* has been repeatedly challenged for centering and celebrating men who loved men, women

Photo credit: Joanna DeGeneres

who loved women, people who loved without regard to gender, and people who lived outside the gender binary. It is included in the anti-book banning resources offered by Unite Against Book Bans, an initiative of the American Library Association.

He is also the author of the young adult novels *A Different Kind of Brave* and the crowdfunded *Queer as a Five-Dollar Bill*, winner of the National Indie Excellence Award for Best Book, LGBTQ for Children & Young Adults. Picture books he has authored include the upcoming *Love of the Half-Eaten Peach*, illustrated by Jieting Chen, and the acclaimed *Red and Green and Blue and White*, illustrated by Paul O. Zelinsky, which the *New York Times* called "Beautiful . . . a message the world can use, throughout the year."

With day jobs for the Independent Book Publishers Association (as their chief content officer) and the Society of Children's Book Writers and Illustrators (as their official blogger), Wind's superhero job is storytelling that empowers people to shine with their own light.

Visit leewind.org to subscribe to his newsletter and continue the journey to discover our past and live your future.

"This is a fascinating book that challenges the simplistic history we have been taught to believe for far too long. Lee Wind illuminates the complexities of historical figures, and through them, readers are given permission to be their true, complex selves. . . . An important book for readers of all ages."

—Lesléa Newman, author of *Heather Has Two Mommies*, *Sparkle Boy*, and *October Mourning: A Song for Matthew Shepard*

"Fascinating, ambitious, diverse, rigorously researched, and much-needed—this book will save lives."

—Kathleen Krull, winner of the Children's Book Guild Nonfiction Award for body of work, and author of the *Lives Of* series

"This work serves not only to educate everyone who reads it, but also to help LGBT youth feel seen, to know people like them exist in the world, and to have role models that are among the most revered of leaders. Do I wish I'd had this in junior high school? You bet!"

—Dr. Judy Grahn, author of *Another Mother Tongue*

"Lee Wind has done a fabulous job pulling back the curtain to reveal some long suppressed history. Not only is *No Way, They Were Gay?* fascinating reading, I firmly believe it is a book that is literally going to be a lifesaver for some young readers."

—Bruce Coville, author of the groundbreaking short story "Am I Blue?" as well as *My Teacher Is an Alien* and more

"I think as a teen I might've chosen to major in History if I'd read Lee Wind's fun, fast-paced, and thought-provoking book. I love how it lays out the evidence about some of our past's greatest heroes, invites us to draw our own conclusions, and inspires us, regardless of our sexual orientation or gender identity to be true to who we are."

—Alex Sanchez, author of *Rainbow Boys* and *You Brought Me the Ocean*